A Newnham Anthology

A Newnham Anthology

EDITED BY

ANN PHILLIPS

FELLOW OF NEWNHAM COLLEGE, CAMBRIDGE

*

*

PUBLISHED FOR NEWNHAM COLLEGE

CAMBRIDGE UNIVERSITY PRESS

CAMBRIDGE

LONDON · NEW YORK · MELBOURNE

Published by the Syndics of the Cambridge University Press
The Pitt Building, Trumpington Street, Cambridge CB2 1RP
Bentley House, 200 Euston Road, London NW1 2DB
32 East 57th Street, New York, NY 10022, USA
296 Beaconsfield Parade, Middle Park, Melbourne 3206, Australia

First published 1979

Printed in Great Britain
at the University Press, Cambridge

Library of Congress Cataloging in Publication Data
Main entry under title:
A Newnham anthology.
1. Newnham College. Cambridge, Eng. – History – Addresses, essays, lectures.
I. Phillips, Ann, M.A. II. Newnham College, Cambridge, Eng.
LF797.C34N48 378.426'59 77-95448
ISBN 0 521 22068 8

CONTENTS

ILLUSTRATIONS

INTRODUCTION

The idea of an anthology mainly made up of reminiscences of former students of Newnham arose when the College was discussing the commemorative side of its centenary celebrations. Although it was realized that the Anthology would not be completed in time for the centenary itself (in 1971), the Governing Body gave its approval to the idea and the collecting of material was begun. It took some years for all the material to come in, and the editing of it has been a slow process: nevertheless, this volume is a part of the College's celebration of a hundred years of its own history.

It was always our intention that the Anthology should present a student's-eye view of the College. There is little here, accordingly, of the kind of history which is made in meetings of the Council and Governing Body; and I have made very little use of the writings of any non-members of Newnham, although there were one or two items I could not resist.

I have in every case tried to let the contributors speak for themselves. Where two people have made the same point in different ways, I have kept both; where two accounts of an event or a period differ in ways it would be impossible, or improper, to reconcile, I have left them to do so. Editing has been restricted to cutting the uninformatively repetitious and adding occasional notes. In particular, contemporary material, such as letters, diaries and minutes, has been left with its idiosyncratic spelling and punctuation, and not subjected to the mild degree of standardization used for later writing.

Editorial conventions are simple. The few interpolations in square brackets in the text, and notes in small type at the foot of some items, are editorial. Dates at the head of pages are those most appropriate to the subject-matter, as are those in the contents list; dates following the names of authors at the foot of individual items are those of their coming up to Newnham.

Besides the contributions especially written for the Anthology, material composed for earlier occasions and stored in the College archives was combed through and drawn upon: so that the 'present day' referred to by the writers of reminiscences may not always be the nineteen-seventies or even the nineteen-sixties, as is apparent from the text itself.

I drew also upon *Thersites*, the Newnham students' magazine (running from 1909 to 1938) and the North Hall Diary, a handwritten account of the main events of each term (running from the beginning of the College to 1919).

A general note on the nomenclature may be helpful. The original College building was Newnham Hall (1875); with the opening of North Hall in 1880 Newnham Hall became South (see the map, pages 26 and 27). When the third building was completed in 1888 a new procedure was adopted: South became Old Hall, North took on the name of Sidgwick (after the College's prime founder and his wife, later to be Principal), and the name of the new Hall, Clough, honoured the College's first Principal. Thereafter naming proceeded sedately with the names of founders, benefactors and Principals – Pfeiffer, Kennedy, Peile, Fawcett and Strachey in due order. The other point of confusion is over the titles 'Vice-Principal' and 'Tutor'. Each Hall not resided in by the Principal herself had in the early days a resident Vice-Principal (few institutions can boast a Principal and four Vice-Principals, but Newnham for years had this distinction). In 1918, when the College received its Charter, the title of these officers became Tutor. Before that date, and occasionally thereafter, 'tutor' generally means 'supervisor'; I have tried to separate this usage by giving it a lower-case 't'.

Many people have helped with the work. At the outset, most of the impetus for the planning of the book came from Rosemary McCabe, and it was her enthusiasm which roused the interest of many of the contributors. The organization of the early stages was presided over by Elisabeth Brown, who kept a check on the correspondence and let nothing escape unfiled and uncatalogued. Margaret Grimshaw and Barbara White, with their great knowledge of the College's living history, answered a great many questions beginning 'Who was' and 'When did' and (perhaps most usefully of all) 'Where can I find'.

I am grateful to all these people: to the many contributors who made the book by sitting down to write, by dictating tapes, and by hunting out letters, diaries and photographs; to the College Council, who relieved me of part of my normal duties for a term to give me time to get the editorial work going; to Jane Heal, who took on those duties in my place; to the University Press for its care of the book, and especially to my indefatigable subeditor, Clare Ballantyne; and to all the well-wishers who have written about the Anthology from time to time, remaining patient and hopeful in spite of the length of time the book has taken to come to completion.

I have tried to trace the owners of copyrights, but realize that there is a danger that I have not found them all: if so, I offer my apologies for the failure. Cambridge University Press kindly allowed me to reprint extracts from Mary Paley Marshall's *What I Remember*; George Allen and Unwin and the author's daughter, Mrs J. I. Kellett Carding, gave permission for quotation from Josephine Kellett's *That Friend of Mine*; and Routledge and Kegan Paul and the author, Victoria Glendinning, gave permission for quotation from *A Suppressed Cry*. Dr M. D. Glynne permitted me to use her mother's letter, called here "King's Comes Round". I should like to thank all of these benefactors.

I am grateful too to the people who sent material which for some reason I was unable to use. Even the unpublished has fed our archives, which have been much enriched by the spate not only of writing but of attic-searching which the news of the Anthology provoked. The archives remain open, though the Anthology is closed: new contributions, reminiscences, afterthoughts, and new discoveries made while turning out will all be welcome and will find their place in our records. It would be pleasant if the material were to continue its growth over the next hundred years and produce another volume then.

Ann Phillips

Newnham College

1869

FOUNDERS AND BENEFACTORS

My father, John Peile, was a prominent member of the party of progress in the University. He was one of the founders of Newnham College for women, and was President of its Council until his death. His were the first college lectures in Cambridge open to women.

The need of a college for women was felt, where they could live and avail themselves of the opportunities then possible. Mother used to describe the first meeting about Newnham, held in the house of Professor Henry Fawcett, the blind Postmaster-General, when Mrs Fawcett (afterwards Dame Millicent) sat on a little stool by the fireside, next to her husband, in order to give an informal air to the proceedings, which were felt to be revolutionary!

A small company was formed, a little house taken, and Miss Clough, sister of the poet Arthur Hugh Clough, was brought from Liverpool to be its head. I can just remember, as a tiny child, going with mother when she went to welcome Miss Clough on her arrival. (The temporary quarters on Miss Clough's arrival were in Panton Street.) She used to tell with amusement how Professor Henry Sidgwick came to her lamenting the 'unfortunate personal appearance' of the first students! They were all remarkably good-looking women, and the founders of the movement were anxious not to be conspicuous in any way. (Most of the first women students wore pre-raphaelite garments.)

Miss Clough was a somewhat formidable person, and approached her duties as head of a women's college in more of the spirit of the schoolmistress than of a college don; but it is difficult now to realize what need there was for wisdom in avoiding opposition as much as possible. She was very careful of the health as well as the intellectual training of her students, and I remember an unfortunate student who was in bed with a bad cold when Miss Clough discovered that she did not possess a red flannel petticoat.

H. M. Kempthorne (Peile). Extract from a notebook, *c.* 1869

*

1871

THE FIRST FIVE STUDENTS

In 1870 I was startled by receiving from the Secretary of the Cambridge Syndicate a suggestion that as a result of my success in the Local Examinations* I should come up to Cambridge to continue my studies. So in 1870 I was installed in a tiny bedroom in a girls' boarding-school on Parker's Piece. I didn't know anyone in the place and my brother who was up at Corpus was so annoyed with my venture that he wouldn't speak to me! At first there appeared to be no one else in my position but

M. Wright (Kennedy)'s drawing of Henry Sidgwick lecturing to the first women students: she entitled it 'Ye great philosopher delivering his lecture'

after two days I was joined by Felicia Larner and then by a Miss Wood. I had another year of Local Exams in view. We could choose our own subjects and no curriculum was suggested. In the light of what followed I always looked upon myself as the very first Newnham student. I found the lectures absorbingly interesting but life at the boarding-school was

* The Cambridge Local Examinations, run by the Local Examinations Syndicate, were opened to women in 1864. Passes in the Higher Local Examination would gain exemption from the Previous Examination (see note, p. 14). The papers for this examination were arranged in lettered Groups, not all of which were defined by a single subject category as, for instance, Group C (Mathematics); and from time to time the Groups regrouped. Further references to the Higher Local are made below, especially by E. M. Sharpley and B. A. Clough.

austere and dull. After two terms of it I decided to take a term off and come up again in October. This I did and entered myself as a boarder in the new house in Regent Street which was opened to receive girl students from the provinces. Henry Sidgwick was the leading spirit among those in Cambridge who sought to advance the women's cause. He it was who took this house, furnished it from his own pocket and arranged for Miss Clough, an old friend, to come and act as housekeeper for the students. There were five of us who came up in 1871 – myself; Mary Paley, who was to become my life-long friend; Edith Creak, a clever sixteen-year-old; Ella Bulley, and Annie Migault. One day Alfred Marshall, our lecturer in Political Economy, stopped Mary Paley and me in the street and asked us if we had ever thought of working for a Tripos examination.* He explained that this would mean at least three years' study, specializing in one or two subjects. We accepted the challenge lightly, not realizing what we were undertaking. Mary and I decided on the Moral Science Tripos for which we were devotedly coached by Henry Sidgwick and Alfred Marshall. Eventually we both obtained a Second Class. Edith Creak took both Classical and Mathematical Tripos and Felicia Larner who had rejoined the little band got a Second in the Historical Tripos in 1875.

M. Wright (Kennedy, 1871)

* Before their formal admission to Tripos examinations, women took the examinations informally by special arrangement with the examiners, who might mark their papers as a favour.

74 REGENT STREET

74 Regent Street had been taken for us by Mr Henry Sidgwick who had spent his Long Vacation time and money in getting it ready. In a letter which he wrote in 1871 he says: 'I am not going to take any real holiday this Long, I have no money. The cares of a household being incumbent, I find myself estimating the expenses of Plate, Linen etc.' So of course we wanted to be economical as well and my first recollections of Mr Sidgwick and Mr Marshall are the evenings when we sat round and sewed the household linen in Miss Clough's sitting-room. This was my first sight of Mr Marshall [whom she later married]. I then thought I had never seen such an attractive face with its delicate outline and brilliant eyes. We sat very silent and rather awed as we listened to them talking to Miss Clough on high subjects. But not always on those,

for Mr Sidgwick was the most delightful conversationalist on any subject. I have known only one to equal him, Henry Smith of Oxford. Every subject Mr Sidgwick touched upon was never the same again. As someone said of him: 'If you so much as mentioned a duster in his presence he would glorify it on the spot.' His conversation made him sometimes inattentive to ordinary affairs and one day when he was helping us at dinner after using a tablespoon for the soup he pulled out the entire contents of the apple pie with the soup ladle, to our great delight. Though we were only five he found us rather troublesome. In another letter he writes: 'There is such a strong impulse towards liberty among the young women attracted by the movement that they will not submit to maternal government.'

Perhaps in those days Miss Clough was rather inclined to treat us like schoolgirls and in the small house we were at close quarters and of course had our meals together with her. But she was a woman with great power of growth and adaptation, and from being the mistress of a school in the North she gradually developed into the ideal Head of a College. Mary Kennedy and I were the worst offenders. For instance, one day we said to Miss Clough: 'We are going to spend the day at Ely and are not sure when we shall be back.' She did not say anything, but a rule appeared soon after in the *Report*: 'Students wishing to make expeditions in the neighbourhood must ask for permission from the Principal.' As it was we spent a happy day, chiefly in the Cathedral, and we ended by climbing the tower in the company of an agreeable young man but parted from him before returning to Cambridge. Mr Sidgwick, determined that the scheme he had so much at heart should not suffer from our troublesome conduct, came and gave us a good talking to and I as spokeswoman promised that we would turn over a new leaf. This turn was made easier because, with numbers increased to twelve, our next two years were spent at Merton Hall, with a dining-room large enough for separate tables, with its lovely garden where the nightingales kept us awake at nights and with its ancient School of Pythagoras supposed to be haunted, though the only ghosts which visited us were enormous spiders.

M. Paley Marshall (1871). Reprinted from *What I Remember*

*

NEWNHAM HALL

1875: October. Newnham Hall opened.*

The following were among the terms of admission.

'No Student is admitted under the age of 17.

The Principal may require any Student to withdraw, who in her opinion is not profiting by the course of study at Newnham Hall.

The Charge for board and lodging is at present £20 per term of eight weeks. Students intending to become teachers are received at present at a charge of £15 per term. (About half the Students at present in residence are received on the reduced terms.) The only extras are wine, and fires in Students' rooms; fires are charged 4 guineas a year to ordinary Students, and 2 guineas to those intending to teach.

The payment for instruction varies slightly, according to the line of study taken up, but rarely exceeds 4 guineas for ordinary Students, and 2 guineas for those intending to become teachers.'

Extract from the North Hall Diary

* See Introduction, p. xii.

INNOCENT GAIETY

7 May 1876

My dearest Mamma,

You talk about enjoying the country; it is just like country here. We are completely private in our garden, and quite surrounded with country sights and sounds – cows and sheep in the fields round us, and birds of all sorts just outside the hedge. I think I have mentioned these said birds before, but I have never heard a word from any of you on the subject! I expected you to have been quite delighted at the idea of our hearing the nightingale, even in the house!

The lawn-tennis has come, and I have played several games. The Bander asked me the first evening, and was exceedingly gracious to me during, and after the game; of course, after; I play better than she does! We are rather put out about our cricket. Some of us, notably Miss Benton, Miss Ellis and I wanted very much to play, so Miss Ellis asked Miss Clough's permission, wh. was granted at once. Whereupon we collected money for a bat and Miss Benton and I bought it yesterday morning. Well, yesterday evening we were just going to play, when Miss Clough came out and said she was sorry but she could not possibly let us play. She said it would spoil the grass, and after a little hesitation, said there were other reasons. We have not, of course, the slightest wish to do what she does not approve of, but I wish she had thought of her 'other reasons' when we first asked her. We hear now, that they used to play at Merton [Merton Hall, home of the College 1872–4], but that it was stopped, probably 'Mr Marshall's friends' objected.

We had a very interesting debate last Tuesday (little debate). The subject was Theatres as a means of Education. When I went into the room I had no intention of speaking, but I had to do so after all. Mary Ellis begged me so hard, and no one had said anything wh. at all suited my views. Evelyn began, very well indeed, but she was so nervous that she broke down in the middle, leaving her sentence unfinished. Miss Green came next. She stood up and spoke as if she had been accustomed all her life to Public Speaking. She said nothing worth hearing, however, uttering about two platitudes, wh. had no bearing on the subject, in an exceedingly forcible manner. Then Conny Brodhurst, and little Miss Hunt spoke, for a very few minutes, and then there was no one else. So I had to get up, and I made, I think, the best speech I have ever made in the little Debate. I really was intensely interested in my subject, and I did so want some of them to agree with me, and the result was that I spoke for some minutes without the slightest hesitation or difficulty, and, a thing I have never done before, spoke of my own feelings on the subject – I mean, what I really feel, not what I feel when I am asked my opinion. You may imagine how glad I was when Miss Benton rose and said she had come into the room, not caring much for the subject, but thinking that, on the whole, theatres were bad, but that she had been entirely convinced by what the last member had said. I am afraid I had rather offended Miss Green, for I had said that I thought no one except the first speaker had kept to the subject, for after Miss Benton's speech, she rose again and said she thought her anecdote (one that she told) was to the point, for it showed that 'the lower orders' could not appreciate Shakspere, whose plays were certainly of a 'lofty and elevating tendency'. This sentence was aimed at me, for I had said that it must do us good to have our feelings moved by plays of an elevating tendency and had gone on to say that by this I meant, plays wh. roused in us impulses towards good, wh. showed us the evils around us and the remedies for those evils. Of course I had to answer, and I said that I thought I had distinctly explained what I meant by 'elevating' and that in the sense in wh. I used the word, I admitted that Shakspere plays might not be of an elevating tendency to the mass of the people 'or as in our assumed superiority we choose to call them the *lower* classes', for they are often incomprehensible to them.

All the evening Evelyn kept saying 'I do admire you so, I never knew you were so nice. I am so glad you said what you did about theatres', and they were all (my friends, I mean) amused at my speech about 'the lower classes'. Conny Brodhurst said: 'I knew you would be up at that, I was sure you could not stand that'.

15 May 1876

I said in my last letter that I was going to none of the May gaieties, but I find I was mistaken, as Mrs Bumpsted has asked me to lunch there tomorrow and go to the flower show in King's grounds with them, and Mrs Raynes has insisted on Miss Benton and I going to see the boat races with them on Thursday evening. However I have declined all the concerts, and flower shows and boat races are very innocent gaiety; they do not keep one up at night, and Tuesday and Thursday are my free days.

That sentence in my letter means if Papa does not promise to come up I shall overwork myself, in wh. case I shall look like a walking shadow, in wh. case Miss J and Miss Graves will write to him to come up in wh. case he will have to come; so that whether he decides to come or not eventually he will have to come, whether he likes it or no.

I will ask Miss Clough about lodgings. I daresay she will know of some.

13 November 1876

My dearest Papa,

I meant to have written to you yesterday but I had not time, so I do so to-night instead. I think I had better tell you what I do on Sundays or you will wonder how it is I cannot find time to write. Yesterday morning, I stayed in the dining hall after breakfast talking to Miss Jeffery, Miss Tovey, Evelyn, and May, till half-past ten. Then I read the papers, *Athenaeum*, *Spec.* and *Saturday* and wrote to Mamma; that took up the time till 1 o'clock. Then I went up to get ready for dinner. Directly after dinner Miss Ritchie asked me to come and see her, so I went and stayed till four o'clock, for just as I was going, about three, she insisted on my staying for tea wh. she was just going to make. So Miss Harrison came up and we had a delightful little party. Then from four till tea at a quarter past five, I practised. Then after tea I came upstairs to write but suddenly I thought I would hang up my pictures, wh. I did. It was great fun. I had to put a chair on my bed for one, get up on my chest of drawers for another and put a chair on my table for the others. I very nearly upset once. In taking the chair off the table, I forgot to keep on the middle part and stepped on the flap, whereupon the table tilted up and I had to make a bold jump with the chair in my hand into my armchair wh. was near, and so just saved myself and the table. I have put up my brackets and the paper rack with pins wh. keep them firm and cannot possibly hurt the walls, and as I have now stained and varnished my cupboard and bookcase, my room really looks very nice. Over the side of my bed is the water colour sketch and the large bracket under it; the large picture of the woman and child is over the mantelpiece, and on each side of the window come the others. My small brackets are on each side of the fireplace, and on the mantelpiece are Mendelssohn, the two groups, two upright vases, the flower basket and filter that Isabel gave me and a small china jar.

I have succeeded in 'humbugging' Mr Archer Hind, so that he does not dream of dismissing me to the other class, on the contrary he treats me with great respect, always asks my opinion of a difficult passage, etc. The other day I was bold enough to strike out a new idea. I did not at all like the meaning that was given in the notes of one passage so I told him that I had taken it as so and so, wh. interpretation the passage might bear for the word χῶρις means distinct and independent. They took the former and read 'But the honour of the gods is distinct, i.e. we may not mingle words of ill omen with our praises of them'. I read 'But the honour of the gods is independent; i.e. whatever subsequent calamity may have befallen us, honour is due to the gods for the blessings they gave before'. He was very much interested when he heard my idea was original, and said it was a very good one. At first he seemed disposed to adopt it, but finally he said that the ordinary interpretation was perhaps more in accordance with Aeschylean ideas, tho' one might bear mine in mind. Wasn't that a triumph. After learning Greek about two months, to strike out a new interpretation of the *Agamemnon* and be told that it was a good one! Shan't I get conceited? And last time in giving me back my Berkeley he said: 'Well, Miss Merrifield, considering you have never read any Plato, you have done this as well as could possibly have been expected. I shall give you a much harder paper some day.'

Miss Ritchie does go to the Greek class; she did not go the first time, but she does now and she also has a coach, a Mr Jenkinson, for Latin and Greek. She gets very 'depressed' over her work and comes to me to be consoled. This coach is a great friend of her brother's and told him that she was 'very sharp but hopelessly inaccurate'. She was in a most melancholy state at the news, especially as she knows it is true. She gets at the general sense of a passage at once, and goes on with a sublime disregard for gender, number and case. Mr Jenkinson also teaches Miss Cann and Miss Tovey Latin and he says they are hopelessly stupid; so I asked him who would please him, whereupon he answered immediately: 'You, for you are so accurate and you have a tremendous enthusiasm too and appreciation of the subject'. You see, I have not got a character for inaccuracy as I had when I was younger, so I suppose that I no longer have the habit. I do not think I have. I think my mathematical training has cured me of that.

I like Miss Ritchie very much indeed. I have seen a great deal of her lately. She is so simple and gentle, and childlike, in fact she is a perfect baby in some things, and yet she has read so much and knows so many nice people, and is so interested in everything – not merely in classics, but in the questions of the day, and political economy, and almost everything you can speak of.

I must begin work now, so Goodbye, love to all.

M. de G. Verrall (Merrifield, 1875). Extracts from letters home

KING'S COMES ROUND

19 February 1878

Hurrah for womens rights!!! – We have another triumph – Now you know the people of Christs College have allowed Natural Science students to attend the lectures for the men but Miss Clough must go too, that is one of the conditions. Well Mr Oscar Browning has been lecturing on History to about 4 of our girls & also giving the same lectures to the men of Kings – so he asked the Provost if the girls might attend the men's lectures to save his time – The Provost called a college meeting & the result is that Kings has opened its arms to the females – They went yesterday for the first time & Miss Clough went just to the first but is not to go in future. They were met on Kings Bridge you know where Mary [the writer's elder sister] – by an undergrad – he directed them where to go then another met them & took them to a third – The third took them into the hall where they were put into lovely leather chairs – with a lovely table pens & ink & there they were 4 of them & Miss C. – surrounded by about 50 men. It is jolly to think of Kings coming round the richest college in Cambridge & once one of the most inveterate enemies of the 'forward minxes'.* And to think of the undergrads receiving them so cordially within their sacred precincts.

Tonight there is to be a grand affair at Girton a dance & heaps of undergrads are going. I do want to go – I am now going to help Miss Bettany to dress. A blue cashmere princess, snowdrops etc – she will look jolly. A little Miss Gell is going & will have necklace & bracelets of snowdrops. She has such a merry little sparkling laugh – I do want to go – Bohoo!!!

Last night we danced in the dining room – Lancers with 8 couples – Schottische – Waltz etc – It was jolly –

Now I am afraid you do not believe in the difficulty of our Geological lectures – I will therefore quote a sentence or two to show you. 'Therefore it is perfectly clear that local catastrophic action is not inconsistent with continuity of causation.' Also that the 'strike of beds is at right angles to the dip in the plane of the bedding' etc. etc. etc. etc. etc.

P.S. The excitement tonight was immense. Miss Bettany wore a very pale blue cashmere trimmed with silk, a fan, gold bracelet, snowdrops & heath in head & dress –

Miss Gell who is about 5 feet nothing wore a white lama with snowdrops in a chain all round the square body & on the elbow sleeve & fan & in her hair. She looked a regular little doll – I wished I were a man to dance with her. She takes *ones* in black shoes & stockings – & black gloves 6″. She did look lovely – Miss Prideaux a *long narrer* lady wore a dark green velvet dress – Miss Harrison white silk & gold beads on neck wrists & head. She is very graceful. Miss Richmond wore pink silk with white crocuses – Miss Clough wore grey slate silk so pretty – They are expected home at 12. It is now 11 so goodnight.

D. Ll. G. Jones (Davies, 1877). Extracts from a letter to her family

* Professor Adam Sedgwick had called the girls seeking admission to the Higher Local Examination 'forward minxes'.

AN INCONSPICUOUS STUDENT

In January 1879 I came to Newnham in mingled joy and terror. For two terms I was in lodgings and worked for my Group A. Miss Marion Kennedy had charge of the out-students, and she had placed me in Grantchester Street with a Mrs Steinhilper, the widow of a recent teacher of German in Cambridge. She had a little girl called Ella, to whom I used to read Hans Andersen. I arrived in dark blue French merino on a wintry afternoon and was informed at once that Mr Smith had brought a message from Miss Clough that she would be glad to see me to dinner at six, and that Mr Smith would fetch me and bring me back. Not, I need not say, 'Ignatius', but Mr Jonathan Smith, the Newnham 'man', who did a variety of things including looking after the pigs – for we kept pigs in the early days – and Miss Clough's hens cooped down by where the Chemical Laboratory stood later. His grave is green in Grantchester churchyard. This invitation frightened me very much. But Mrs Steinhilper gave me tea and a globular German pancake, I tied a red ribbon under my turn-down collar, and all in the blue French merino was escorted under those dark elms you know, though now much shorn of their overhanging gloom, and was left ringing at the front-door bell of Newnham Hall.*

Miss Clough was a vision of comfort and great interest. It was because of her name that Newnham and not Girton had become my College. At dinner I sat beside her and she called to sit upon my other side at the end of the High Table (which was just as Miss Dale has it now) the only person that I knew, then Fanny Hoyle, now Mrs Rowe, who said to me, 'Miss Sharpley, the last time we met you were reading Herbert Spencer's *Education*.' She was a school-friend of my cousin, at whose house I had met her, and who had supplied me with that serious treatise. After dinner Miss Clough showed me the pictures on her walls and said, 'That is my brother. He wrote poems', and I think she was pleased to find I knew them. She said she sometimes thought that people did not read them very much, and she may have felt that if they were read in darkest Lincolnshire this could not be so much so as she imagined.

My second term, the May Term, was spent at Crofton Cottages, where Miss Sarah Harland, afterwards Lady Napier Shaw, had charge of half a dozen Newnham out-students. The rooms at the back of the house were exceedingly delightful, looking as they did on the then unravished Grantchester Meadows and the long line of poplars, with Eltisley Avenue still unimagined. In those days Arithmetic was an integral part of Group A of the Higher Local. Miss Harland was a splendid teacher and she got me through that, and in the summer, to my great surprise, I won the Group A scholarship. Scholars had a right to rooms in College, but I did not know that; there was great pressure for entrance into the

* We don't, alas, know the elms any longer: they used to grow south of Old Hall.

Hall and I had every expectation of remaining an out-student. Now Miss Clough, as some of you remember, was sometimes rather *rusée* in a good cause, and she wrote me a kind letter to say that as the list for entrance was a long one and as I was so comfortable at Crofton Cottages she thought I should like to stay there and waive my claim to come into the Hall. How I had the courage I have never known, but I did write and claimed my privilege, and in October I inherited the top floor north room next the bathroom through which you may remember the rope of the Old Hall bell passes and wakes you up remarkably completely. I had many other rooms after that, and I visit them all at night, upstairs and downstairs and in my lady's chamber. Next year the North Hall, now Sidgwick Hall, was opened. I remember going across the road* at the end of my first term to say goodbye to Miss Clough, who with Mrs Sidgwick was walking about upon the planks among the foundations of the new building.

I was an inconspicuous student, very bad at tennis – our only game – but fond of gym, and I could row a little, and once I coxed in 'the scrimmage' in a boat taken down to the races by Mr and Mrs Cox, of Cavendish. I was no doubt horribly studious, but also I had many friends, among them by degrees the resident lecturers, Miss Crofts, Miss Martin and Miss Merrifield. The resident lecturers used to chaperon us at lectures, and it was Miss Crofts (Mrs Frank Darwin) in that capacity who said she must sit at the end of the bench 'to ward off attack and prevent escape'. My first sight of Miss Martin (Mrs James Ward) was of her nursing the Old Hall cat at three o'clock tea in Hall. My chum in all work and in discussion of things in general was Constance Black, now Mrs Edward Garnett, the Russian scholar and translator. I knew some fragments of Latin and Miss Day had started me on the Greek Testament, so when Group A was over I elected to read Classics and was interviewed by Mr Archer-Hind. No thought of a Tripos ever entered my head, or indeed his until later. As I remember the interview he simply asked us each which class we wished to join, Greek I or the more advanced Greek II, the former being an excellent elementary drill administered by Mr Jenkinson while the latter was going to read Aristophanes with Mr Archer-Hind. I voted for *The Frogs* and was thereupon enrolled without test or protest. After that it was pure enjoyment; I was an easy laugher, and the lecturer took great pleasure in 'putting me on' when he saw me giggling helplessly. For you know *The Frogs* is very funny indeed.

* See p. 25.

Later in the year he said, moving his pencil up and down as was his wont, 'Do you know, Miss Sharpley, I think you might think about the Tripos.'

E. M. Sharpley (1879). From the Roll *Letter*, 1930

*

THE SIDGWICKS IN RESIDENCE

In the fall of 1880 when the time came for Newnham College to open, Dr Trumbull, my escort across the Atlantic, took me from Liverpool to Cambridge and established me there. I try to picture what the College was like in those faraway days, so different from what it was in my visit fifty-five years later.

South Hall being full to overflowing, the next step was a companion building across the street. No second Miss Clough was available but the head of the new North Hall must be a person of distinction. Professor and Mrs Sidgwick had been married for four years; so, as there were no children, the problem was solved by their coming to live in tiny quarters in North Hall – a bedroom, a small study for Mr Sidgwick and a large combined living-room and office for Mrs Sidgwick, who became Vice-Principal.*

As I arrived, North Hall was just opening; I remember that we students, at our first breakfast, had to carry down the chairs from our bedrooms. The dining-hall had at one end a High Table at which Mrs Sidgwick sat and to which different students were invited from the four tables which filled the rest of the room. Mr Sidgwick usually sat at her right and it was a joy to hear his talk, like a mountain stream, full and sparkling, pouring along regardless of the nature of its banks. He had a very serious stammer; I recall the remark of one of his friends, 'When the words don't come, you involuntarily finsish the sentence to yourself but always find when he completes it that he has made it better than you could.' He had a fine vein of humour. I remember when I was visiting at their house afterwards and there had been a little dinner party; after all the guests were gone, Mr Sidgwick leaned against the mantel and, balancing himself on one foot upon the coping about the hearth, kept his wife and me intent as he discussed the maladjustment of the universe as evidenced by the fact that when your dress shoes begin to be comfortable they cease to be presentable.

* See Introduction, p. xii.

As I had come to England for a definite purpose, it seemed wiser to take only the subjects that would further my plan. That meant that I could not enter for a Tripos – the examination that crowned and tested the three or four years of work. A preliminary to entrance for the Tripos was a successful passing of the Little-go,* an examination in Classics, Mathematics and Paley's *Evidences of Christianity*. My time was spent entirely on Anatomy, Biology and Physiology. About five years earlier Huxley had succeeded in introducing laboratory work into his course at South Kensington. Dr Michael Foster, dubbed by Huxley 'the Archangel', had been one of his assistants and now was at Cambridge. To him I had written at the suggestion of Mr Agassiz; he justified his name by his kindness to me. It was under his guidance that Huxley's *Elementary Biology* was used in our little stone-floored laboratory at Newnham. I still quiver with cold as I remember those raw days in the laboratory barely tempered by a little grate fire in one corner.

I had a course in the Anatomy of Invertebrates under Mr Frank Balfour, brother of Mrs Sidgwick, and one in Anatomy of Vertebrates under Mr Joseph Lister, a nephew of Sir Joseph Lister, who hoped to follow in his uncle's footsteps. The days were all alike – lectures and laboratory work, varied by a five-mile bicycle spin through Grantchester and Trumpington or, at the proper season, through the Madingley woods for primroses. As Newnham is about fifteen minutes' walk from the centre of Cambridge we were in the midst of open country with hedgerows all about. In the early evenings we had our feeble imitation of the Cambridge Union, or a colourful dance. Those were the days of 'high art', when the vogue among the initiates was for the beautiful silks and velvets to be had from Liberty or from the theatrical supply shop of Burnet. Instead of the prevailing fashions we copied the long graceful lines of costumes in old paintings. I do not expect to see again such rich harmonies of colour and line as now come before my closed eyes.

The only people who meant much to me were Mrs Sidgwick and Miss Gladstone. Mrs Sidgwick I worshipped. She was always remote, as I suppose happily married people are wont to be, and one felt in her the long line of privilege behind her as the sister of Arthur Balfour, then in Parliament and later Prime Minister. She was like an exquisite alabaster

* The Previous Examination (or Little-go) had to be passed by all candidates for Cambridge degrees, either before or after they came into residence; there were papers in Classics, Mathematics, and the doctrine of the Church of England (conveniently embodied in Dr Paley's book). Over the years the examination was modified in many ways (including the acceptance of passes in Local Examinations in lieu of passes in the Previous itself), and it was abolished in 1960.

vase with the soul shining through. I think she came to care for me partly because she divined how very much I cared for her, but we never had the personal chitchat common between friends who are equals. It was during my stay at Newnham that the Society for Psychical Research was formed and we talked often of it and its possibilities. I visited her twice later, once in her Cambridge home in the outskirts and once in her Newnham quarters after she became Principal and had accommodations for guests.

Miss Gladstone was her secretary, and in training to succeed her. She was an open-hearted woman, always eager to talk, not only about the father [then Prime Minister] whom she adored, but about all her relatives and even about family problems. She was younger than Mrs Sidgwick and, while never forgetting her position, she associated with the students much more on terms of equality. I always felt that knowing her enabled me to understand the hold of Mr Gladstone on his constituents. She was aloof to anyone whose mind did not go along with hers in her worship of her father, so sure he was right that she had no comprehension of another point of view. It was a tragedy for her when she was recalled from the Vice-Principalship which she was adorning to take the place at home of her older sister Mary, a very brilliant woman who had married one of the Hawarden curates years younger than herself. Both she and her husband felt after a few years that he could never have a fair chance so long as he was under Mr Gladstone's wing. Her departure meant that the other daughter must come home to relieve her mother. It meant not merely giving up Newnham but going to a home where she was constantly contrasted with Mary whom her parents and others considered her superior. After her father's death, the situation became very trying; the strain over the departure of the family from Hawarden was severe. After the break-up of the family, she took another headship, but it was not successful, and when I last saw her she was living in London alone with her memories.

Some of my happiest late afternoons were spent at the home of Horace Darwin. His wife, only a bit older than I and a most sweet woman, had divined that I was lonely and made me free of her house. At the time between tea and dinner I used often to slip down and have a romp with the little Erasmus, then about two years old. I remember calling there later when he must have been eight or nine. He took me out to see his pigeons and showed me the pride of his heart – a beautiful feather. 'I had a prettier one,' he said, 'but I gave it to my sister because she is a girl.'

It was through that acquaintance that I had an opportunity of seeing

Charles Darwin. He did not come down often during term-time because he feared the strain of seeing his many friends. During my three years at Newnham, he made one exception to his rule and Mrs Darwin asked me to dine with them at that time. I was too careless to write an account of it, but I do recall his humorous account of coming into his dining-room one night after dinner to find his big sons testing the current statement that a wine glass falling to the floor squarely on its rim would not break. Their experiment had not been successful. I remember also a remark that showed his modesty. He had been over to see Mr Gladstone 'and he greeted me just as if he had been one of us'. And another answer, 'Yes, I have patience'.

When he sat down beside me, he asked, as everybody in England had a fashion of doing, if I knew any one in St Louis. My answer – that St Louis was farther from my home in Boston than London was from Constantinople – amused him greatly. And then – it must have been about eight o'clock – his wife said, 'Charles, I think you had better go to bed', and he disappeared.

M. A. Willcox (1880)

THE THREE GRACES

Dear Sir,

Three Graces embodying the proposals of the Syndicate printed below are to be submitted to the Senate at 2.30 P.M. on Thursday, Feb. 24. Although the majority of the speakers in the Arts School on Feb. 11 were favourable, there is likely to be considerable opposition, and it is understood that if this proposal is rejected, it will be rejected not on points of detail, but on grounds which are equally valid against any scheme which has been advocated for extending to women the advantages of education at the University. Further, the rejection of this proposal will not leave women in the same position as before, but will undoubtedly involve the cessation of the existing informal system under which female students are allowed to enter for the University Examinations. The occasion is therefore obviously a critical one for the future of female education, and the attendance and support of those Members of the Senate who have signed memorials in favour of the admission of women to the University Examinations are urgently requested.

J. C. Adams
R. D. Archer-Hind
W. H. Bateson
G. F. Browne
Robert Burn
A. Cayley
E. C. Clark
N. M. Ferrers
W. H. H. Hudson
Henry Jackson
B. H. Kennedy
G. D. Liveing
P. T. Main
J. E. B. Mayor
John Peile
S. G. Phear
G. W. Prothero
Henry Sidgwick
James Stuart
Sedley Taylor
Coutts Trotter

GRACES

CORPUS CHRISTI COLLEGE LODGE. *February* 14, 1881.

At the CONGREGATION on *Thursday*, February 24, at 2.30 P.M., the following Graces, among others, having received the sanction of the Council, will be offered to the SENATE:

1. *That the Report,* dated Dec.* 3, 1880, *of the Syndicate appointed June* 3, 1880, *to consider four Memorials relating to the encouragement to be given to the Higher Education of Women, be confirmed, with the exception of paragraphs* 8 *and* 9.
2. *That paragraph* 8 *of the same Report be confirmed.*
3. *That paragraph* 9 *of the same Report be confirmed.*

N.B. The voting will take place punctually at 2.30 p.m.

* The main recommendations of the Report, confirmed in the first Grace, were that women should be admitted to the Previous Examination and Tripos examinations of the University; that women students should be able to fulfil the conditions of residence at Girton or Newnham colleges, or within the University precincts under the regulations of these colleges, and that certificates of residence issued by Girton and Newnham should be recognised by the University; that class lists of women who satisfied the examiners in the examinations of the University should be published; and that women successful in Tripos examinations should receive certificates to this effect.

Paragraphs 8 and 9 were as follows:

8. That in each Class of female students in which the names are arranged in order of merit, the place which each of such students would have occupied in the corresponding Class of Members of the University shall be indicated.
9. That the Examiners for a Tripos shall be at liberty to state, if the case be so, that a female student who has failed to satisfy them, has in their opinion reached a standard equivalent to that required from Members of the University for the Ordinary B.A. Degree.

Thus it was the passing of the second Grace which made Philippa Fawcett's triumph possible (see p. 33).

⁎

HURRAH! WE HAVE WON!

24 February 1881

I am writing to you now in the interval of awful suspense, for I am so excited I really cannot work. In less than an hour the voting takes place, & none of us can settle our minds to anything else. I daresay to you all this sounds very strange but if you were up here you would be sharing the suspense we are all in. I do not think (from what Miss Morton says) that you understand quite what is to be voted on, so I will expound it for the public benefit. What the Senate is to decide is this – that women who have hitherto been admitted to tripos examinations by the favour of private examiners, are now to be admitted formally, & to receive a formal certificate as to what they have done. I hope you will all read the *University Reporter* I sent home as it has the full discussion in it. If that does not interest you at any rate you will be amused to hear of our efforts. I wrote seven letters & post cards, but that was nothing to what some did. Miss Gladstone wrote 19, & someone else 17, & daily promises of votes have been coming in. Mr Collis is the only one I am certain of, & he is by common consent declared to be 'a dear sweet little man'. (I am sorry to say he is not coming to lunch, but I yet hope he may drop in to tea. This is however irrelevant.) The Vice-Chancellor has been working hard to get up his party. This morning we heard that they are confident of victory. But the devotion of the men to our cause is truly touching. They are coming from gt. distances, St Bees, Sheffield, and Newcastle! And best of all many M.P.s who *must* be in the House to-night are among our advocates. Yesterday we were alarmed by a telegram from Mr Pennington, father of one of our students, & an M.P. to say that there wd. be a division in the H. of Commons this evening wh. he feared wd. prevent many. Therefore Miss Gladstone at once telegraphed, to her father, her brother & Mr Pennington, & Mr Pennington telegraphed back this morning. The result is – *a Special Train* has been put on to take back the M.P.s in time to London. And this is announced in this morning's *Times* under the heading of 'Female Wranglers at Cambridge' – I suppose to attract attention. We shall soon be famous in the eyes of the world, for the *Times* has already devoted two Leading Articles to us, & there will probably be another on us to-morrow or Saturday. The 1st one was ambiguous, the 2nd, that of yesterday was nasty & mean. Mr Sidgwick foamed over it & telegraphed incessantly to people to tell them to come all the same. We have been in two weeks' *Punch*, who is our ardent partisan, but his last joke was silly for it confused Oxford & Cambridge exam terms. Mrs Garrett Anderson has written to the *Times* & to the *Cam. Review* in our favour, so at any rate people will know what is going on. I must stop for a minute. I am going out with Miss Morrison, & under pretence of getting a book, I am going to a shop opposite the Senate House to see the friends & foes in their gowns going to battle. It will be fun!

5 p.m.

Hurrah! we have won! We had 398 against 32 for the 1st Grace, a large majority for the 2nd, & the 3rd was not opposed at all! I must relate to you in order, so that you may have a correct idea. Miss Morrison & I went out and passed down the street leading past the Senate House by accident of course! But we met a number of students doing the same, wh. was strange. I counted every intelligent looking man as a friend. After a few perambulations we called on a lady, & missed the éclat of the great announcement. It was arranged as follows. Mrs Sidgwick's sister Lady Rayleigh was at the Senate House with her pony carriage & was to drive with the news at once. But some of the students had another plan. One was to get the news directly it was out, she then went to Clare Bridge, waved her handkerchief to another on King's Bridge, who signalled to another on horse back, at the back of King's. She then galopped here at once with a white handkerchief tied on the end of her riding whip. Whereupon two others hoisted a flag on our roof, the gong was sounded & every one clapped. For about an hour a crowd of students stood outside the gates, waiting for news about the 2 other graces. The man who brought it was a classical lecturer who had been specially injured by the Vice-Chancellor's speech. We clapped him violently, then when Mr Sidgwick came in sight we clapped still more, & he not knowing the cause ran on into the house, but afterwards waved his hat violently & seemed too delighted to keep still. After that we came into the house & clapped Miss Clough. The men at Ridley got on the roof & surveyed us with amazement thro' eye glasses. I am told the opposition gave up all hope yesterday, & the Vice-Chancellor telegraphed to his men not to trouble. Some did not even care to go to the Senate House, they were so sure of losing, altho' only this morning one of their party predicted certain victory. I believe the scene in the Senate House was too amusing. It was so crowded many could not sit. So they reserved one little spot, & each sat down for a second, gave his vote & jumped up again. They have to vote sitting on a piece *of wood*! We heard the odious Vice-Chancellor had hired all the M.A. gowns, but the procters were all on our side so they must have secured some for our women. When women get the Degrees (for this is only the thin end of the wedge) it will be nothing to this. We all feel it is the great crisis in the history of women's colleges. (If this does not interest you I'll never write to you no more! I think Miss Lizzie Tiddeman wd. like to know all about it, so would you shew her this letter. Many thanks for Mother's this morning. I am glad she is better.)

E. A. Andrews (1879). Letter to her sisters at home

*

A LETTER TO MR A. J. BUTLER*

Dear Sir February 26 1881

Both for ourselves and on behalf of the resident lecturers and students of Newnham College we are anxious to express our gratitude for the trouble you took on Thursday, and the benefit we feel you have done to the cause of woman's education. Could we have foreseen the almost total collapse of the opposition we should of course have begged friends who could only come at great trouble and inconvenience, not to do so.

At the same time we feel not only that that collapse was due to the strength we were perceived to have in the enthusiasm of distant friends, but that the overwhelming majority by which the graces were carried will be of lasting advantage to us in strengthening our position here, and throughout the country.

We are

Yours faithfully
Anne J. Clough
Principal
Eleanor Mildred Sidgwick
Vice Principal

* A former Fellow of Trinity.

*

EPIGRAM ON THE PASSING OF THE GRACES

'The first Grace for admitting women
to the University Examinations was
carried by a majority of 366 to 32.'

The votes by which the ladies won
Were as a Leap Year's days:
A month's brief tale would all but tell
The number of the Nays.
Thus, as the sun in heaven, our cause
Is dear to men of sense:
The adverse tide is little more
Than lunar influence.

Dr Jebb (later Sir Richard Claverhouse Jebb
and Regius Professor of Greek), 1881

*

1881

A COLLEGE WITH STATUS

The first students were pioneers; they were, for the most part, women of mark, who had come up to Cambridge probably with a good deal of difficulty and determination, perhaps even with a vision. Their memory lived on, and I think in South Hall the students felt they were part of the 'haloed' past. Certainly they had Morris papers in their rooms, and were rather Pre-Raphaelite in dress.

At the North Hall things were different. Nearly all the students had come up with a view to getting a job in the teaching profession. There were many of the high-school-girl type, and how they did work! Morning, noon and night. So far from having Morris papers in our rooms we had none at all, just the plaster. I remember Maggie Cobden coming in to see me and looking at the wall, and saying, 'How beautiful.' She was Pre-Raphaelite in dress too.

Mr and Mrs Sidgwick had rooms on the ground floor at the 'going-to-be' garden end. Above, there was Miss Gladstone's room, Mrs Sidgwick's secretary, and above that Miss Martin's, the one and only lecturer in our Hall. Miss Gladstone soon had a group round her, shall we say, of the more serious students. Older than some, she herself was very religious and, to our way of thinking, perhaps mistakenly, tinged the lot.

Miss Martin had two or three friends, perhaps serious in another way, very attractive, and I was handed on to her by Sarah Prideaux and had the run of her room. Miss Martin was a perfectly delightful Irishwoman, delicate and swift in both wit and humour, and so kindly to me, the young intruder. I never felt in the way, or not clever enough. I had another group of friends, Gertrude Bevan, Lilian Sheldon, Lily Radford and Lily Pennington, who were all out for the athletic side of life, and as far as I remember we got the first tennis court going at the North Hall, and very soon had a fair number of others keen to play. Lily Pennington was a really good player; I believe her mother, Mrs Pennington, had been one of the first people to play lawn-tennis at all. The South Hall had a court too, so we played matches with each other, and Mr Arthur Balfour, Mrs Sidgwick's brother, coming on a visit, gave us a cup to be played for between the two Halls (singles). Later, Mr Colman gave us a cup to be played for in the same way (doubles).

My friends and I used to run across to the gymnasium at the South Hall and have great times there. But apart from this there were no outdoor games such as there are now, and of course no bicycles. One might say there was the river. But it was a law, unwritten I think, that students should not go on the river without a chaperon. It was a great temptation; there was the Freshman's River gliding away among the meadows, willows dipping in the water. Lilian Sheldon never would go, she was loyal to the backbone, always. True, one had to pull past the men's bathing sheds, and what might one not see there? When mixed parties went up in a boat together, the ladies were landed just *before* the bathing sheds, and walked round behind. By the time my own daughter went up women students had their own bathing shed, likewise bicycles. I remember once getting Miss Lee, a don at South Hall, to come with us as 'chap' [chaperon] on the Backs. Miss Lee was *not* an oarsman in any sense of the word: she steered. I always liked Miss Lee very much; I believe she knew sixteen languages, one of them Sanskrit, (she said she would teach me Sanskrit if I would learn the alphabet first). Well, we paddled away under the bridges, and then something seized me and I said, 'Let's go through Jesus lock and on for a bit.' Miss Lee consented. We went. I knew well enough all the house-boats would be just beyond the lock, and the men getting into their eights for the afternoon's work. They were. We paddled on, Miss Lee's eyes getting larger and larger it seemed to me. It was such fun, the river crowded with boats, and men shouting and the coach on the towpath. Miss Lee said, 'Don't you think, Miss Dixon, we had better turn round and go back?' 'Certainly, Miss Lee,' I said, and back we went. But we *had* done it.

One reckoned at Newnham to read for a couple of hours after dinner, and then there were gatherings in each other's rooms for cocoa etc. For some reason – I forget what – one changed into a dressing-gown in one's room after dinner. It was very comfortable, anyway.

Sometimes two or three of us would go out for the whole day (with leave no doubt), and go by train to Ely and up on to the Dane's Dyke, where a purple flower grew called Dane's Blood, coloured they said by the blood of the Danes after a battle there. Then lunch, on all the nice unwholesome things we had bought at Smith's. Then the Cathedral. Mrs Paley Marshall describes her day at Ely with Miss Mary Kennedy. She says they climbed the tower in the company of an agreeable young man! Well! We of a later generation were more circumspect, we only went up with the verger, and rang the bell for Vespers.

I never knew, indeed I don't think I ever thought about it at the time, why I was allowed to stay on for three years without taking a Tripos. I think I must have been almost the last student allowed to do so. I suppose in those days there wasn't so much of a queue. Since then the whole system has been more regularised. It was during my time that the 'Three Graces' were passed by the Senate admitting women formally to the examinations.

After that, Newnham and Girton had a distinct status in the University; they were officially acknowledged, their students no longer received instruction and took examinations by the kindness of certain professors (all honour to them), but took their places with the men, and when the results of the examinations were posted up on the Senate House door, the women's names were bracketed with the names of those men they had equalled.* I always considered at the time that Newnham and Girton had been accepted as official colleges of the University. I put it to the test one day. Trinity was giving a concert in the chapel by invitation to members of the University. I and another student made up our minds to go. We streamed through the quad with all the swells, and at the door the verger, or someone in authority, said, 'What college?' 'Newnham,' I said firmly, and we passed in. Perhaps I was right, perhaps, however, the verger wasn't sure, and thought it best to let things go.

One episode of my life at Newnham I must close with. The daffodil had been really accepted as the Newnham flower. Students could be seen any day in spring gathering them in Grantchester Meadows by the river. I don't think a student's room in Newnham was without its bunch of daffodils. One year there was a big function, I forget what, and flowers were needed for the tables and everywhere. Daffodils were over. What to do? A kind professor who lived at the Gogs, and specialised in irises, said he would give us a cartload if we would come and fetch them. His name has quite escaped my memory. Two of us hired a dogcart, drove over to his house, and he filled the cart to overflowing. His daughter was there, afterwards Mrs Rowe, whom I knew in later years. We drove back in triumph, the irises were a huge success and superseded the daffodil, becoming the Newnham flower. Some years later I went up to Cambridge again for a Newnham function, and was met there by a young student with a basket of irises. She offered me one, saying, 'The iris is the Newnham flower you know.' I received it with smile and thanks, but thought to myself 'sic transit'.

K. M. Rathbone (Dixon, 1880)

* See note, p. 17.

1884

THE MAKING OF SIDGWICK AVENUE

I have been commanded to write something for the *Letter*, and I am told that this something may suitably consist of my recollections of the College during the various stages in which I have known it. I am afraid they will be very random recollections and that I shall be sure to leave out the most important and interesting things and to talk too much about things that everyone knows. Still I must do as I am told and try.

I will begin with very early recollections indeed, before Newnham was Newnham and long before I was a student. I became acquainted with the infant College in the Long Vacation of 1873, when it was two years old and was established at Merton Hall, a most attractive rambling old house, of which there is a picture in Miss Gardner's history of the College. The house is still there at the end of the Backs, tucked away out of sight behind walls and cottages, sitting in its large old garden which runs down from the road to the ditch which is the boundary of St John's on the west side. One can peer in through the slatted door in the wall on the road or look across St John's ditch, but otherwise it is quite hidden. It was a very nice place for a summer holiday; the garden was full of gooseberries and currants, and a great deal of jam-making went on alongside of the studies of the few students who were up. I remember that among these few were Miss Creak, the great Miss Creak of King Edward's, Birmingham, and Mrs R. T. Wright – then Miss Mary Kennedy – with both of whom we were privileged to play croquet. I remember one thing concerned with the future College, and that is driving up with my aunt to see the proposed site of the building which was then being thought of. We drove up past Professor Liveing's house [The Pightle, Newnham Walk] to a field gate which I suppose was about where the letter-box now is, and looked into a large grass field – the space now occupied by the College buildings and garden.

When I next came to Cambridge Newnham Hall was built and well established. I came up two or three times before I became a student, in order to take Groups of the Higher Local, and finally in the May Term of 1884 I was taken in for some weeks to prepare for the last Group for my certificate, the once celebrated Group C, Mathematics. I always held that the examiners must have mixed up my papers with someone else's, as this alone could account for my having passed, but anyhow, my name appeared in the list and all was well.

Of course recent generations hardly know what the Higher Local was, but to many earlier generations it bulked very large indeed. Hardly anyone in the earlier days took the Little-go. The Higher Local was a better examination, and if you never got as far as a Tripos the Higher Local certificate was something solid to put in your pocket, and in those days was a valuable qualification. It was not essential then to complete your preliminaries before coming to College, and therefore wretched Language people struggling to pass in Mathematics and miserable Mathematicians fainting over their French were a painfully common spectacle.

It was in October 1884 that I formally entered College as a student (I came up intending to stay one year). There were then only the Old Hall and Sidgwick Hall, then called South Hall and North Hall, and the North Hall had just got its west wing and thirteen extra students. My aunt was Principal and presided in the South Hall, and Miss Gladstone was Vice-Principal, in charge of the North Hall. Miss Sharpley and Miss Gardner were lecturers in the South Hall, and Miss Marshall was my aunt's secretary. In the North Hall were Miss Jane Lee and Miss Collier, and Miss Gladstone's secretary Miss French.

There was one outward feature of those times which made a very great difference indeed, namely the public way which ran between the two Halls and cut the garden into two parts. This road continued what is now called Newnham Walk past where the archway now is, and ended at a point about opposite to the Clough Hall front door. There it became a footpath between thorn hedges, the line of which is still marked by the older thorn trees in front of Peile Hall. The lime trees opposite Clough Hall were young trees then, hanging over the wooden paling on one side of the road, and on the other side was a wall, the traces of which can still be seen in the dry turf in hot summers. Sidgwick Hall was divided from the road by a low wall and iron railing, and Old Hall by big wooden gates at the end of the wall. Sidgwick Avenue did not exist, and the only driving way to the College was by Malting Lane. There were only 100 students then instead of over 200, but it may be imagined that at the beginnings and ends of terms many difficulties arose in that narrow channel.

Many members of the Roll will remember this state of things, but it is thirty years, more than half the life-time of the College, since it came to an end, so I hope I may be forgiven for describing it and for calling up the horrid picture of what the College would have been if it had continued to consist of two gardens with buildings on each side of the road. And I can't resist telling about the great struggle which was needed to bring about this vital change.

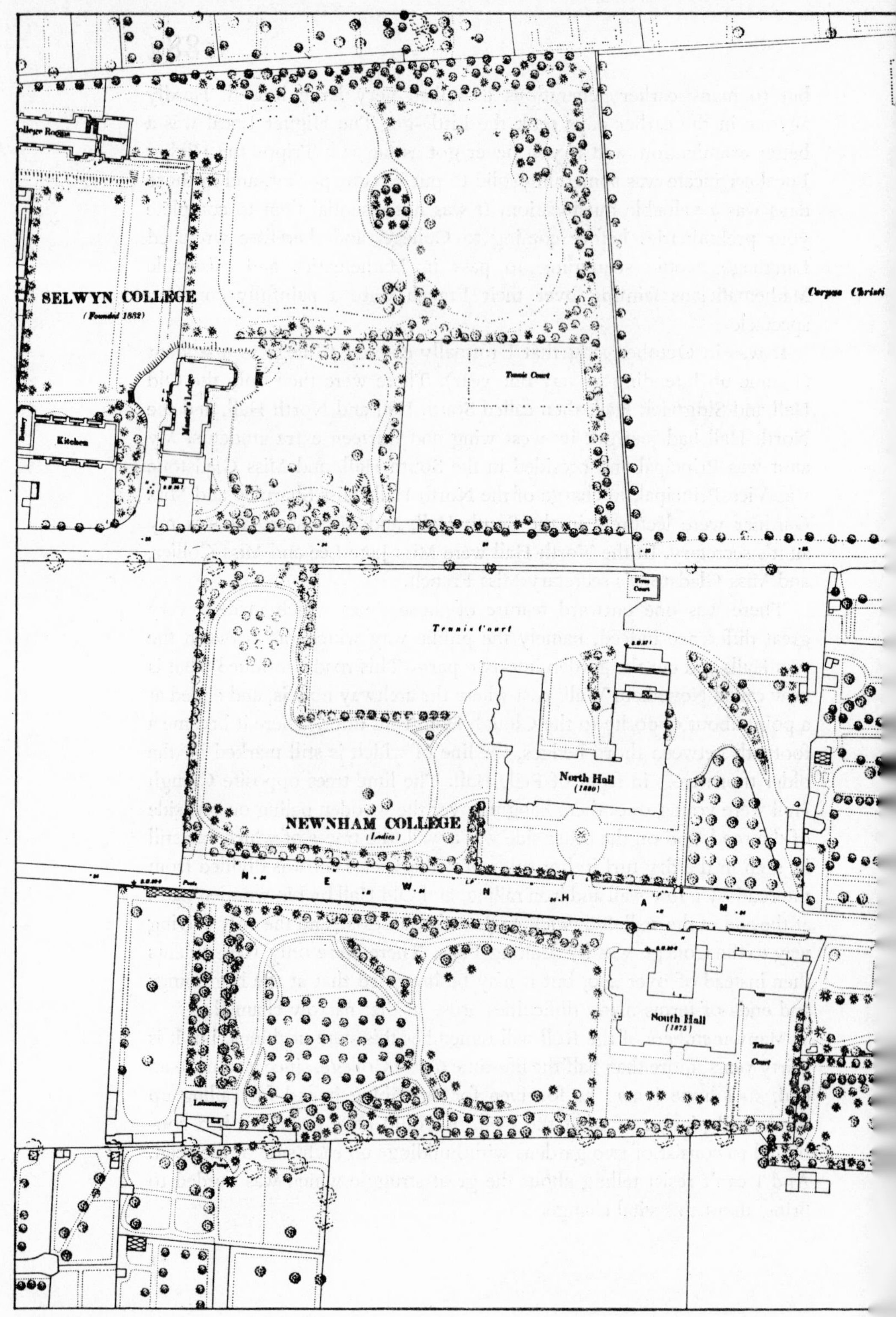
SELWYN COLLEGE
(Founded 1882)
Kitchen
Master's Lodge
Tennis Court
Corpus Christi
Fives Court
Tennis Court
North Hall
(1880)
NEWNHAM COLLEGE
(Ladies)
N E W N H A M
South Hall
(1875)
Tennis Court

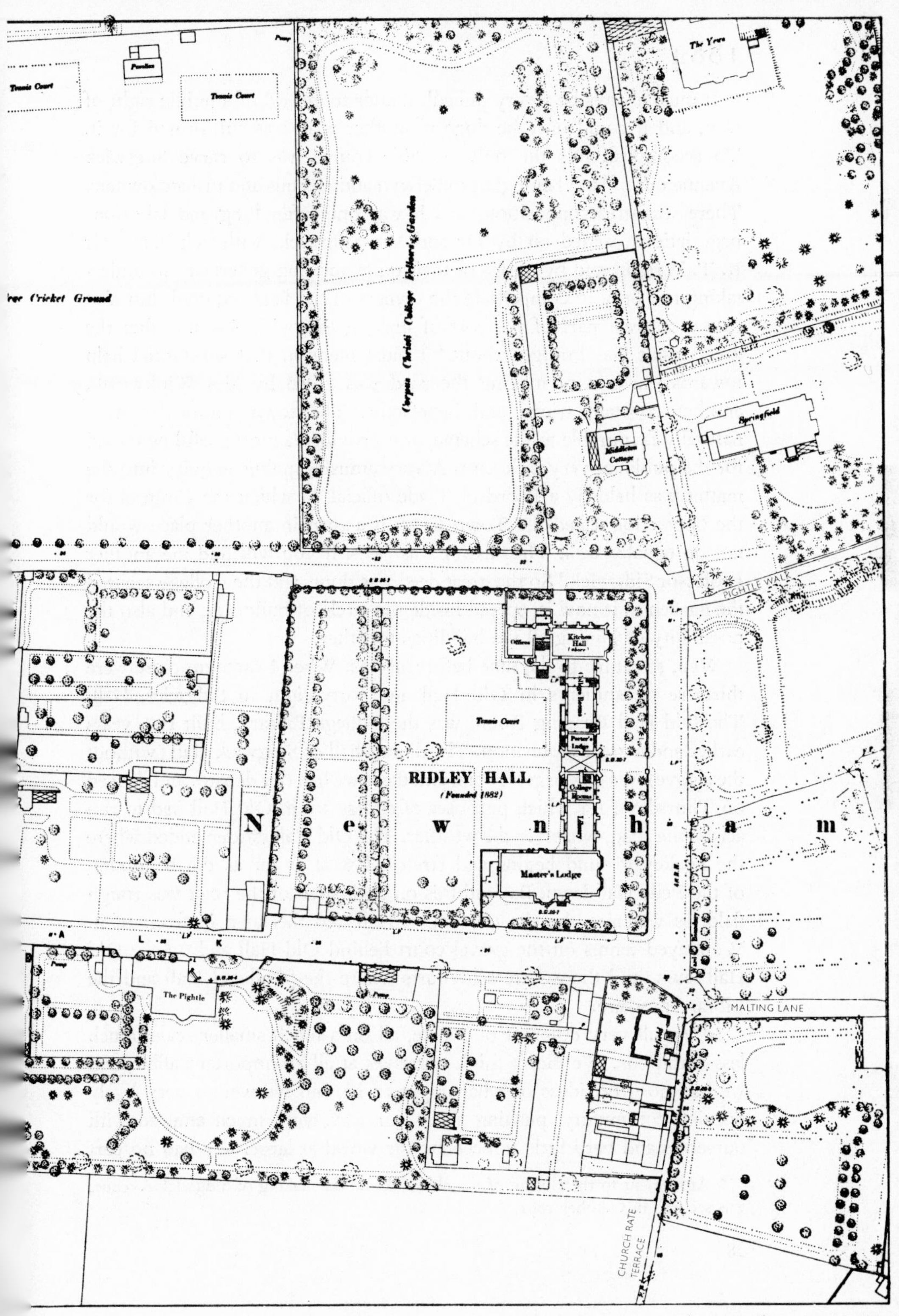

The Newnham area, 1888

It must always be a very difficult matter to get rid of a public right of way, and it could only be done if another road was substituted for it. To accomplish this the only possible course was to carve Sidgwick Avenue out of land belonging to Selwyn and Corpus and private owners. There was great opposition, and it was only after long and laborious negotiations carried on by Dr and Mrs Sidgwick, with help from Mr R. T. Wright, and by means of their quite amazing generosity in undertaking not only to compensate the owners of the land required, but also to pay a great part of the cost of making Sidgwick Avenue, that the great result was brought about.* I must mention that substantial help towards the cost of making the road was given by Mrs Winkworth, another constant friend and benefactor. The town authorities were naturally favourable to the scheme, as it provided a most useful new road for the public at very little cost. A very amusing public enquiry into the matter was held by a Board of Trade official, at which the Counsel for the opposition asked the Town Clerk if a road in another place would not do equally well. The answer was 'Yes, if you will find me another Professor Sidgwick.' So the great deed was done, and the College secured the garden as it now is, spread inside the circle of buildings, and also the possibility of joining all the buildings together.

Well, to return to the time before all this. When I came up there were thirty-seven students in Old Hall and forty-eight in Sidgwick Hall. The Old Hall Reading Room was the College Library, built two years earlier and a great acquisition. The dining-hall of Sidgwick Hall (without the alcove) was our largest room, and there we had our debates and danced on Thursdays, for which purposes of course we in Old Hall had to run across the road, whatever the weather. The Old Hall garden ended where the hockey ground begins and stretched west as far as the beginning of the Peile Hall lawn. Beyond this on both sides of the road was rough field, as was also the site of Clough Hall and the lawn in front of it. We played tennis on the gravel court behind Old Hall and on the Old Hall lawn, and there were ash courts where the [College] Hall and the Library now are.

It was all very different of course, all on a much smaller scale, much less ambitious. We didn't think ourselves at all an important affair, and we had no great ideas of what ought to be, but we were a very lively buzzing community, pushing along our way, very much amused with ourselves and very little noticed by the world at large. We had no part

* Agreement to the closing of the old road, and the making of Sidgwick Avenue, was secured in October 1891.

or lot in University societies except the Ladies' Discussion Society and I think C.U.M.S. I think there must have been very many fewer University societies then, and in any case the University generally were hardly aware of our existence. But we ran our own societies very vigorously; we were very keen about our debates, which seemed to me then and for many years after I had ceased to be a student to be almost always stirring and stimulating occasions even if there was not a great deal of eloquence displayed. The Political Society was started in my first term and was an immediate success. It almost at once took the form of a Parliament, with Speaker and Government and Opposition and members for constituencies, and for twenty years and more it flourished like a particularly green bay-tree. One of the Newnham *Letters* I see describes it as 'the absorbing interest of all the competent'. Much time and thought was spent by members of the Government in preparing bills and by the Opposition in discovering their weak points. We learnt to be familiar with parliamentary procedure, and we learnt a good deal about public questions. We were full of zeal and fury and fought joyfully and hard. On occasions when a close vote was expected everyone in the College was canvassed hotly and the Whips have been known to drag absentees out of their beds to vote. Miss Gladstone never attended the meetings in case her presence should be embarrassing sometimes, but on particular occasions she was induced by the Liberal Whip to sit in some near spot and was brought in when the division came. The Political was a very good training ground, and five of the candidates at the last election began their political life there – Mrs Corbett Ashby, Mrs Dimsdale, Mrs Hamilton, Miss Susan Lawrence and Mrs Strachey. It is amusing to remember that Miss Susan Lawrence, who has been returned to Parliament as Labour member for East Ham North, was Conservative Prime Minister in her Newnham days.

I have said that the University generally were hardly aware of our existence, but there was a little band of very distinguished University people who were our constant friends and helpers, as members of the Council and of our committees, as lecturers and otherwise. I hope it will always be remembered that the College was founded by members of the University and the wives and daughters of members of the University, and grew up under their hands. I should like to mention and talk about them all, but there are too many, and there would be too much to say.

When Clough Hall was built in 1888 and we had another fifty students and a real College Hall which would hold us all, the College began, as it seems to me, to be a good deal more like what it is now. Three

Halls seem so much more than two, and when there was also a common meeting place the whole thing was drawn together and became clearly one community. Up to that time we had to have our Commemoration dinner and speeches in two parts, though we met afterwards and danced in Sidgwick Hall. The supper on trestle tables in the new Hall on the evening after it had been opened by the then Prince of Wales was our first real College Feast. There were numbers of Old Students there, and Professor and Mrs Adams and Professor and Mrs Caley looked down on us from the gallery.

By this time I had ceased to be a student, and had been appointed secretary to my aunt, who moved across from Old Hall to Clough Hall in 1888. I remember that when we were preparing for the students to come in at the beginning of the Michaelmas Term I showed my competence for my new duties by counting wrong, and leaving one room unfurnished and one student (it was Miss Neroutsos) without a room. It was discovered a few hours before she arrived, and she found a bed and other necessaries. I never knew whether she thought her room rather unfinished in appearance.

B. A. Clough (1884). From the Roll *Letter*, 1924

THE KINDEST OF KIND CREATURES

Tuesday, 13 October 1885
Your letter the other day was a great solace – I read it by the sitting-room fire, whither I generally repair after breakfast until my room has got quite warm and comfortable.* Our letters are laid out on a table in the dining-room, where also is kept the book in which we have to mark ourselves as present. On Sundays we are marked at all three meals, I suppose that if I was absent at two an enquiry would be made, if at the third I was still absent a telegram would be despatched to you to ask if I had run away! Miss Clough is the kindest of kind creatures. The other night she lectured the students in her room on being late for Prayers, and then whispered to me '*You* needn't come down punctually, a quarter or half-past eight will do *quite* well for you!' As you can imagine, I am only too glad to take the extra quarter of an hour in bed in the morning!

* Miss Seebohm was ill during her short time at Newnham and died in December 1885.

We may be as late as nine, but of course it is preferred that we should appear at Prayers.

Tonight nearly everybody has gone across to the North Hall to a debating meeting. At the end of dinner Miss Clough rang her little bell and then said she hoped all students going to it would wrap up thoroughly this cold night and that those who had colds would not go at all. Then fearing lest I should not class myself in that category, she waited for me outside and said '*You* won't go, Miss Seebohm'. Yesterday as I was coming out from lunch she called me back and said 'Now Miss Seebohm dear, you aren't going to work, are you?' 'No, Miss Clough, not just yet.' 'I should take a little rest after lunch, if I was you'. Which is what I always do. She also always either comes herself or sends a message by an old [probably third-year] student to know last thing whether I am feeling alright for the night – I am generally preparing my bed when she comes.

Getting to bed is a matter of some time here. The sofa has to be converted into a bed, the cushions changing their hue from red to white; the bureau has to be cleared for a dressing-table, and books, blotter and pens exchanged for brush and comb, hair-pins etc; the screen has to be removed from the washstand, and the towel-horse brought forth from its obscurity; and lastly the easy chairs have to be pushed against the walls to make room for the bath, which is brought in in the morning by a feminine duplicate of the lazy, cat-faced violinist of our Maloja band. To give you some idea of my days here, I will describe one to you in detail.

Tomorrow will be spent as follows, if all is well: I shall be called at 7.30, and go down to 8.15 breakfast, cocoa-tin in hand. If Miss Clough does not ask me to sit by her when I say Good-morning, I shall go down near the other fire, making my cocoa at the coffee stand. Then I shall mark myself in the book and look for my letters (and I hope there will be one!). At nine, muffled in several coverings, I shall run across to the North Hall for Miss Gardner's lecture on Constitutional History, *which* I don't care for much yet. I shall be back in my room soon after ten, and shall light my fire, get out my books, *take my medicine*, and sit down or recline with my books till twelve. Then I shall take some Brand's Beef (unless Mrs Marshall orders me milk and bread and butter downstairs) and go to Prof. Seeley's lecture on Political Philosophy. Hugh will be there, and I think of having lunch with *him* tomorrow. When I get back I shall rest, and go to 3.30 tea (or rather cocoa for me) with Margaret Powell. From four till six I read to myself or write my papers, and dinner is at 6.30 after which I do no work. At nine I make cocoa and am well in bed by ten. I have one lecture on Mondays and Fridays, and two on Tuesdays, Wednesdays and Thursdays, and none on Saturdays. Prof. Seeley's on Wednesdays are the only ones in the town. Most are with Miss Gardner, so I hope I shall like her better soon. Three times a week Constitutional History, and twice a week French History for which I am not going to read unless I have time begging. Twice a week Political Economy with Mrs Marshall, and I don't know yet how much work she requires, because she has a bad cold at present and cannot lecture.

Tuesday, 20 October 1885

You *should* see Miss Gardner's get-up – droopy straw hat, shetland shawl thrown on without any grace, and big heel-less felt slippers in which she shuffles along. Then she evidently uses no mirror for her toilet, for this morning she came down with the ends of her hair sticking straight out like a cow's tail – she drags it back tight, twists it and sticks one hair pin through. The style of dress here is certainly *not* elegant – tho' I have hope for the future as most of the new students are neat and ordinary. Meta* and I count the numbers of turned-down lace and stays – the former are numerous, the latter scarce.

Wednesday, 21 October 1885

Harriet is becoming a very devoted attendant, and asks me now when she calls me what sort of night I have had and whether she shall bring my breakfast up. She amuses me immensely – she is too well-mannered to speak unless I address her first, but if I begin she is very loquacious, and pours out her troubles with Miss Tuke who is continually breaking her lamp chimneys. Harriet thinks she will be quite ruined if she goes on breaking three in a fortnight. She quite alarmed Meta by this suggestion so that Meta enquired humbly how much they cost – and learnt to her infinite relief and amusement, twopence each!

Mrs Marshall was as nice as before this morning, but she has given us a fearful paper to write – four long questions and we mayn't read up about them nor will she tell us anything about them till afterwards, we are to answer them from our own Common Sense and by thinking them out for ourselves. Happily she doesn't mind a bit whether our conclusions are right or wrong so long as we *do* think them out to some conclusion. So this afternoon I have been sitting down to *think* for two hours, but alas I can reason most of them to two exactly opposite conclusions – a sadly unnecessary fertility of brain I have got!

* Meta Tuke, later Lecturer in French at Newnham and Principal of Bedford College.

Friday, 30 October 1885
Oh! just think, I have broken two lamp chimneys! Meta is beginning to crow, but Harriet says I couldn't help it!

We all went across after dinner to the North Hall, the room was full. All the proceedings were amusingly formal and solemn. Miss Rickett was in the chair and looked so nice in a yellow silk frock. But oh dear! I *wish* I could describe the costumes to you! You never saw anything like it in your life! It might have been a fancy dress evening. Why can't I draw like Judy? The miserable attempts at Greek robes and hygienic dresses – I hope my new Sunday frock is being made *very* neat and fitting – that is all I am particular about in it – nothing slouchy, bunchy or draggledy about it, *please*!

W. Seebohm (1885)

Extracts from letters to her sisters at home, reprinted from *A Suppressed Cry* by Victoria Glendinning

P. G. FAWCETT*

Hail the triumph of the corset
Hail the fair Philippa Fawcett
Victress in the fray
    Crown her queen of Hydrostatics
    And the other Mathematics
Wreathe her brow with bay.

If you entertain objections
To such things as conic sections
Put them out of sight
    Rather sing of the essential
    Beauty of the Differential
Calculus tonight.

Worthy of our approbation
She who works out an equation
By whatever ruse
    Brighter than the Rose of Sharon
    Are the beauties of the square on
The hypotenuse.

* In 1890 in Part I of the Mathematical Tripos P. G. Fawcett was placed 'above the Senior Wrangler'.

Curve and angle let her con and
Parallelopipedon and
Parallelogram
    Few can equal, none can beat her
    At eliminating theta
By the river Cam.

May she increase in knowledge daily
Till the great Professor Cayley
Owns himself surpassed
    Till the great Professor Salmon
    Votes his own achievements gammon
And admires aghast.

Anon. *c.* 1890

COLLEGE FOOD

12 October 1889

My kettle and candlesticks came up yesterday; the College supply us with one reading lamp but of course that isn't very much for two people to work by. I have already invested in candles and I am going out to get tea and sugar this afternoon. I have also bought a box of shortbread; one gets rather hungry at half past nine and no one goes to bed before half past ten or eleven – in fact I believe that from 10 to 11 is the great hour for coffee parties, but I think the reasonable people prefer those entertainments from 3.30 to 4.30.

I boiled some water for my hot water bottle last night and had great fun over it; I do not understand the management of a kettle and the wretched thing boiled over and made an awful smell.

15 October 1889

I had a latin lecture today; I forgot the lecturer's name, but I didn't think much of him. We only construed a chapter of Livy, and as we shall have to do eight chapters a week to get through the book, it didn't seem much good. I am working hard at my Greek, both Grammar and Testament; I spend about three hours a day at it; in fact I did a whole chapter of St Matthew today. I am also struggling with Jevons' Elementary Logic. The Chemistry is nothing like so interesting as the Electricity at College [University College, Liverpool]; but I think the lectures are fairly good; the worst part is the undergraduates who talk incessantly the whole time.

The food is distinctly not good, everyone is agreed on that; the puddings are practically untouchable, the preserved stewed fruit is often fermented, the meat is sometimes raw and generally semi-tepid; vegetables few and far between; people say they only give us what is grown in the garden; these are for the most part turnips.

No one goes to bed before 10.30, and the baths which are next my bedroom, go on till about eleven; luckily they don't disturb me much. I have now made my bed fairly comfortable with rugs and pillows; it only wanted a little careful adjusting. Our working hours are 9 to 12, 3 to 6 and 8 to 10; three days a week I am only back at 1.20; so between that and three I get in lunch and a walk. Of course we can take any hours we like for work, only at the stated hours the house is kept quiet and that makes a great difference; besides one is liable to have interruptions from callers; and it is not etiquette for freshers to put up 'engaged' on their doors.

24 October 1891

We are going to hold a dancing class in the big Hall on Tuesdays. To our dismay we discovered about half the freshers cannot even waltz. We are to begin by teaching them their steps all round the room, and about twelve or fourteen have already applied although we only stuck up the notice this afternoon. I shouldn't be surprised if we had from twenty to thirty pupils in the end; I rather fancy myself doing Mme Michan. You will be shocked to hear that I have succeeded in introducing the Kitchen Lancers and the Pas de Quatre; the latter was an immense success and was danced last Thursday with furore. I have instructed about ten people and taught another person the music, so that one may see some twenty to thirty couples prancing up and down the room. It is an awfully funny sight; people in all sorts of garments and of all sizes hopping and skipping round the room; and appealing to me to settle the relative merits of various kinds of kicks and jumps.

3 December 1891

I am suffering from the effects of two bumper suppers. Our team carried off the Hockey cup on Saturday after a tremendous fight, by 1 goal to nil. I never played in a harder or faster game. On Sunday we gave ourselves a tea; Monday evening Miss Thena Clough entertained us, and we went on with speeches and cheering till half past eleven or twelve. Last night the Sidgwick team and Miss Gladstone gave us a supper, and we had more speeches and then songs and finally cheered ourselves hoarse and separated at a very late hour.

1892

18 May 1892

Those hateful Tripos Exams began today – and will continue to the end of term. Helen Chamberlain has three days this week and three about a fortnight hence. The Mathematical is fearfully hard work; the poor victims are very much exhausted after their papers. I took Helen down to both papers; the Exam: is held in the Hall of the Y.M.C.A. and a most objectionable 'legend' runs round the ceiling – 'If thou do well, the pain fades, the joy remains. If ill, the joy fades, the pain remains.' – I can't imagine anything more dispiriting for Exam: purposes. Miss Scott begins on Saturday and continues through the beginning of next week. We have elaborate feeding arrangements; administering soup before hall each night, and giving victims a good supper. We have just got a cold roast chicken from the pastry cook's and eke it out with asparagus or tomatoes which I boil. On the whole, the College food is less sufficient than ever this term.

C. D. Dampier (Holt, 1889).

Reprinted from *Letters from Newnham College, 1889–1892*

A RAG DANCE

Having been entered for Girton, I decided to go to Newnham, as the result of a talk given by Miss A. J. Clough to the sixth form of the high school I attended. So I went up in March 1892 for an entrance exam and having passed (*not* with honours) I went up for the May Term to Newnham. Some time previous to my entrance exam Miss Clough had died and practically all the College was in mourning. My sister and I stayed in rooms in Newnham Village but went to Hall at Sidgwick, where Miss Gladstone was Vice-Principal. The ground was covered with deep snow, there was no street lighting and we were given lamps to light us along the way. Everybody was most kind to us. I longed to go to Sidgwick Hall but it was full up, so I landed in Old Hall. Miss J. Lee was Vice-Principal there and I got very fond of her.

We were very decorous in those times – lights out at *10 p.m.* on landings etc.; all students in their own rooms, and no further activities.

We had a rag dance occasionally, with a prize for the most original outfit. I remember that Miss Gladstone went as 'Cambridge Butter' in a crackerlike appearance of some yellow stuff – and caused great amusement by dancing with one of the dons, Miss Collier, I believe, who had got herself up as a loaf. Miss Gladstone was tall* and the other very dumpy.

In Clough Hall there was a unique occasion, when Lady Ulrica Duncombe was allowed to have her maid in the room next to hers.

Anon. *c.* 1892

* Cambridge butter used to be sold by length.

A CHANGE OF FRONT

I am glad that the last touch to the beauty of this College is one of which no lapse of time is likely to mar the appropriateness. Nothing seems more unchangeable than a great building: Mr Champneys* and we know by experience that the aspect of a building can vary with circumstances. Newnham has twice executed that often fatal manoeuvre – a change of front. The beautiful front of the Old Hall looks now, not as we expected, upon busy streets, but on quiet fields. The avenue which preserves another name which will live in the memories of Newnham, does not command the most attractive view of either of the other Halls. But the new gateway can hardly be turned inside out.

Dr Peile, Master of Christ's College

Extract from a speech at the presentation of the Clough Memorial Gates in Newnham Walk, 3 November 1894

* Basil Champneys, designer of the Clough Memorial Gates, was the College's architect for all the earlier buildings (up to and including Peile).

WOMEN ON SUFFERANCE

We had to go up a few days before term began in order to take Little-go. There were so few in residence the first night that at dinner we all sat at the High Table in Old Hall and we were overwhelmed with awe when we found ourselves sitting opposite Miss Helen Gladstone and Miss Philippa Fawcett. At that time Mr Gladstone was a legendary figure and his little grand-daughter, Dorothy Drew, was almost as well known, and to hear Miss Gladstone talking familiarly of her home and of Dorothy, who had just been given a tricycle, seemed marvellous! I don't remember much of Miss Fawcett's conversation, but it must have had some connection with going abroad, for I remember her mention of Boulogne as:

'You know, that place we can none of us pronounce.' I felt she was quite human even if she had been 'above the Senior Wrangler'.

Cambridge in October was a revelation of autumn beauty such as a girl from industrial Lancashire had not seen before. The golden tints of the trees in the Backs, the scarlet Virginia creeper covering a wall of Clare and the clear light over all, are a most lovely memory.

Women students in Cambridge were there at that time more or less on sufferance. We were allowed to take the Tripos examinations, but we had no status as undergraduates and were not granted a degree. We were given certificates to show that we had passed the Tripos examination and had resided in College the required number of terms, so that if and when degrees were granted we should be qualified to receive them. Many members of the University disapproved of women's colleges and of higher education for women generally, so the authorities of Newnham and Girton liked us to be as unobtrusive as possible. We did not take much part in the life of the University, and we suffered many restrictions. We were asked always to wear gloves in the town (and of course hats!); we must not ride a bicycle in the main streets, nor take a boat out on the river in the day-time unless accompanied by a chaperon who must be either a married woman or one of the College dons. In the May Term we could be on the river in the early morning, without chaperon, between the hours of six and nine, and as some of my friends were keen on rowing we often left the Silver Street boathouse soon after six o'clock, rowed down to Baitsbite where we had breakfast, and were back in College by nine o'clock. It was very lovely gliding along the Backs past Queens', Clare, King's, John's, Trinity, etc., under the beautiful bridges in the quiet of an early summer morning. During the Long Vacation we could go on the river at any time unchaperoned and we had several lovely long days taking lunch and tea with us, idling along quiet backwaters. When we watched the Lent and May Races on the river we were not supposed to go on the towing path, but to stand in the meadows on the opposite side.

We were not allowed to entertain any men friends in our own rooms. When fathers or brothers visited us, we could give them tea, but could not invite any of our friends into our room to meet them, not even if our mother were there as well. Smoking was forbidden and so were amateur theatricals in term-time; but acting was allowed in the 'Long'. I remember I was 'a simple village maiden' in a pink cotton frock and a sun-bonnet with my hair streaming down my back, in a play we acted in the gymnasium in the Long of 1898. Winifred Cullis (later famous as a Professor and Doctor of Science) and Ida Smedley (afterwards Dr

Smedley-Maclean, a well-known research Chemist) were respectively the hero and villain of the piece and fought a duel on the stage in my honour. They also wrote the play.

I was a keen hockey player and we had to wear navy blue serge skirts that must come down to within twelve inches of the ground, to hide our legs as much as possible. Tennis was played in long white piqué skirts that almost touched the ground. But I have never seen better women's hockey than was played at Newnham in the years from 1896 to 1899. These restrictions did not trouble us much; they were all part of the general Victorian attitude to women, and College life was full of interest and in many ways was a very free life in comparison with our home life.

Mrs Sidgwick's mother was a sister of the Lord Salisbury who was Queen Victoria's highly respected Prime Minister, and her brother was Arthur Balfour, a later Prime Minister. She herself was quiet and unassuming, but had the poise and unselfconscious dignity of a great lady. Arthur Balfour often visited her at Newnham and I have a vivid memory of seeing him and Dr Sidgwick walking along the Backs, Mr Balfour tall, willowy and silent, and little Dr Sidgwick trotting along talking most volubly. Dr and Mrs Sidgwick were two of the best friends Newnham ever had, giving generously of time and money. Once a term each student was supposed to pay an afternoon call on Mrs Sidgwick, and in our third year we were each invited at least once to breakfast with them. Dr Sidgwick had a slight stammer: he used it with great effect when telling a funny story, stammering just before coming to the point.

Miss Gladstone had great personal charm and was well beloved. On the first morning of the Tripos examination she presented to each of us a sprig of sweet-briar from the hedge in Newnham garden planted either by Miss Clough or in memory of her – I am not sure which. There were nightingales in the garden in those days and sometimes in the May Term their music went on until dawn.

I had read very little Latin and Greek when I went up, and my tutor, Miss Sharpley, suggested that I should find the work for either the Modern Languages or History Tripos easier, but my Lancashire obstinacy (or grit) refused to acknowledge defeat. I often worked late. Once a term Classics students had to write an English essay to be corrected by one of the University dons, and it must be given in before 9 a.m. on a certain day. There was a pillar-box in Newnham which was cleared at 2.30 a.m., and letters posted before then were delivered at breakfast-time in Cambridge. My essays were usually posted about 2.25 a.m.!

C. Crowther (Kenyon, 1896)

*

1898

AN ENDLESS FOUNTAIN

I went up to Newnham in 1898, absolutely ignorant of the ways of the world, with no inhibitions, and a happy home behind me. It seemed delightful to me to be going to study English Literature, which I thought of as a compound of delightful tales, plays and romances:

> An endless fountain of immortal drink
> Pouring unto us from the heaven's brink.

On my second night sitting by my little fire in a top north room in Sidgwick Hall, I was startled by a loud knock on the door. The visitor told me she had come to take me to a Secret Meeting of First-Year Students! Lights were out and we traversed a lot of dark passages and finally reached a room where a handful of young women were standing about. The door was fastened and a tall gangling kind of girl began to speak. She was very plain and badly dressed and seemed to have a grievance against life. It was agreed that we first-year students would be kept in our place and that we needed an association to protect ourselves. Other speakers also urged that we should stir up other members to resist all kinds of aggression at the hands of Authority. All this was very seriously discussed and we were called upon to sign a portentous-looking but grubby document with our blood. I heard the whole business with astonishment and distaste. I pricked my finger but could not produce a single spot of blood. However, I promised to write a poem for the magazine which was to be produced.

Having no personal injury to write about I resolved on a poetic ancient history of a nun immured in the wall of an old convent. Nothing else happened except that a very thin little magazine, handwritten, appeared on the tables beneath the notice-boards in all the Halls, a few days later.

When lectures began my love of tales and romances was fully satisfied by the lecturer in English Literature who talked to us twice a week in a dark old lecture room near the Cam. He was a very untidy and what I thought an elderly man, with a bald patch on his head. When he spoke he seemed to me to have access not only to Elizabethan literature but to the enchanting lands of Oberon and Titania, of Balder and Arthur. It was the custom of the students who wished to ask a question to put a little note on his desk – anyone who did so was called up after the lecture and given an answer. One day I ventured to do this; my question was answered quickly and I volunteered the information that I had found a beautiful book which I was reading in a top cubicle of the Old Library. It was a child's Book of Saints. He was much interested and said it was written by one of his own friends and would I like him to borrow it for me. The next week he arrived with the book, which contained the stories of the ancient Valorous Saints and adventures of the old Celtic World. So began a friendship with Israel Gollancz who was a liberally-minded Jew, later to become Sir Israel Gollancz and a bright star in the intellectual firmament. He left Cambridge shortly afterwards, but remained my friend until his death and gave me many rare and beautiful books. He was only thirty-three years old when I first met him.

Society at Newnham in my day was formed of small circles from the big public schools (one of which I myself had come from); they held together and were watchful of one another's interests. There were a few students who had never been to school at all, but had been educated at home. We had only one American girl, whose slender education and immense self-reliance caused us to wonder. There were more students studying Natural Science than there were Arts students. A few odd individuals from the North seemed to have no scholastic connection. We also had a few aristocrats. They never stayed for long or took a Tripos but were ornamental.

The dons were interesting. There was Miss B. A. Clough who was reported to walk about the corridors at night smoking (a thing strictly forbidden to all) and often overhearing discussions which were going on at cocoa-parties. Another lady was a complete enigma, my tutor in French, little Miss Tuke. She it was who encouraged me to write a French play and offered a prize for an English sonnet, which I won. Once she took me to a concert – this was at St John's College. A nice-looking undergraduate sat on my left and offered me a programme and chatted a little, but Miss Tuke availed herself of the interval to separate us.

Miss Steele Smith was a very quiet person who taught the dull subject of Mediaeval German grammar. I got to know her after visiting her one night when she was ill. Her profound knowledge of German was due to family circumstances. Her father, a Unitarian minister, was thrust out of his community for heresy and went with his boys and girls to live in Germany, where they all enjoyed a good education at no expense. The reason for her often misinterpreted quietness and plainness was want of money – for she was educating, by her own efforts and earnings, her brother's children. She was to become a dear friend of mine.

I was a member of our Debating Society which had been declining in popularity and in my second year I was asked to ginger it up. I was told to shock the assembly by some means. I looked up the minutes of the Society and decided upon a comic picture of early meetings – one of which was held in an old garden with the President sitting in a cherry tree. Without any thought of malice in my mind (for I greatly admired the Pioneers of the first Hall) I launched into a comic account of serious young women in earnest pursuit of ridiculous subjects for debate – all this was delivered without fear.

As I sat down an elderly don, without the least sense of humour, sprang up and angrily accused me of being an ungrateful daughter of Newnham. When she sat down other speakers sprang to their feet and a real quarrel began. I shivered in my seat and wondered how I was going to sum up, but rescue was near, Miss B. A. Clough rose majestically and with great good humour reminded the audience that laughter was the prerogative of love and that we often laugh most at those we love most. She went on to show the advantages of a debating society and hoped that this one would take new life. So my character was cleared. I summed up happily and rejoiced I had lost the motion.

There were two famous ladies connected with Newnham life – the Misses Kennedy. Miss M. Kennedy had acted as Honorary Secretary for many years. Her sister Miss Julia took English students for coaching in *The Anglo-Saxon Chronicle* in her beautiful dining-room. One wonderful day we were taken by Miss Julia to the May Races. First we had an elegant luncheon – with a memorable pudding – and then we all climbed up into a wagonette with beribboned horses and drove away to the river bank. I had often run up and down the river path after the boats, but today I sat still and aloof, high up above the crowds.

Social life in 1898 was extremely restricted. No men could visit us without a chaperon – as to our visiting them, such a proposition was unthinkable. Once and once only did I break the rules. Walking down Sidgwick Avenue, I met a young man whose home was close to mine. A dull awkward fellow, I had never spoken with him before. But now he smiled and stopped to greet me. He was at Selwyn – and invited me to come and have coffee with him. I said that I would, not liking to snub him. So at eleven o'clock the next day I crossed the road from a back gate and walked into Johnny's rooms. To my horror it was full of his friends – I was the attraction. I took a chocolate biscuit and some coffee and could get no further. Ten men at once was too much for me. In less than ten minutes I was back in Newnham.

The Musical Society gave one concert a term.* There were no dances, I believe, because we were not permitted to go to them. But famous people sometimes came to lecture, Edith Sitwell, for example, and Bertrand Russell.

In summertime we liked to give parties in the garden, chaperoned as usual. I had an elderly friend who never refused to come to an impromptu party. She was a Cambridge lady, mother of a first-year student who was one of my best friends. Sometimes the garden was so full of people that we had to set the tea-table in the middle of bushes or sit upon the grass. On Sundays in spring we delighted to ride out on bicycles to Hardwick woods to pick primroses, or to walk to Grantchester Meadows; in fact we were perfectly free to go wherever we wanted, on bicycles or on foot. In winter there was hockey – though my niece (Newnham, 1943–7) finds it difficult to believe that I was a very swift attacking left wing.

Having been encouraged by my success in the poetry competition, I began to think seriously of what next I should write. And during my last week at Newnham, sad to be leaving it all behind and feeling very uncertain of what was going to happen to me when I got out into the reality of the world, I wrote the following allegorical poem:

When on an ancient highway winding far
Across the moors and mountains to the sea
A holy pilgrim seeking Gallice
Comes when the sun is hot, where green trees are –
Tall pines, whose ancient solemn branches meet
Above a silent glade, safe from the light
And white dust, cool as rainy summer-night –
How gratefully he sings, while with swift feet
Thinking upon his vow and heaven's bright Maid
He sweetly walks beneath that happy shade
Forgetful of the weary leagues that lie
Beyond his little wood. So undelayed
By toil and strife this three-years day have I
Been kept from dust and heat in which men die.

This is a truthful picture of my thoughts on leaving Newnham.

G. M. L. Thomas (1898)

* The College Music Society was founded by K. A. Raleigh (1883) and was later given her name; it has now reverted to its original title.

*

1899

‘STUDENTS MAY RIDE THE BICYCLE’

There have been many changes in Cambridge since 1899. To mention some of the most conspicuous: there were no motors, few bicycles, no aeroplanes, no cinemas, no wireless, and no women smokers.

C. S. Rolls when an undergraduate at Trinity startled Cambridge with his little 4 h.p. Peugeot in 1895; when he went along Trinity Street everyone rushed to their doors to see. No car was registered in Cambridge before 1904, and that was a Co-op van. The Rover ‘Safety’ bicycle was ousting the penny-farthing in 1885. Ladies’ bicycles were still novelties and special College regulations had to be made for them. These laid down: ‘Students may ride the bicycle with certain restrictions. The art may not be acquired at College. Only inveterate proficiency is countenanced. This is tested by a searching examination in corner-turning etc. before candidates receive a diploma’ (1894). I well remember the cumbrous skirts covering trouserlegs firmly secured to ankles with broad black elastic. Not many students owned bicycles, though some clubbed together and shared one. By 1895 bicycling had become a ‘marked phase in Newnham athletics. Competitors cram feverishly before breakfast to prepare for the fatal test (of coasting round the hockey field). In 1896 a bicycle shed had to be erected. In the same year one of the events at the Newnham and Girton joint garden party was a bicycle tournament which we are told afforded great entertainment to the spectators.’

Aeroplanes came much later. First to land in Cambridge was a Blériot piloted by a Mr Moorhouse who landed on Parker’s Piece for a wager in the summer of 1911 or 1912, and took off early next morning.

No cinemas – but there was the New Theatre in Regent Street, viewed with stern disapproval, though students of English were allowed to go to Shakespearian plays. I remember one occasion when a friend and I had taken tickets for *The Merchant of Venice* and at the last moment the programme was altered and a non-Shakespearian play substituted. The College authorities heard of the change and a don was sent forthwith to the theatre and we were ignominiously extracted from our seats just before the curtain went up.

No wireless – but there were gramophones on the market. One couldn’t dream of owning one but they could be hired from Millers at, I think, 2s 6d a night. Gramophones might be thought innocuous enough, but I can remember the only time when I indulged in the extravagance and was enjoying a music-hall song, 'A little bit off the top', when there was a knock at my door and the Vice-Principal came in to ask me to turn it off. My room overlooked Sidgwick Avenue and an undergraduate had been observed stopping beneath to listen to the strange sound.

Smoking was strictly prohibited. This wasn't owing to objections by the staff, for some of them smoked, notably Miss B. A. Clough herself. It was forbidden because it was pointed out that parents wouldn't send their daughters to Newnham if they thought that they might get contaminated by the pernicious habit. It was also pointed out that Miss Clough used to hire a hansom when she wanted a smoke, and drove out into the country or to a friend's smoking-room. We couldn't afford such a luxury. Prohibitions are provocative and we were occasionally in trouble. Tobacco smoke is remarkably penetrating.

Finally I may note briefly what seem to me the most conspicuous contrasts between the Newnham of my day and the present – the attitude of the students towards *dress* and towards *men*. Remember I came up just after the first clear sign of the hostility of the University towards women students. So the chief aim of the College was to be as inconspicuous as possible. Anything conspicuous in dress or behaviour was strongly disapproved.

Few of us had any money to spend on clothes. There were no shops where one could buy ready-mades as now, and perhaps we were also influenced to some extent by the example of the Principal, Mrs Sidgwick, who succeeded Miss Clough. Her tastes were simple and her dress was unimaginative. One little anecdote is characteristic. There was some discussion in the common room about how much luggage one had to take for a week-end, and someone complained how much space a dressing-gown took. 'Oh, do you take a dressing-gown?' said Mrs Sidgwick. 'I always wear my macintosh.' And a macintosh was her usual garb by day too. As the sister of the Prime Minister she had sometimes to go to smart functions, but then we were told she used to borrow a dress. Our long skirts, stiff collars and tight waists were very uncomfortable and even on the hockey field we were expected to have skirts below the knee. One of our team had to write home for permission to leave off her flannel petticoat when playing hockey.

The gibes about women students as husband-hunters are innumerable and will continue as long as there are male and female students in Cambridge colleges; but my impression is that they used not to pay much attention to each other. We didn't take much interest in the men and they were certainly terrified of us. If you wanted to be a social success you concealed the fact that you came from Girton or Newnham.

Our lives were so excitingly novel. We worked, some of us, ten hours a day, and there were so many College societies and preoccupations that there was little time or energy for anything else. There were the Political, Debating, Sharp Practice societies, the Historical, Classical, Scientific societies, the Browning, Shakespeare and other Literary societies, the Sunday Society, the Musical Society and many others. Those were recognised by authority, and there were many not recognised and indeed concealed from authority. (I remember my special contribution was a secret society called the L.S.D. And the letters hadn't the significance they have now; they didn't even mean pounds, shillings and pence. They merely meant 'Leaving Sunday Dinner'. A small group of us signed off for Sunday dinners and we hired a room in Grantchester Street, I think for 7s 6d a term. Each of us had in turn to provide a meal for the group. And there I may add we used to make our own cigarettes after a fashion.) For athletics there were tennis, hockey, cricket, fives, boating and the fire brigade. Life was never dull.

I don't think I spoke to a man my first year. I had cousins at various colleges but we never met. It wasn't done. There were romances and flirtations of course, though opportunities were few. Chaperons were omnipresent. One of the rendezvous for assignations was an astonishing one – the old University Library [in the Old Schools]. But anyone who remembers its mazes and intricacies will realise its potentialities. Only a select few third-year students were permitted to use the University Library, and I never heard of this misuse of it till my husband told me years later. In my time one student got engaged while she was still up, and we were all rather disapproving. She was a research student and got engaged to the lecturer who was coaching her. We felt it was a breach of academic propriety. One of the first breaks of strict segregation of men and women was made by the Tennis Club. We represented to the authorities how much improved our play would be if we had the advantage of playing with men, and the suggestion was favourably received. We, the Tennis Six who played in inter-college matches, were allowed to invite men on certain days, brothers, cousins or old family friends and of course carefully chaperoned. The Tennis Six interpreted the term 'cousin' rather liberally.

M. A. Quiggin (Hingston, 1899)

*

1900

QUEEN ANNE AND MARY ANNE

Shut your eyes and what do you see of Newnham? I see the grounds with the double-blossom cherry trees all white, the red buildings with the undergraduate's libellous quip 'Queen Anne in front and Mary Anne at the back', the long corridors within, especially the ground-floor one in Clough because my first room was at the end and looked out on the garden. There was the Library with Jane Harrison's Charioteer* at the entrance; also Jane herself was on hand and you had to go down to dinner early for the privilege of sitting at her table, but it was worth it. Naturally you think of Miss Clough, Vice-Principal of Clough, 'B.A.', enjoyed by us all, with her inevitable tweed coat and skirt, her chuckle and the twinkle that did not miss much. Then there was Mrs Sidgwick, the Principal and very special, not so easy to talk to, some people thought, but always sympathetic: the old-fashioned word 'revered' seems to express best how we thought of her.

It's amusing to remember how young we were at eighteen. Early in our first term some of us, finding the intellectual clubs and societies rather overwhelming, petitioned a slightly amused 'B.A.' for use of the Blue Room once a week so that we could play games. That urge was short-lived, though I do remember occasional ballet practices when a few kindred spirits shared our meagre accomplishments.

I've heard students of a later day boast of secret and complicated ways of circumventing regulations and slipping in late at night, but we had a simple plan – we found we could lie down flat and roll under one of the iron gates (though actually, as far as I know, it was used solely to get out early enough to watch the sunrise or to cook breakfast out of doors). In the early part of the century regulations were kept. We were still very much on probation. When Professor Marshall, father of today's Political Economy, called his three women students to his home to return some papers, his remarks, though kindly, were caustic. He said the amount I had written was in reverse proportion to the importance of the subject-matter; and to someone else, 'Your writing takes longer to read than anyone else's, and the result is not worth it.' He then proceeded to express doubts that he had been wise in opening his classes to women students, and wondered whether perhaps the type of German hausfrau wouldn't serve our nation better. His lectures were tremendously stimulating, and though I never became an economist but turned to teaching

* Miss Harrison presented to the College a copy of the Charioteer of Delphi.

and later got caught up in a world of art, what I learnt from them and from Dr Keynes's lectures on Logic gave me some idea of how to reason and that I suppose is one of the aims of education.

There is one small prank I remember. Chaperons were much in demand, and once my cousin, a little younger than I and at Girton, impersonated her own mother so that my friend and I could entertain at tea some undergraduates who wanted to see Newnham. It was fun and we carried it off successfully: the young men left very much impressed with my charming aunt.

F. M. Brown (Sturton, 1900)

*

'TO ESCORT, SIXPENCE'

I was a student at Newnham from 1901 to 1904, reading History, attending lectures by such giants as Dr Cunningham, Professor Gwatkin, Dr Reddaway, and of course Miss Alice Gardner and Miss Mary Bateson. Never-to-be-forgotten hours. I also had the privilege of attending what I think must have been Professor Benians's first course of lectures, when he came to Newnham to take a few of us through a Special Period on France under Richelieu.

In those days of the controversy between Free Trade and Protection, we used to listen to Dr Cunningham in the afternoons, only to have all our new-found convictions overthrown by Dr Keynes in the evenings. Opinions were less divided over the question of Women's Suffrage, and I remember one very thrilling debate [of the College's Political Society] when Margery Corbett (later Dame Margery Corbett Ashby) was Liberal Prime Minister. A less serious debate was on the motion 'That Personal Charm is better than Moral Worth'; the Proposer, again Margery Corbett, beautifully dressed in pink with rosebuds in her hair, I think gained the victory over Patty Craske in a severe black gown and wearing an arum lily.

Regulations were strictly observed in those days. I remember going with a few others to a twenty-first birthday party, given by an out-student who lived with her parents, I think it was in Grange Road. At the stroke of 9 p.m. a maid announced, 'The gentleman from the College has called for the young ladies.' We meekly said goodnight and followed the majestic black-coated porter, who carried a candle-lantern to lead us the short distance back to the College. At the end of the term I received a note: 'To escort, 6d. I am surprised you have not paid me before. Signed, T. Smith.'

In my third year the long-planned bathing sheds were erected on a muddy backwater up the river, but what a joy they were! I really think that being elected the first swimming captain and winning the first swimming cup brought me the proudest time of my life.

My contemporaries in Old Hall will remember Sunday evenings in Miss Rickett's room when she read *Gryll Grange* to us; coffee parties in Miss Stephen's room in Sidgwick, when we struggled with delicate handleless cups wondering what to do with the large-size water-biscuits which refused to balance; and above all, the solitary early-morning breakfasts alone with Mrs Sidgwick in her room in Pfeiffer, just before we went down.

On Thursday evenings we used to dance in Clough Hall if we could find anyone to play the piano for us. Once a term there would be fancy dress. One evening there was a sudden pause while two white pedestals were carried in and the Charioteer from Delphi, accompanied by the Greek maiden, solemnly walked in from the Library Corridor and took up their well-known positions, perfect reproductions effected with the help of whitening from the tennis courts. I missed these two statues from the Library Corridor when I last visited Newnham in 1969; I hope they still enjoy a place of honour somewhere in the College, with their memories of Jane Harrison!

I sometimes wonder if present students find time to enjoy pleasures like those wonderful 'Trip' [Tripos] tea-parties under the lilac trees, summer afternoons in hammocks in the avenue of trees opposite Clough, before the building of Kennedy or Peile, leisurely games of croquet, Sunday evening walks over the meadows to Grantchester church, and many other delights of those days. Do they still skate on frozen, flooded Coe Fen to the music of a barrel-organ? Do they still ride bicycles along the road to Ely? There used to be a cottage by the roadside where you could have a wonderful tea of cress sandwiches, cakes, and jam for fourpence each!

M. W. Balcombe (1901)

REGULARITY AND MODERATION

The next motion before the house was *That Newnham is in need of complete reform.* The proposer T. Gosse. Opposer M. Hattersley spoke of the wonderful perfection of Newnham. The regularity and moderation of the life. She implied she could not have opposed the motion if 'Newnham' had meant the buildings. M. Duff spoke in favour of the motion. She devoted her attention to our table manners. She passed to our roughness on the hockey field. D. Byrne supported. Defined 'Newnham' as the spirit of the place. She thought complete change was necessary but she would retain the College buildings. She advocated increased kindliness and pass degrees. This motion was lost by a majority of two.

From the minutes of G.A.P.S. ('Gradus ad Parnassum' or 'The Gentle Art of Public Speaking'), 30 January 1901

*

IN NEWNHAM WALK

I went up to Newnham in 1901 and had a room in Old Hall in what we then called 'the second-floor slums'. The window looked down on Newnham Walk leading up to the entrance gates, and I remember two occasions on which I saw something very amusing.

One was the sight of Miss Jane Harrison, the distinguished Classical scholar, wheeling a very old-fashioned pram in which was a Greek statue of a female figure, I suppose of a goddess. This had an outstretched left arm but as it was on its back in the pram the arm was held up to high heaven and the effect was most extraordinary. Miss Harrison had wheeled this through the streets of Cambridge completely unperturbed.

Another interesting thing I used to see from my window was parties of American sightseers being driven by 'cabbies'. In those days American tourists used to come by train to Cambridge arriving about twelve o'clock and going on by a three o'clock train to Ely, so that they did the sights of Cambridge in three hours; and as there were no cars they hired a horse and open carriage. On one particular day I remember a party of Americans being driven up and being addressed by the cabby in a loud voice: 'This 'ere's Newnham, the lydies' College. This is what they calls the Hold All.'

In those days we had horse-trams up and down Cambridge streets, but if we needed to go out after dinner we had to go in a hansom cab.

E. G. Brown (Parsons, 1901)

*

Newnham Tripos candidates, 1885

The hockey team, 1891. On the extreme left are (back row) M. Steele Smith (later Tutor of Clough Hall), and (middle row) C. D. Holt (see page 34). In the front, seated, are G. L. Elles (left) and P. G. Fawcett, both later College lecturers

The 'staff', about 1890. (Standing, left to right: A. Gardner, B. A. Clough, E. R. Saunders, M. E. Rickett. Seated, middle row: H. Gladstone, A. J. Clough (Principal), K. Stephen, J. Lee. Front row: M. J. Tuke, E. M. Sharpley, A. B. Collier)

Four Principals of Newnham.
(Standing, J. P. Strachey, 1923–41; K. Stephen, 1911–20.
Seated, B. A. Clough, 1920–23; E. M. Sidgwick (Balfour), 1892–1910)

The newly built Newnham Hall (later South, now Old, Hall) standing in isolation, 1875

North Hall (now Sidgwick), showing the public road between it and South Hall: about 1890

Tea in South Hall, about 1890

A student's room in Clough Hall, about 1900

The damaged gates at Pfeiffer Building (see p 150), October 1921

Warwork in the College gardens, 1941 (Ridley Hall in the background). E. M. Chrystal leads the team

Fire-fighting drill on Old Hall roof, 1941

In the Library (the upper bays were not given a floor until 1967; before that access to the books was by a narrow catwalk)

Dinner in Clough Hall

1901

A REVOLUTIONARY AT HEART

When my parents decided to send me to College they had never met a College girl, so our friend Miss Eckenstein produced Tessa Gosse, talented and charming daughter of the famous author. She seemed to have removed any doubts. But a hitch occurred. My brother Adrian was to follow my father to New College and would of course have two rooms. My father was incensed that I should be expected to do with one, and insisted on two. The authorities allotted me the two smallest rooms in Sidgwick: equality betwen the sexes was gained.

On home tuition I seem to have passed the entrance exam easily, but when I chose to read Classics the authorities advised Languages or History. Languages I refused, as I was practically bilingual in French and fluent in German. History seemed to me not a strict enough discipline for a girl who had never been to school. I felt I needed to be up against a tougher discipline. Sent to London to consult my father, he asked, 'What do you want to read?' 'Classics.' 'Well, read them; and come out to lunch' (oysters at Pimms). The result: a poor Second, but a wonderful world of beauty, history and philosophy had opened.

Newnham was my first experience of community life, and I found it very exhilarating. My chief interest was in the Political Debating Society, as I had already helped my father in his election fights. There were Liberal and Conservative 'Governments' in power in alternate terms. Bills were introduced and debated. I was fortunate to coincide with two staunch Liberals, Victoria Buxton and Eglantine Jebb. Less austere was the other Debating Society, where I horrified the dons by arguing successfully 'That Personal Charm is better than Moral Worth'. If the dons were alarmed at me, I was horrified with their attitude of opposition or indifference to votes for women, in which campaign my parents, brother and sisters had already been active. How could women with their privileges of learning be so reactionary?

Of course we were carefully chaperoned when attending lectures in the men's colleges, even if there were several of us, so that it was hardly surprising that later on I had another disappointment. My brother's friend Edwin Montagu (later Secretary of State for India), proposed an inter-college debate between Newnham and his college. I welcomed this as a step towards equality and integration into the University, but Mrs Sidgwick turned it down as dangerous and impossible.

Looking back I now see that I was a revolutionary at heart. My close friends and I were as interested as any student of today in the social ills of society, but we did not expect any attention to be paid to our views until we had left College and had had some more experience of life. The dons I could whole-heartedly admire were Jane Harrison, the unorthodox Classicist, and Anna Paues, Lecturer in Old High German and specialist in mediaeval Bibles. She came from Uppsala's co-educational university.

Another clash occurred when my brother came over from Oxford. Our hockey team contained the Pennycuicks, who played tennis for England and had been our home guests. Having survived mixed hockey in the Christmas holidays, he wanted to watch the match. I was furious when Miss Clough turned us back, presumably because hockey skirts showed our ankles. 'Horrid mind' was my reaction. I felt ashamed in front of my brother. My spiritual development was also unorthodox. I attended the Presbyterian church with its outstanding preacher in the morning and the University Sermons in the afternoon, though my eyes would prick with sleep on a hot summer day. I added an occasional 8 a.m. service at the C. of E. church near by.

I waged constant war with the authorities over meals. The cooking was a disgrace. I came to the sad conclusion that the dons did not know or care what they were eating. I remember half a dozen legs of good English mutton black outside and red inside, and when prunes arrived at every meal getting squashier and squashier as the bottom of the barrel drew nearer. I led so many delegations that I was finally consulted in private as to remedies. Experience in catering for a large and hospitable country house proved useful.

Social life in Cambridge had been brightened by the fairly recent introduction of married Fellows, some of whom were contemporaries and friends of my young uncles, so I visited their wives. Undergraduates would arrive and depart in small batches to keep up their courage. The only sphere of life in which we could meet undergraduates was the political parties, and there if a woman was elected on to the committee or as an officer another one had to be elected as a chaperon. I felt quite experienced as I had made my first political speeches on Free Trade, education and land reform helping my father in his election campaigns, and when he came to help in a Cambridge election I found myself taking the chair at a village meeting for the Liberal candidate.

I thoroughly enjoyed my Newnham days but was glad when they were over and I was part of the adult world of men and women.

M. I. Corbett Ashby (1901)

*

SOCIAL CUSTOMS

In my time at Newnham there were only three Halls – Old, Sidgwick and Clough – and Pfeiffer Building, in which the Principal, Mrs Sidgwick had her rooms. The legend ran 'Clough for games, Sidgwick for brains and Old for silk petticoats'*, but I do not remember that it appeared to fit the facts of the case particularly well. Outside Old Hall there was an orchard, where those who could afford it swung in hammocks, occupied, I fear, more by romantic musings than by serious study; beyond the orchard lay the hockey field. In front of Sidgwick there was a croquet lawn, used perhaps more by dons and fourth-years than by ordinary students; I was a player myself and for some time Secretary of the Croquet Club. Across the garden from Clough [where the Mound is now] there was a small observatory, where Miss Stephen, Vice-Principal of Sidgwick Hall, made mysterious observations every morning after breakfast, and beyond this lay the lawn-tennis courts; behind Sidgwick there were fives courts. The trees were fairly well grown and afforded pleasant shade, but I cannot remember much about flowers in the garden, except a fine bed of delphiniums near the orchard.

Our rooms were for the most part a fair size and heated by open coal fires; most students ended by providing their own wardrobe curtains and bed covers, to give the room the air of a sitting room rather than a 'bed-sit', and we all had outsize biscuit-tins, kept under our beds, to hold eatables and what-not. When the College was still young a benefactor left a sum of money to provide a lady's maid for every five young ladies, but most of the young ladies had no idea what to do with such a creature, and the benefaction was changed into half a pint of milk to be drunk at night by each young lady on finishing her studies: hence the custom of giving cocoa-parties, the guests bringing their own milk and the hostess supplying food, often of a very indigestible nature. I can remember eating extravagantly buttered muffins and cream buns between ten and eleven at night.

In those days we all wore long skirts lined at the bottom with brush-braid, a term probably unfamiliar to most of my readers, and black shoes and stockings. Anything 'fancy' about one's feet or ankles was considered 'fast'. Hats were very large and heavily trimmed; in the summer black crinoline straw hats trimmed with flowers, many flowers, were very

* Each Hall had its own version!

popular. The first evening dress I had made for me was of black satin, with large puffed sleeves to the elbow and a skirt that billowed out to a train at the back (very inconvenient for dancing), the whole trimmed pretty fully with deep cream lace. When I stepped out of it, it stood up on the floor, and fifteen years later some of it was still leading a respectable existence as a princess petticoat. Things were made to last in 1902.

There were various social customs connected with meals. Breakfast was at 8 a.m. The Vice-Principal and other dons occupied the High Table, and short prayers were said before breakfast was served; if you were down in time for this, well and good, but if not you had to go up to the High and shake hands with the Vice-Principal. The only way to avoid this was to come in very late when she had gone, and risk being late for a nine o'clock lecture. At lunch-time I think only dons and perhaps fourth-years sat at the High, but at dinner in the evening (for which we dressed) each don took a table and students sat at them in no prescribed order. Freshers and august fourth-years might sit side by side; no permanent groupings occurred. I never gave this custom a thought at the time, but looking back on it I think it was good social training; we were accustomed to conversing with people younger and older than ourselves, much older in the case of the dons, and with people of very varied interests, opinions and social and geographical origins. Also the practice discouraged the formation of permanently exclusive sets.

Once a week Mrs Sidgwick dined in each Hall, and students sat at the High with her: I have entirely forgotten how this was organised. Some time in our third year we were invited, two or three at a time, to breakfast with Mrs Sidgwick in her flat at 8 a.m., not the hour of one's social best, but fortunately cut short by lectures at nine. We had immense respect for her; she was soft-voiced, slight in figure and generally pale in colouring, but in her grey eyes shone the light of the pure intellectual, quite unconscious of itself, but making one painfully aware of one's own amateurish inferiority.

My most lasting memory of our studies is that we were made to feel responsible for our own progress in them: we were no longer schoolgirls but adults, and we were proud of our independence. With much of our syllabuses we had no help from above at all: if a student proved unequal to the strain involved by this treatment, she was invited to retire as unsuited to University life, but it hardly ever happened. We had some lectures in the town at the Divinity Schools, which men undergraduates also attended, but we sat in separate blocks. On the way back to Newnham we passed the tempting Buol's Café, but none of us ever stopped for coffee; we could not afford the expense nor the time it would have taken. It must be remembered that at that date we were very much on sufferance in the University and not yet members of it, therefore we had much in mind the necessity for proving our worth and our equality with men when it came to examination results. We had lectures in College as well, also seminar classes and personal coaching. Here I cannot resist inserting an anecdote characteristic of the atmosphere of the time. I was being coached by Dr Breul, and we were studying Middle High German lyrics and came across a love-song that I thought particularly charming and wanted to say so, but Dr Breul turned the page very firmly and said, 'Es ist nicht erbaulich' (not edifying). Is there anything left that would be thought 'nicht erbaulich' today? We looked upon our lecturers with great respect for their knowledge and with affection for their personalities. They were not all equally good teachers, but they all had something vitally individual about them. For instance Miss Gardner, Lecturer in History, who always spoke at debates and presented both sides of the case so convincingly in her quiet voice that it was hard to know which way to vote after hearing her.

I do not remember anything that could be called supervision of our work. There were study hours during which there was supposed to be quiet, if not absolute silence, in the building, but there was no rule about 'lights out': if you wanted to work all night you could. There were first- and second-year 'Mays' examinations, a sort of mock-Tripos, and our papers were returned and marked. As we had no statistics by means of which we could compare our performances with those of other years we were left rather puzzled by our results, and no one dreamed of asking for enlightenment: this was rather characteristic of Newnham at the time. If we could not swim we must drown.

E. Terry (1902)

TO AN INVIGILATOR

When I go up to Heaven on high
And pass within the door,
At last, I think that you and I
Will settle up our score.

For you shall sit in Satan's grip
And I at Heaven's gate,
And *you* shall do an endless Trip
While *I* invigilate.

K. K. Pinsent (Radford, 1903)

*

'POLITICAL'

I remember the thrill of coming down to dinner each evening in my first term and looking on the table under the clock in Sidgwick Hall for the little notes of invitation to cocoa that waited there for the freshers. It was so exciting to meet crowds of new people at these festivities and at meals and at the College societies. I can't imagine Newnham without Political. To join one's party and choose one's constituency and attend the interesting debates was a source of great pleasure. In my last year a somewhat dramatic incident was staged in the 'House'. A bill to abolish the House of Lords was brought in, and a number of Liberals who disagreed with the measure walked across the floor to join the ranks of the Liberal Unionists on the crossbenches. The originator of this incident was Miss Lynda Grier, and it fell to me to make the speech in which the disaffection was declared, and to lead the small band of seceders. Afterwards doubts were cast on the possibility of such a thing happening in Parliament, but the deed had then been done.

There were numbers of small Hall societies as well as the College ones. I was a member of a debating society called G.A.P.S. (I don't remember what the initials stood for!)* It met in the room of the President, and each member brought a motion written on a piece of paper, all of which were put into a box and drawn out by a Proposer as directed from the chair. One motion I have always remembered – 'That flying machines would add a new danger to life'. Nobody suggested their use in war and the danger of bombs, as no one imagined war was practical politics!

But the society whose membership gave me the most pleasure was 'The Minor Poets', a small and select group, of which among others Helen Verrall and Georgette Bowden-Smith were members. We all took turns to produce verses which were criticised and discussed in a very pleasant atmosphere. Applicants for membership submitted poems which were carefully considered by the meeting. Our contributions were

* See p. 50.

all entered in a large book kept by the President. When I was last at Commemoration in 1946 I enquired about the society which I was told had lapsed, but no one could tell me what had happened to the book. I should have loved to see it. But the chief performance of the Society was to produce a delightful parody of *Everyman* under the title *Every Tripper*.*

I read History, and most of our lectures were in Cambridge in various colleges where we joined the men, sitting well apart at separate tables. At Trinity we listened to Mr G. T. Lapsley whose lectures on Constitutional History we much enjoyed, and my friend Hilda Roseveare and I derived much amusement from his brightly coloured silk handkerchiefs. We also had Professor Gwatkin at Emmanuel, a most original old gentleman whose sight obliged him to hold notes so close to his eyes that his nose almost touched the paper. He also had an engaging habit of walking about among us asking questions and sitting on the edge of tables and swinging his legs. We had lectures from Professor Bury in the Divinity Schools, and in my third year from Professor G. Lowes Dickinson on Analytical Politics which were most interesting.

What I remember most of my life in Sidgwick is the personality of dear Miss Stephen the Vice-Principal. She radiated goodwill and interest in our doings and was charmingly natural in her conversation and contacts. She gave one a sense of security and peace. Miss Collier and Miss Saunders were the other two dons resident in Sidgwick, for whom we entertained deep respect and affection. I personally knew little of the dons in other Halls, except for dear Miss Alice Gardner, beloved by all her students, who gave us lectures in Roman History and corrected our essays.

One of the pleasant features of everyday life was a kind of 'dole' that was issued every evening after dinner for any who wanted it, of half a pint of milk and half a loaf of bread, providing a basis for the fare of the nightly cocoas. I particularly remember it because there was available a loaf called 'Standard Bread', a sort of not-quite-wholemeal with a most delicious flavour which I have not met since. It was at this time that I and my friends would look in at the room of Miss Michie, Sidgwick's housekeeper. We would foregather there when she was not too busy, to enjoy little chats with her. She was always so kind and friendly and ready to give us any advice or help we might need. She was small and active and bright and we loved her. Our cocoa had to be brewed over our small open fires which resulted in various accidents at

* See pp. 69ff.

times, but it was wonderful what one could do in those conditions. One evening I and a few friends borrowed a frying-pan from the 'common stock'* at the end of the passage and had quite a successful feast of pancakes, efficiently tossed!

The garden was a joy in summer. Those who managed to secure a place in the orchard slung hammocks and enjoyed peace and fresh air. A few had garden space and did their best to produce flowers. My friend and I had some very fine pansies, to which we gave the names of some of our favourite lecturers! Another of the summer features was sleeping on the roof of Clough. There was not much space, and armfuls of cushions had to be collected to make it sufficiently comfortable. I remember my surprise when I woke up to find my pillow wet with dew.

On the athletic side I had the good luck to be included in the Hall hockey team, and in my first year took part in some 'freak' matches. One was Heavy v. Light and I was the heaviest of the lights! I did not qualify for a place among the Beauty v. Brains teams.

M. Wolstenholme (1904)

* The College's original name for a gyp-room or shared kitchen derived quite simply: from the 'common stocks' of crockery etc. available there for use by any member of the Hall.

TO TRINITY UNCHAPERONED

One reason for the care that the authorities thought necessary to exercise was because at that time women were not recognised as members of the University and were only there on sufferance. We attended a lecture if the lecturer agreed that we should, and I remember Mrs Marshall, who was my Director of Studies (I was working on the newly instituted Economics Tripos), anxiously asking if I wanted to take Currency and Banking in the second part because, she said, Professor Foxwell did not accept women. Fortunately I didn't, but at the same time Professor Foxwell was giving a course at the London School of Economics where he was allowed no choice and had to have women students if they opted for his subject. There was a mixed – but not large – group of students taking Economics. Several men – Walter Layton was one in my year, and a Chinese student and a Hindu.

At the beginning of 1908 one of our lecturers, a Fellow of Trinity, Mr McGregor, had to give his course in a building known then as the Literary Lecture Rooms in Trinity Street because he could not get a room in college. After the first lecture he announced that the following week he would be lecturing in college as he had managed to get a room. It never entered my head that this made any difference to my going there. I was the only woman taking that course that year, but halfway through the term Miss Clough sent for me and said she had heard that I was going to Trinity unchaperoned. I explained the situation, said that the group of students were the same as those who went to other lectures, namely at King's, and that I not only went to King's unchaperoned but that I went to Mr Lowes Dickinson's room to get my papers back. 'Oh,' she said, 'King's is quite different. We promised the Master of Trinity that our students would never go to his college unchaperoned', so for the rest of the year an unfortunate don had to bicycle down from Newnham and sit at the back of the room and listen to a by no means easy set of lectures on Monopoly. Nowadays it is difficult to think that that state of affairs ever existed. Once the battle for women's degrees had been won and they were accepted like men as members of the University, all was changed.

I do not blame the Newnham and Girton authorities. There was, we were told, a group of Cambridge ladies – wives of Professors – who kept an eagle eye on our behaviour and every lapse would be immediately reported to the University and would delay the granting of equal rights.

D. S. Simon (Potter, 1904)

*

LETTERS TO A SISTER

30 October 1904

When I got in from Girton yesterday I found my fire on the point of going out. I am always having exciting times with it. You see in this cold weather I want it in the morning, and if I stay out long in the afternoon it is pretty sure to be expiring when I get back, but it has never gone quite out yet. I coax it round with paper and sugar. When I go into town for my lecture tomorrow I am going to buy a lot of luxuries for it, sifted sugar, firelighters and sticks. It is more trouble than a gas stove, but much more interesting. I am getting awfully fond of it. I don't know what I shall do without it when I come home. I shall be home very soon now, in a month and ten days.

You asked me to tell you how the Political was managed. Well, there is a very beautiful chair, which stands in a recess in the Hall. This is brought out on Monday nights directly after dinner and set on the dais. The Speaker (Miss Fulford) sits in it, and on her right, rather behind her, is her secretary, sitting at a table with paper, ink and a clock.

The Liberals sit all down one side of the Hall on the Speaker's left, the Conservatives, that is, the government, on her right, and the Liberal Unionists across the end of the Hall facing her.

They sit on rows of chairs, and the leaders and whips of the party sit on the front row. The sitting lasts from a little before eight to half-past. No member may speak for more than ten minutes (I can't remember the parliamentary words properly) and during the last ten minutes no one may speak for more than three. When anyone has spoken their full time they have to stop, and the Speaker asks the House whether it is their pleasure that she should proceed; of course it generally is. I am not quite sure how they vote, as I did not wait for it last time, but I think they go behind the chairs on the two sides of the Hall.

17 November 1904

I am so sleepy I can scarcely write, but I have to sit up because I am to go to a cocoa at half-past ten; it is fearfully late, but it is being given by very dissipated people. I went to a cocoa last night at which neither of the hostesses turned up for about a quarter of an hour after the time they asked us. They had left a friend to receive us, who was very sleepy and anxious to go to bed.

These are freshers' cocoas you understand, I think the second and third years have about finished asking us now. I am rather sorry, because several girls I like have not asked me.

Miss Clough has been away all today, and will come back some time tomorrow. Everyone is very sad when she is away. Miss Tuke reads prayers and says grace, and it isn't nearly so nice somehow.

22 January 1905

I have got a pink hyacinth in a pot. I wanted a white one, but there were none to be had. When it fades you shall have the bulb for the garden, unless I get a garden here. This term I have been given new curtains and a new carpet. The curtains are very nice, a pattern in dull yellow and dark blue on a dull green ground and made of velvet; unfortunately one pair is about a foot shorter than the other, but still they are a great improvement on the old ones, and make the room look much nicer. The carpet is an improvement too in a way, as the old one was very shabby and not pretty, but the new one is bright red, and as my walls are yellow, and my bed, etc., blue, both very bright, it makes the room exceedingly gay. My bed-spread is in rather an unhappy condition at present, as we were cleaning the silver yesterday with a mixture of jewellers' rouge and water, and poor Miss Johnson managed to spill it over herself and the bed. She was very much distressed, and tried, rather unsuccessfully, to wash it out. However it doesn't show much when the spread is the other way up, with a cushion over the place.

6 May 1905

The weather is perfect here, and the river is covered with little canoes. We had tea out in the garden this afternoon, in the orchard. There was a cricket match going on, the freshers' match between Sidgwick and Clough, but by most astonishing good luck I am not playing in it. The match is still going on; I don't know when it will end, but Clough is losing I am afraid.

27 July 1905

Yesterday the swimming gymkhana was held, and I am wildly anxious to learn to swim with one arm. They had various races. The most exciting were the umbrella race, where they had to swim holding up open umbrellas, the egg and spoon races, and the candle race. The last was frightfully exciting. They had to swim down the bath holding a candle and matches, light the candles, and swim back keeping them alight. It was frightfully difficult, as it was rather a windy day, but the bath is very sheltered. Lighting the candle was very hard, and no one succeeded in keeping it alight all the way back, but one girl got about three-quarters of the way.

Last of all there was walking the greasy pole. The pole was laid across the bath and greased with soft soap. Everyone tried to walk it, but no one got far. They were allowed three tries. During the first round it became clear that the only way to do it was not to attempt to walk, but to slide down as far and as fast as possible, of course the pole sagged a little in the middle. The second trier in the second round was an enormously tall, big girl, who balanced herself on the end, shot down to the middle, and then the pole broke in two and in she went. So of course no more could be done.

12 October 1905

The College is very full this year. All the rooms are occupied except the spare bedroom. I had some of the freshers to cocoa last night, but they were not very nice ones. I didn't mean to begin to have parties till next week, but circumstances have been too strong for me.

I went to my first lecture this morning. It was in Trinity College dining hall. The men sit at the High, but we are only allowed to sit at the tables below.

Yesterday I went to the evening service at King's. It begins at five, and when we went in it was almost dark in the ante-chapel, but the chapel was lighted by rows of tapers set on the stalls. From the ante-chapel you could see the vaulted roof of the chapel lighted up beyond the screen, and the angels of the organ dark against it. There was a lovely anthem, and all the singing was just plain singing without an organ, it might have been awful, but it was beautiful.

15 October 1905

We are designing to start a new society. The membership is to be exceedingly select, as it is to consist at present of Marjorie Ferguson, Marjory Stephenson, Myra Curtis and myself. But we are thinking of admitting one or two others. It is a literary society, as yet nameless, and is to meet between tea and supper on Sundays. During the week the members are to read some essay, poem or other literary work, and to meet to discuss it. At each meeting the members draw lots, and the one on whom the lot falls chooses the subject for the next meeting. It is to meet for the first time today, the subject chosen being an essay of Emerson's on Compensation. It has nothing to do with trade unions and employers' liability, but is very interesting. The society is to be kept a dead secret, but when you come I will try to get the others to a meeting, if you are discreet.

There have been all the usual meetings, and I am very stiff from playing hockey.

12 November 1905

On Thursday night there was a tremendous rumpus. Cambridge University played the New Zealanders you know, and lost of course. To celebrate their defeat, apparently, and also it being the King's birthday, there was a large and prolonged rag that night. Crowds of undergraduates came up Sidgwick Avenue, shouting and cheering and throwing crackers. They threw one into the library, and a girl sitting there had to chase it all over the place, putting out the sparks, but not daring to grab it. They carried off the boarding over the doors of the new buildings [Kennedy] to make a bonfire. There were four bonfires in various parts of Cambridge and great rows all over all night.

A select party of us were doing the wine-glass in Marjorie's room. We asked it what college it was that was leading the rag, and it immediately spelt Clare, very quickly. We heard next day that two Clare men had been taken to the police station.

3 December 1905

There was the inter-college debate at Girton last night. The subject was 'That fanatics have done more for progress than moderates'.

We drove over to Girton in buses and cabs, about eighty-five of us. There was great agitation at both ends in case there should not be enough room for everybody, but I don't think anyone was left behind either time. The debate was a very long one, Myra and Gladys [Johnson] both made short speeches. The motion was carried finally, but I don't agree with it myself. After the debate there was dancing and refreshments, very good refreshments, and then we went home. There was only room for six people in our bus, but they insisted on putting in eight, so we had a lively drive home.

4 February 1906

I spoke at debate last night. It was perfectly awful. However I got through and didn't break down, which was a great comfort. It was rather a good debate on the whole.

Several people spoke for the motion, although very few voted for it, but the few were keen. I think I told you that it was 'That no individual should have an income of more than £500 a year'. The proposers argued on socialistic grounds. I don't know anything about socialism, but I managed to say something. I wanted to bring in the wage limit in football, but it didn't come in very well, so in the end I left it out. I quoted from the 'Imperial Rescript'. Do you remember that poem? It is in *Barrack-Room Ballads*, it begins:

> Now this is the tale of the Council the German Kaiser decreed,
> To ease the strong of their burden, to help the weak in their need.

Speaking in public is perfectly awful and I will never, never do it again.

18 February 1906

There is a competition in the *Granta* this week to discover the handsomest undergraduate in Cambridge. A coupon is provided on which his name and college are to be written and your own signed. It would be rather sport to send one in from here, but I am afraid it might lead to trouble, and besides I don't think there are any handsome men in Cambridge, at least I don't see them; on the whole undergraduates are a very poor-looking lot.

6 March 1906

I went to Political but I did not find it very exciting, so I came away. People were very noisy, certainly, and kept shouting 'shame' and 'query', but the most exciting thing that happened was that as I was sitting knitting in the gallery, one of my needles shot off my knee down onto the floor of the House. Before I could go away I had to go and pick it up, which was very embarrassing, but not many people noticed.

1906

11 March 1906

Nothing really interesting has happened since you left, I think. There was the debate, however, last night. The motion was 'That the works of Bernard Shaw are morally and artistically false'. Everyone had been cramming up the works most desperately, but even so there were long gaps between the speeches. The ones that were made were good and interesting though; Myra spoke very well. The motion was carried by a large majority, rather an unexpected result. After that there was dancing, and then we made cocoa in my room, and were V-Ped*, for the first time! It was not really late, considering, and we were not at all noisy, but I had forgotten to shut the ventilator.

I have proposed† to Miss Mutch. Marjorie and Myra have been very much excited over the event for some days, and it came off today.

7 May 1906

It is very hot here, and I have been lying in the hammock a good deal. There is a new shop in Cambridge where you can get fruitarian goods. Shena Potter gave a supper of them last night, and she came to ask me to it, but I was out, and so I didn't go.

However several people had indigestion after it so perhaps it was just as well.

11 November 1906

The worst has happened and Marjorie has proposed to Miss R—. I was afraid it was bound to come, but I thought perhaps when she had got so far she might refrain till the end.

18 November 1906

The truth party was a great success, and most hilarious. It was done something like consequences. There were as many sheets of paper as there were people present, and each sheet was devoted to one person's character. Each person wrote her opinion of the character and folded it over and passed it on. When they were finished they were collected and read out. Some of them were good, some bad; mine was not very nice but Myra's was the worst, so she was given the prize, a beautiful black golliwog, with an appropriate inscription.

M. H. Dodds (1904)

Extracts from letters written between 1904 and 1909 to a younger sister at a boarding-school in London

* Called on – for disciplinary reasons – by the Vice-Principal.

† To propose (or 'prop') to someone was to suggest the use of Christian names.

*

RULES OF NEWNHAM COLLEGE (AS REVISED)

1 Students may walk unaccompanied about any part of Cambridge until 8.30 on Sundays. On weekdays they must be chaperoned after 7 by a don, or a cab-man.
2 Students may ride bicycles in Silver Street and other dangerous parts of Cambridge, but must walk in the less crowded and wider streets for fear of accidents.
3 Students may entertain male visitors for from three to four hours in the waiting-room or garden. The Vice-Principal must be informed if a man is to be entertained in the music room, and on no account must he eat or drink anything unless a chaperon be present.
4 Students may not go up any staircases in men's colleges unless there is a lecture room at the top. Any student may come down any staircase in men's colleges alone and unchaperoned.
5 Uncles are fathers or brothers.
6 Anyone who does not attend breakfast or Sunday supper, must state that she has attended them by marking her name in a book provided for the purpose. If she is unable to mark it herself someone should do it for her.
7 No man is a competent chaperon but a certified cab-driver, father or brother (see Rule 5).

E. Radford (1905)

Contribution to an undergraduate notebook collection of verse and humorous items, 1906–8

FRIENDSHIPS

As far as my life in Cambridge goes, I was born at the right time. At the age of seventeen I took the College entrance in Classics. I had only had six months of Greek, but dear Miss Sharpley thought that I showed promise. Miss Sharpley was still the same 'thin, pale, girlish creature but so nice and clever' that she was in 1885 when Winnie Seebohm went up.* Newnham seemed glad to have me. In later years I should never have squeezed in.

When, in 1906, I came up I changed from Classics to History for then, I imagined, instead of a corner of the world, the whole world would be at

* See *A Suppressed Cry* by Victoria Glendinning, and pp. 10ff.

my feet. (My love was for literature, but reading other people's criticisms would, I thought, take the bloom off.) It was the worst choice I could have made. History, in my day, was a dead subject in Cambridge. We had no tutorials. My tutor, the learned little Miss Gardner, was not inspiring. She returned our essays with a few comments, made in indistinct speech that invited no controversy. In and out of one's studies, she shuffled in her felt slippers and shapeless gown without leaving any historical impression except the cruel concept of a 'blue-stocking'. University lectures on English Economic and Constitutional History and the Outlines (alas, completely lifeless) of European History were all dust to me. As 'shop', as one's subject was called, was taboo as a topic of conversation I never discussed any historical theory or character with anyone during all my three years at Cambridge. The waters of learning were bitter. Although I would not have admitted to the treachery, knew that with History I should have done better in Oxford with its splendid system of tutorials, with dons who stung one into thought.

My education in Cambridge came entirely from my fellow-Newnhamites. It was a remarkable period. True, although many young women had come up to qualify to earn their living by teaching and there were many featureless among them, there was an élite from a larger world. To me, coming from a narrow puritanical background, this larger world opened new horizons. Not that I penetrated it for some time. My first months at Newnham were the unhappiest of my eighteen years. I was isolated. The 'riff-raff', as we arrogantly called them, would have accepted me into their obscure ranks, but I would have none of them. To the élite I was an outsider: shy, half-baked, inarticulate, with no convictions of my own. (How did one gain convictions? My contemporaries seemed to have them.) I had nothing to contribute.

Yet the sun also rises. In my second term, my neighbour in Old Hall, Jessie Cameron, coming in to borrow my kettle and blushing deeply said: 'May I propose?' (that is, call you Francesca). Jessie was an independent down-to-earth Scotswoman, uninfluenced by other people's opinions, and she had decided, as she put it later, that I wasn't so bad after all. Moreover she was a second-year, infinitely superior to us poor freshers, and immensely popular. She was so droll, so different from everyone else and far more interested in the world about her and in other people than in herself. Like her brother John, later Vice-Chancellor of the University, she was a mathematical genius. Mathematics seemed to have washed her mind clean, while ours were cluttered up with useless facts. Brought up in a Perthshire village, where her father was schoolmaster, and one of eight children, she was forthright, unsnobbish, free of the Victorian sentimentality and humbug, the rags of which still clung to most of us. Jessie's 'proposal' gave me status. Soon after, I was adopted by Marjorie Leon. She came from St Felix, with a band of girls who were in the vanguard of culture.

The girls from St Felix had come from the enlarging influence of its Head Miss Silcox, from whom, they told me, they had learned much more than they ever did at the University. The leader of the old Felicians was Ka Cox. I went to History lectures with Ka, for whom I developed a profound, though hopeless, admiration. She swam in an upper aether, far above my sphere. She was an aesthete – wore loose, diaphanous clothes with Peter Pan collars (not stiff high ones with bones sticking into the neck like ours) and had silver baubles in her hair. She belonged to the Fabian Society, went with Marjorie Leon on unchaperoned walking-tours with Justin Brooke and Jacques Raverat, rode horseback with Lowes Dickinson, boated with Rupert Brooke (who intermittently was in love with her), acted in *Comus* with him in the Long, conversed with Darwins, Cornfords and Keynes (the élite of Cambridge), had her College room papered with plain brown, knew the poems of Meredith and Francis Thompson by heart and talked of art, philosophy and literature like an initiate. At nineteen she was a miracle of poise, maturity and charm.

In Ka's orbit there were other aesthetes: Eleanor Enfield with her quiet uptilted face that looked as if awaiting enlightenment (which she was soon to obtain with her husband Emile Burns, in the Communist Party); Dorothy Lamb, sister of the painter Henry, and very exclusive; Evelyn Radford, later to promote the love and practice of music all over Cornwall. As well as these poetic figures, there were splendid women, like D. Shena Potter (later Lady Simon), Agnes Conway, Eva Spielman (Mrs Hubback) and Lynda Grier, 'all people of strong individuality whose public spirit in their various careers withstood the disasters and disillusion of our time'.* But I, alas, knew these splendid girls but slightly. They were in Clough Hall, much superior to Old in my time, for the quality of both its students and its dons. Here, B.A. Clough's deep voice and endearing chuckle could be heard; the Swedish Miss Paues, as large in heart as in body, brought warmth into donnish contacts; and Jane Harrison with her originality and her penetration into the world of Ancient Greece brought glamour into scholarship. (There

* See Newnham *Letter*, 1970, obituary of Evelyn Radford.

was a society for damming the Jordan, in my day. Miss Jordan, an earnest student, was monopolizing the seat next to Jane at dinner; Jane's admirers set out to thwart her and share out the honour. They had to get there early.)

More accessible to me, although she was not in Old, was Osmy (Dorothea Osmaston). Her flower-like face can be seen in photos, along with dozens of Ka, in Michael Hastings's *Rupert Brooke*. Osmy, in spite of her vast energy in every direction – music, sport, economics, politics – seemed still a little girl and not at all alarming. We could laugh at her childlike pride in her Greek dresses and her figure-skating and she charmed me by the candour with which she announced, over cocoa, that her ambition was not for a career but to marry and have six children. As soon as she left Newnham, she married Walter Layton and had seven. Later I noticed her watching their antics with the same sort of innocent surprise that she had shown over her own manifold achievements.

We had the pleasant habit in those days of going to reading-parties in the country in the Easter Vac, ostensibly to swot for the Tripos. Here I got to know the bright mocking-bird, Lyndall Schreiner, niece of the celebrated Olive, the beautiful Margot Hume with her voice full of tears and her gay laugh. We didn't know then what a distinguished scientist she was to become: how she was to increase our knowledge of vitamins and of how to treat monkeys in captivity.

At Newnham and on reading-parties we discussed unashamedly everything under the sun, all the old problems: free will and predestination, the place of women (the Suffrage was 'in', Ray Costello made many of us converts and even go on processions). Even highbrows discussed everything with unabashed seriousness. Amber Reeves in a lecture to our Philosophy Society proclaimed the relativity of morals – a shattering assumption. To me Amber was intellect personified. When, soon after her speech, it was whispered that she had run off to Paris for a week-end with H. G. Wells, a story the dons were trying to hush up, she became more dashing than anyone else we knew. We thought of her with awe.

I had never heard of H. G. Wells when I caught a glimpse of his loud checks disappearing round the corner of Newnham corridors, but Marjorie Leon explained him to me. The only daughter of an enlightened Liberal, Chairman of Education in the L.C.C., Marjorie belonged to the modern world. Will Beveridge was a frequent guest at her luxurious home near Hindhead (now given to the Ockenden Venture). Marjorie was vital, maternal, domineering; she needed someone to instruct and to boss, and found me virgin soil. She took me to my first two plays, the

Greek *Oresteia* and *You Never Can Tell.* She explained Darwin to me and some of the ills of society and how Lloyd George was going to tackle them, and Beveridge, always going on about Labour Exchanges.

To the modern Newnhamite how unbelievably naive and inexperienced we must seem! I look at the old photographs of us in our enormous hats and long skirts, hair done up with a hundred hair-pins in buns at the back of the head or on top if it, and it seems we lived a hundred years ago. Were we young, then? We felt rather old. I don't see 'the triumph set on youth' on any of our brows, except perhaps on Osmy's. The modern Newnhamite, living in an almost mixed society, with the stimulus and excitement of male companionship, must think of us with pity. This is misplaced. Many of us had lived through lonely schooldays. For the first time we made friends. The slow exploration of another human being, the discovery of shared perplexities and interests, the delight in our new companions' gifts and, maybe, beauty (for beauty was not wanting in those years) – these were excitements. Many of us made friends who remained faithful to us all our lives. There were other things – tennis, hockey, boating on the Cam, debates, Evensong at King's, skating on the fens with an undergraduate cousin or Philip Baker – but to me it was the friendship with other girls that I think of, and the springs and autumns of Cambridge with their almost unbearable beauty.

F. M. Wilson (1906)

'EVERY TRIPPER'

E.T. Now, by my fay, I am undone.
Oh, to whom shall I make my moan?
O wretched caitiff, whither shall I flee?
  For help in this world whither shall I turn?
Sith that ye two* have forsaken me
  And joined with this my foe to make me mourn.
There is none to succour me by the way,
And I see my time is nigh spent away.

Virtuous Principles *enters*

V.P. Every Tripper, how low art thou brought!
  Yet mayst thou still delivered be.
How oft hast thou my counsel set at nought

* Midnight Oil and Crambooks.

Yet now will I abide with thee.
I will not forsake thee indeed,
Thou shalt find me a good friend at need.
All earthly things are but vanity.
Games and Cocoa and all fly,
Save Virtuous Principles, and that am I.
Would thou hadst called me ere thy doom was ripe.
Then had I driven this Microbe* from thy side,
But now methinks he hath thee in his gripe,
And help is vain! Yet shall not these twain abide.
Away! Aroint ye! dasters both,
To leave your prey ye are full loth,
But well ye know that such a power
Is given me in this latest hour
That ye must seek that place whence ye were sent.
Fly! Get you hence, incontinent! (*They fly.*)
Thou hast rejected me, and trusted fickle friends,
But now thou seest how their fair speaking ends.
Thou hast despised me,
And scorned me in my heart.

E.T. But now, most excellent V.P.,
I see thee as thou art.
Take example, all ye that do hear and see,
How they that I loved best have forsaken me,
Except my Virtuous Principles, that bideth truely.
But wilt thou not forsake me also?

Chant of Examiners behind:

Mathematical Tripos,
Classical Tripos,
Moral Sciences Tripos,
Natural Sciences Tripos.

V.P. Yea, Every Tripper, when that dread door you pass,
Through which I may not go with thee, alas!
But not yet for no manner of woe.

Chant of Examiners rises:

General European History, Political Economy,
Comparative and Analytical Politics,
Latin Prose.

* Tripos Microbe.

T.M.* Nay, now the hour cometh verily.
Hark!

Chant of Examiners:

Historical French Grammar, Elements of Anglo-
Saxon, German Translation, International Law.

Hark! Thy high judges do chant solemnly
The trials that thou needs must undergo.

V.P. Farewell! Farewell! Thou art of help bereft,
This—for remembrance—is my parting gift.

(*She gives her rosemary.*)

T.M. But constant to thy side *I* still will come!
Thy fearful end doth now before thee loom.
Behold the door! Go forward! meet thy doom!

(*He points to the door whereon is written* '*To the Tripos*'.)

The Examiners chant:

Pure Mathematics, Natural Philosophy,
Natural Philosophy, Pure Mathematics,
Pure Mathematics and Natural Philosophy,
Natural Philosophy and Pure Mathematics.
Problems.

(*The Examiner putteth out a hand from the door and haleth*
Every Tripper *through.*)

The Chant:

First Class – Second Class – Third Class,
Standard of the Ordinary Degree,
Excused the General Examination.

(*A Hollow Groan.*)

Extract from *Every Tripper*, written, produced and privately printed by 'The Minor Poets', an informal College poetry society (see pp. 56f.), 1906

* Tripos Microbe

*

MISS FREUND

In those days the gates were locked at six o'clock. One could of course get permission to be out later, but had to sign at the Porters' Lodge on return. It followed from this rule that the Vice-Principal (in my day Miss Rickett) marked a register during dinner. From this arose a custom that students at the end table in the bottom alcove had to send up a list of names because they could not be seen from the High Table. In my time, and especially in my third year, it became quite a habit to send up the list disguised in some way – anagrams, limericks, other languages. I think Miss Rickett and the High Table looked forward to some puzzle to keep them amused.

In my day Miss Freund reigned supreme in the Chemistry Lab. in the garden. She was a great character – Austrian by birth, she wrote excellent English but never managed to speak it. She would break off a sentence and say, 'Have I got you wiz me in zat?'; and on one occasion when a student had had a little argument with her she said, 'Now, Miss X, have I got you wiz me in the hydrochloric acid?' In her youth she had a cycling accident and lost a leg; she had an artificial one which she was apt to put firmly on one and then ask one to fetch something. Every year just before the Tripos she would summon her Chemistry students to do some special study. It was of course a hoax. In 1907 she urged them to go to the lab. to study again the lives of certain Chemists. They found large boxes of lovely chocolates from Buol's with a different life-history and picture of some famous Chemist in each. In my year we were requested to go and make a further study of the 'Periodic Table of the Elements'. We found a very large board with the Table set out. The divisions across and down were made with Edinburgh Rock, numbers were made of chocolate, and the elements were iced cakes each showing its name and atomic weight in icing. The nonvalent atoms were round, univalent had a protruding corner, bivalent two, trivalent triangular, and so on. We divided it up between us!

H. Wilson (1905)

INVITATION TO THE PERIODIC TABLE

Your attention is drawn to the desirability – in fact the necessity – of perfecting your knowledge of the Periodic System of Classification of the Elements. Whether considered from the point of view of theoretical or of descriptive and classifactory Chemistry, Mendeleef's system demands extensive and detailed knowledge, and such time as you can still give to revising (= cramming??) in Chemistry might, it is suggested, be advantageously spent on this subject. Since however it has always been recognised that a well-arranged and well-spaced-out table which allows one to take in at a glance as many facts and relationships as possible, is a desideratum in this matter, you will find at the laboratory such a table provided for your use. This table, whilst in the main following the usual lines, tries to bring out, by means of a tentative symbolism, more facts than it is usual to try and convey. Whether however it is of a kind that would lend itself to extended use as an adjunct to the study of Chemistry must be considered doubtful.

I. Freund (Girton College, 1882)

THE MAY RACES

There was considerable rivalry between the three Halls, not only in games (hockey, cricket, tennis and fives; lacrosse was introduced only in our last year) but also between the Hall fire brigades, each Hall having its own, complete with hoses etc. Practices were frequent and the sound of the fire-bell brought the brigade members running from all directions. We learnt to run out and join hoses, and the quickest route from one part of the College to another. Our chief desire was to have a real fire in order to show our prowess. One Sunday there actually was a slight fire in Clough; the brigades were summoned; Sidgwick and Clough rushed to the scene but all of Old had gone to church! We felt let down.

The wives of many of the University dons were At Home to undergraduates on Sunday afternoons, and members of Newnham and Girton were almost urged to come to help entertain; but we don't think the men really appreciated our presence, and conversation was often very halting and strained, as we had very little in common.

Dons' wives also made up parties for the May Races, inviting us to lunch and going by boat to Grassy Corner with usually a picnic tea. Town photographers were very active on such occasions. Those Newnham students who were not so favoured by fortune but who wished to see the races were catered for by the College assigning to an unfortunate don the task of patrolling the meadows as a kind of collective chaperon. On one such occasion it fell to the lot of Miss Alice Gardner, known to all as 'A.G.' As she was crossing from the towing path in the Grind (does it still exist?)* a motor-launch coming down stream ran into it and the occupants slowly descended into the Cam. Three of us who were present ran to the spot in time to hear A.G. say in a calm voice, 'I can't

* The Grind, no longer in existence, was a ferry operating between Chesterton and Stourbridge Common.

swim, but if you'll tell me what to do, I'll do it.' She was brought safely to land by two undergraduates, received by us, conveyed to a hansom which was near and seen off to College. At breakfast the next morning I was called to High to give a detailed account. When I said that one of her rescuers was J. R. M. Butler, one of the dons present exclaimed, 'I'd fall in the river myself to be rescued by Jim Butler.' (I wonder whether he is still alive and whether he knew that he was the idol of a large section of the female population.)*

A.G. was quite one of the outstanding personalities in College, she was small and always wore stockings with white heels. Another striking personality who comes to mind was Miss Clough, 'B.A.' as she was always called. In those days we were forbidden to ride down Trinity Street but had to dismount and wheel our bicylces, really a more risky procedure; the fine for transgressing was one shilling. Miss Clough, one morning seeing one of her Hall cycling in Trinity Street, stopped her and holding out her hand said: 'Can you lend me a shilling, Miss X?'

Mrs Sidgwick always wore a little square of white lace on her head. She had a flat on first floor Pfeiffer, and might often be seen flitting across the garden in her long black dress. She used to give breakfast parties to which we were invited two or three at a time in our third year. When she dined in Hall the invitation to dine also at High was viewed with mingled apprehension and dismay. E.K.B. can't remember whether it was on one such occasion that she upset her glass of water and wanted to sink under the table with shame.

Tradition played its part in our lives. We never bought or took into College daffodils before Commem, but for Commem dinner we all wore them. The Hall which triumphed in a final inter-Hall match placed the cup in the centre of the table at dinner, and those of us given to verse-making composed laudatory efforts and dropped them anonymously in the cup. As far as we remember they were read aloud.

We affected a mannish style in dress in the daytime: coat and skirt, blouse with stiff collar and knotted tie, although our skirts nearly touched the ground. But in the evening we became feminine and wore evening dress, on special occasions having a short train. The prevailing hair-style was to wear it high in front, either over a pad or else furiously back-combed. Hats were always worn, ranging from small ones tipped up at the back to large cart-wheels. Skirts worn for games might be a few inches off the ground, but then no male was ever allowed in the

* This was J. R. M. Butler, later Regius Professor of Modern History; he died in 1975.

field where we played games. Which reminds me: some students who wished to sleep on the roof of Old in the hot summer were told they must come in at a very early hour, six o'clock I think, for fear Ridley men should see them in dressing-gowns.

There was a portress who sat in a little room by the big [Pfeiffer] gates, and a housekeeper whose name I forget unless it was Miss Betts. There was a large number of maids, I think one to each floor, who kept our rooms, brought round hot water night and morning, and washed our china after tea- or cocoa-parties. There was a man in green baize apron who cleaned our shoes and presumably filled the coal-scuttles, for each room had an open fire (which was laid each morning by a woman from outside if I remember rightly, and usually very badly laid); even our beds were made for us.

We went up older than the later generations of students, many if not most of us were twenty or over. We were near enough to the beginnings to realise and appreciate our privileges and accept our consequent responsibilities. It was exciting to be in, if not of, a famous University and to see and hear people of distinction. But perhaps the most important experience was being in contact with brilliant minds, both in College and out.

And as one looks back it is mostly the little things which come to mind: the scent of wallflowers through the open window, cycling to Madingley to pick cowslips, and if we intended going further afield having to tell our V.-P. so that (in the words of Miss Collier) she might know in which direction to send a search-party if we were not back for Hall. There was the glamour of the market, gayer it seems to us than it is now, where we bought flowers and cherries; bathing on a warm afternoon in the rather muddy little backwater enclosed for our use, where the depth varied from day to day; going down to the river muffled up in a cold wind to watch the Lents, then eating eggs on muffins at Matthew's before returning to College just in time to dress for dinner. And last but not least that long unknown sight – the College pony pulling the mowing machine wearing his little leather boots.

E. K. Bradfield (Bawden, 1907) and G. F. Gabb (1907)

*

A DISCREET PERSON

I was attending lectures with a fellow-student and we were the only women at the lectures. When my fellow-student got flu and was unable to go, as I should have been the only woman present, my Vice-Principal, who was also my tutor, felt it her duty to accompany me and sit beside me while I tried to take intelligent notes. This happened twice: after the second lecture she decided that I was a 'discreet person' and to my great relief I was allowed to go alone till my fellow-student was restored to health.

A. V. Clarke (1907)

NEWNHAM SCIENTISTS

My memories are of the Science people from 1908 to 1911: I was fortunate to know some of the great ones. At Newnham, Miss Elles, Miss Saunders and Miss Freund stand out; and among University lecturers, Dr Marr, Professor Bateson, and Dr Haddon. The energy, kindliness and enthusiasm of Miss Elles made her perhaps the most inspiring influence in those glorious years, which culminated in an unforgettable Sedgwick Club trip to Church Stretton.

Miss Saunders, or 'Becky' as we called her among ourselves, lived in Sidgwick when I was there. To some of us she seemed the embodiment of dedicated search for scientific truth. Rather austere in her tweed coat and skirt, with a very masculine collar and tie, yet with such a kindly twinkle in her eye. At dinner her severely plain black silk, with the gold medal on a thin gold chain her only ornament, might look equally forbidding to a nervous fresher seated beside her; but an encouragingly kindly remark followed by a somehow friendly silence was most reassuring. In the old Balfour Lab. we rejoiced in her wonderfully exact and clear teaching, and the orderly marshalling of the facts by which she led us to understand and delight in the ways of plants.

Miss Freund was a terror to the first-year student, with her sharp rebukes for thoughtless mistakes. One grew to love her as time went on, though we laughed at her emphatic and odd use of English. Yet how brave she was trundling her crippled and, I am sure, often painful body about in her invalid chair smiling, urging, scolding us along to 'zat goal to which we are all travelling which is ze Tripos'.

Dear Dr Marr would come stamping into the lecture room, his gown streaming behind him, and cut and slice the country up with gusto. Glaciers streamed slowly down, rivers meandered or were beheaded, such 'noxious spots' as the Fens spread themselves, and only the ancient hills of his beloved Lakeland and Scotland remained to make habitable spots for decent folk. All the same we all panted joyfully after him, filling notebook after notebook with more or less legible writing.

Those were the days when Mendelism was the latest big idea, and though as a Botany student I only attended the more general lectures I did share in a delightful afternoon at Grantchester, when Professor Bateson led us on a Sunday afternoon round of his own farmyard, garden, and poultry runs. As each cockerel and hen that he picked up had its inheritance demonstrated he would look round for some hand to receive the bird, till those of us with a country upbringing found our arms full of protesting poultry, and the procession would go round again returning them to their numbered pens. Some undergraduates in light Sunday suits were not very partial to this form of instruction.

The Geography Diploma of those days included Anthropo-geography, and Dr Haddon's fascinating lectures on the ways of the less civilized peoples of the earth, with perhaps that year especial emphasis on New Guinea, from which he had recently returned. His racy and amusing lectures were packed with first-hand information, and encouragement to follow up further question after question that arose.

We took the first part of the Diploma examination in the Corn Exchange, with pass men, at trestle tables. I remember well how my papers jumped when either the Theology candidate on my left, or the Historian on my right, banged his elbows on the table; and how hot it was. Our Tripos papers were still written in the Nonconformist schoolroom behind the Balfour Lab., but for the second part of the Geography Diploma we were admitted to the cool green silences of the New Examination Halls – a wonderful experience!

The year before, 1910, women were first admitted to work as undergraduates in the University Chemical Laboratories, to the annoyance of the 'lab. boys', who evidently expected us to give them more trouble than the men. I do not think the three from Newnham and two from Girton really did; but the lab. boys took a delight in leaving some essential bit of apparatus out of our lists so that we had to walk the whole length of the lab. to the store to ask for it. An ordeal for some of us, especially as they appeared to be too busy to attend to us for several minutes while we waited at the door.

I have a vivid memory of an afternoon in my first week when I was walking down Silver Street, lost in a fresher's dream, and almost ran into one of 'The Men' who threw away his cigarette and stepped into the gutter to let me pass. 'Well,' I thought, 'whatever I feel like I must look like a grown-up lady!' (Cigarettes were cheaper and manners better then.) We wore almost a uniform of white blouse, and tweed coat and skirt. The blouse should be of 'nun's veiling' and the collar fixed with a plain rolled gold pin; but such blouses were expensive! When I wore my first, my clumsy spilling of acid in the lab. made large holes in the front which no darning would conceal. But it was still all right with the coat on; and not on the warmest spring day might that coat be removed, either at lectures or in the street, so all was well.

M. D. Ball (1908)

*

WOMEN IN LABORATORIES

My first acquaintance with Newnham was in the summer of 1909, when I came to Cambridge to take the Natural Sciences practicals of the Cambridge Higher Local Examination. Until then I had had no ambition to become a student, but this visit, when I stayed in Old Hall, filled me with an intense desire to become a member of the College. I think the appearance of the garden when I entered by the Clough Memorial Gates was what most appealed to me. Round the sunken garden was a hedge of pale pink 'monthly' roses. They flowered almost all summer long, and I felt sad when they were replaced by a lavender hedge. I was soon lucky enough to learn that I was to be given a place in College and was to be in Clough Hall. I spent a very happy first year in a ground-floor room looking over the garden.

At that time Peile Hall was being built and students who would move into Peile Hall in 1910 spent their first year in two nearby houses, Melrose in Grange Road and No. 1 Selwyn Gardens. I remember a nerve-racking occasion when a friend persuaded me to follow her up the ladders to the top-floor common room of Peile. There was a wonderful view over the College, but down below a horrifying void because no floors had yet been put in.

The only domestic job that a student had to do was to make her bed on Sundays. She did not even have to wash up the crockery etc. used in her own room. Shoes were put outside the door to be cleaned by Bowen, the Clough Hall porter, and he filled the coal-scuttles. We were lucky enough in those days to have coal fires.

We were always expected to change into evening dress for dinner in Hall. It was a more formal and probably chillier meal than nowadays. On leaving the Hall, each student picked up a mug containing half a pint of sterilised milk which was usually used later on to make cocoa over the fire in her room. Why this ration of milk was always sterilised was a mystery. Other milk was not sterilised and probably was not even pasteurised. After dark, a journey from Clough Hall to the College Library or beyond was to be avoided by nervous students. We were not supposed to use the Hall as a passageway, and in the days before the present kitchen was built, the passage between the Hall and the kitchen was the haunt of many very lively cockroaches.

During my first year, my room was looked after by Lizzie, who was for many years a valued College servant. Many of the housekeepers and maids remained for a long time in College service. The appearance of the maids was attractive. In the morning they wore print dresses with large white aprons. Later in the day they wore black dresses with small fancy aprons, and they always wore becoming frilled mob-caps. The payment of fees was simple. At the beginning of each term, an inclusive fee of £30 was paid by each student occupying an ordinary room (£32 for a large room and £35 for a set of two rooms). This fee covered all normal expenses, room with fire and service, four meals a day and all normal teaching and examination fees. Any unusual teaching had to be paid for extra, but such payment was rarely incurred. If College bed linen and towels were used a charge of, I think, ten shillings a term was made.

Except for bicycles (I was one of the many students who cycled everywhere), modes of transport in Cambridge were very different from now. Cars were almost non-existent. Hansom-cabs and four-wheelers (often called 'growlers') were used by those with plenty of cash. For others, some journeys could be made by horse-tram. A tram pulled by a single horse trundled slowly from the railway station along Hills Road. At the Roman Catholic Church, you could change to one which went via Lensfield Road and Trumpington Street to King's Parade. In due course, the horse-trams were replaced by motor buses, but the tram-lines remained for a long time after their use had disappeared.

During my three years as a student, changes were gradually taking place in the teaching arrangements. We attended University lectures, segregated to the first row or two of the lecture theatre, and were usually accompanied by a chaperon. For practical work in Biological Sciences, we were taught by College lecturers in the Balfour Laboratory in Downing Place. Practical Chemistry we did in the laboratory in the College grounds, but in my second year we joined the men students in the old University Chemical Laboratory. In my third year I joined the twelve male students and the all-male staff of the old Physiological Laboratory to work for Part II. It was quite a change!

When the present Physiological Laboratory was opened in 1914, the women students joined the men for all their practical work. For some time the women worked together in pairs, but it was not very long before working partnerships between men and women became the usual thing. In 1917, when the teaching staff of the department was depleted by the war, Professor Langley asked me to demonstrate in Physiology, work that I enjoyed doing for many years. At about the same time, Miss Hart came as the first woman assistant. It was quite a long time before the employment of girl assistants became usual.

In 1921, the University decided against making us members of the University, but granted 'Titles of Degrees' to those who had passed the necessary examinations and paid the required fees. One advantage of holding this titular degree was that it now became possible to use the University Library as a right. Until now it had only been possible to use the University Library if the College applied for a ticket for each student thought likely to make good use of the privilege.

In 1948 women were made full members of the University, with the many changes that this involved. We now had to wear caps and gowns. For examinations we sat with the men students and our names were in the same alphabetical lists as theirs. Degrees were conferred on us in the Senate House by the Vice-Chancellor and we became eligible for all University posts and prizes; we were now full members of the University on an equal footing with men.

D. Thacker (Dale, 1909)

COLLEGE MANNERS AND CUSTOMS

Madam,

As humble seekers after knowledge, may I ask a few questions concerning the manners and customs of this College which are at present a little obscure.

1 Is it really true that there are numerous pairs of Siamese twins in College, or is there such serious danger of losing one's friends that it is absolutely necessary to walk arm-in-arm even up Sidgwick Avenue?

2 Is it, or is it not the custom to *change* for dinner? I am quite in the dark as to this.

3 Notes left on Hall tables are intended as light literature for the entire community, aren't they? It would surely be selfish to seal them.

4 To what extent is the humility of a fresher supposed to go?

5 We understand that rules made by the *community* are invariably kept. This does not, we suppose, apply to silence hours, though it obviously does to the rule making the banging of doors compulsory.

6 Need the Library be used as an exercising ground on wet mornings?

7 Of course it is the best possible manners for friends invariably to sit together at meals, but must they entirely ignore anyone else who is unfortunate enough to come to the same table?

8 Need the food occupy our minds as well as our digestive organs at table?

9 Cleanliness is next to Godliness; but need it include the whole bathroom? If so, why exclude the mopping-up cloth?

10 What exactly does the term 'Private Property' mean?

11 Is it necessary for the entertainment of Sidgwick Hall that members of Clough and Old, passing through Sidgwick, should select the ground-floor corridor for their oratorical efforts?

Answers to these problems would be gratefully received by

HUMBLE FOLLOWERS OF TURVEYDROP

('You must borrow me Gargantua's mouth first,' etc. *As You Like It*, III, ii – Ed.)

From *Thersites*, November 1909

AN UNINTERRUPTED VIEW

There can be few places better sited to observe the day-to-day life of Cambridge than Trumpington Street, where it merges into King's Parade. In the terrace of houses, known as Corpus Buildings, opposite to what was then the Bull Hotel, I lived from 1903 to 1928.

From the upstairs drawing-room window there was an uninterrupted view as far as Gonville and Caius College and the Senate House, including the whole façade of King's. The hotel opposite was a constant source of interest, while to the left 'Cats' had an original frontage of enormous elm trees filled with cawing rooks. Between the college and the hotel were a couple of shops with students' rooms above. Small iron balconies gave an excellent purchase to their inmates when arriving back after the official college locking-up time.

Corpus Buildings back on to the Old Court of Corpus – a delightful spot seldom found by the casual visitor. Across a small yard gentlemen in residence could aim lumps of sugar through our back door, if left open, past a breakfast-room to targets in the hall beyond. The Saxon tower of St Bene't's church rises above the Corpus roof-tops, the oldest of all the buildings surrounding the terrace.

In a quieter age the very sounds of the town (long before it received the title of City) were characteristic: the hours, and even quarters, chimed by innumerable clocks; the morning and evening ringing of the curfew from Great St Mary's Church, which still persists above the din of traffic; but long departed are the clop-clop on stone setts of the feet of the horses which drew the trams – the only form of public transport. Two routes intersected at the end of Lensfield Road. One route ran from Great St Mary's to East Road (does the modern Newnham student even know where East Road is?); the other from Christ's College to the station. Thus, the journey from Trumpington Street to the station always involved a change at 'the Cathedral', a spot which has lost some of its significance since those days. Horses were changed on the north side of Great St Mary's and at Christ's. To call a hansom cab, the nearest ranks were outside the Senate House or St Botolph's Church at the top of Silver Street.

The Proctors, accompanied by their Bulldogs, often passed below on their nightly rounds of the streets. The wearing of both cap *and* gown was strictly enforced, and the Bulldogs, porters chosen for their fleetness of foot (is this still the same?), could be led a considerable dance if the culprit did not immediately respond to the demand for 'Your name and college, Sir?'. The sound of a chase was not infrequent, but on Sunday afternoon the measured tread of the trio on their way to the University Sermon presented a more dignified sound – the Proctors in gowns, and the Bulldogs in long capes caught up over their arms and carrying heavy leather books containing records of the University.

In the event of serious misdemeanour a gentleman 'in stat. pup.' might find himself 'sent down', permanently or only temporarily, and at this period such an event was an opportunity for a mock funeral. These processions invariably took a route along King's Parade as 'the corpse', still very much alive and sometimes riding in a hansom cab or four-wheeler, was accompanied to the railway station by a large body of mourners – a 'widow' possibly in voluminous black and a large handkerchief – the number of vehicles and the size of the crowd depending on the popularity of the deceased.

Proctors varied in popularity, as no doubt they do today. One, who had earned an unenviable reputation, found that a crowd of apparently innocent undergraduates gathered in silence outside his college and accompanied him in procession to Great St Mary's for several Sunday afternoons.

Before the First World War rags were completely spontaneous affairs;

it was after this that they became associated with November 11th and the Poppy Day collection. Guy Fawkes, however, was always regularly celebrated. Bonfires on the market square or elsewhere needed fuel. On November 5th the Bull Hotel always removed a large board outside which displayed advertisements for the New Theatre, and their wooden tubs planted with small conifer trees. Our door-mat was always taken in for that evening. It was on such an occasion that we watched a crowd of undergraduates skilfully drive the Proctor and the Bulldogs until their backs were, literally, against the wall of Barclays Bank on the corner of Corpus Buildings and Bene't Street. They took refuge on the steps of the bank and were for a considerable period unable to free themselves from the peaceful crowd which had no intention of budging an inch.

One rag of the mid-twenties stands out from others. It was announced that Howard Carter would arrive to unseal the tomb of Tutankhamen which, for the event, was located in the men's underground lavatory in the market place. Crowds gathered and the eminent archaeologist and his motley entourage duly arrived. At one point in the proceedings an angel descended on a wire stretched from the roof of the tallest building on the east side of the square to the railings of the public convenience. Many and varied were the objects brought from the 'tomb', including numerous mummies strangely resembling tailors' dummies. Tutankhamen himself proved to be Gog (or Magog) stolen from London University for the occasion, which led to further complications before the wooden figure was returned to its original owners.

Another imaginative relaxation of the twenties was the Pavement Club, which flourished for a period on Saturday mornings for some weeks and of which we had an excellent view. Participants gathered from about noon until one o'clock and the rendezvous was King's Parade. Each brought his (or in a few cases, her) own entertainment – cards, chess, tiddley-winks or the daily paper – or merely whiled away the hour in pleasant conversation. Who was participant or who audience was somewhat difficult to determine, but while it lasted all available pavement space was well filled and such traffic as there was in those days was wise to use another route.

Visitors, distinguished or otherwise, to the Bull Hotel provided much entertainment to a small girl hanging out of her top bedroom window, especially during the light June evenings of May Week. Sisters, girlfriends and their chaperons would stay for several days, both for the races and, particularly, the college balls. From eight to nine onwards trim young men in dinner-jackets arrived and emerged with their guests in ravishing creations, only partially concealed under evening cloaks which were as fascinating as the long dresses themselves. Given a fine night, there being no cars, they could be watched up the length of the street. Corpus or Cats, especially when the dance floor was in a marquee, were within sound range until early morning, and King's might be decorated with candles in coloured fairy lights the length of the screen.

The gas-lamp-lighter survived well into the century, poking his metal rod with its flame inside the tip into the small trap-door at the base of the street lamp. The milkman delivered into jugs left on the front steps, using a metal measure which hung by a hook on his polished cans, always adding an extra drop at the end. In the market butter was sold by length – a yard weighed two pounds – and the rolls were brought from the country in long wicker baskets. The 'weight' was cut off by measurement on a cane. Those baskets survived for years after the rolls disappeared and the farm butter was made into one-pound and half-pound pats, the forerunners of our machine packs today.

As a market town Cambridge has always had considerable traffic from the surrounding villages, and until the bus ousted them this was by carrier's cart. These carts came in on Saturdays and usually another day in the week. There were stables in various yards in the town – high entrances can still be seen in Trumpington Street. Many is the time that, as a small girl, I would deliver to the carrier a bottle of medicine, prescribed by my father, to go to some country patient.

Street cleaning was of a different kind – horse-droppings needed to be removed and the street sweepers were constantly passing up and down with their brush and shovel, pushing a small hand-cart. Many Newnham students must remember the one-armed crossing-sweeper at the bottom of Sidgwick Avenue, who features in Gwen Raverat's *Period Piece*. Another Cambridge character was the wooden-legged man who was always around to guide visitors through the colleges.

Our home was always open to undergraduates every Sunday afternoon – a common practice at the time – and we never ate tea alone. In memory it was always crumpets, kept warm behind the brass fender with a good fire in the grate. We are now so accustomed to a wide variety of students from abroad; until after the First World War the only large group from outside Europe were Indian students. These came in considerable numbers – as a British degree was essential for civil servants. My mother's family had a long Indian connection and she herself had lived there until she was eight years old. Thus Indian students were often among our guests and by 1923, when I myself became a student, other nationalities had become more numerous. I can remember the first African student whom I met between 1923 and 1926. We occasionally held lively international evenings in our large drawing-room. The day might be fixed by prior consultation with a young Theology student from St Catharine's, Donald Soper, whose skill at the piano and in enlivening games was a guarantee of a successful evening.

It was therefore natural that, once I became a student, I should come in contact with others similarly interested in international friendship and good relations with overseas students in Cambridge. This developed into a regular fortnightly 'International Tea', open to all students and to some senior members of the University. It was held in various places, particularly the Y.M.C.A. Hall in Alexandra Street. Organisation was simple – everyone paid 1s 6d for their tea and the only entertainment was personal conversation. Friendships were formed and, after a time, the small committee organised a residential gathering at High Leigh, Broxbourne. This proved very successful and became an annual event. Newnham and Girton were both well represented in this activity and students from the theological colleges, particularly from Westminster College and Westcott House, were among the leaders. The good spirit which prevailed owed a great deal to one of the first chairmen, a Westcott House student from Ceylon, F. R. S. Mendis.

Shortly after I had taken my degree we moved from Corpus Buildings to Huntingdon Road; my experience of Cambridge became no different from that of many another local resident living out of sight and sound of the centre of the town. The tram-lines had disappeared; buses and cars banished the comparative peace of the streets but, let us be thankful, not the ubiquitous bicycle.

M. A. Radley (Wright, 1923)

THE LAW OF DIMINISHING RETURNS

In Part II of the History Tripos then one read one's Special Subject, Modern History, and one or two other subjects, at choice. I read History of Political Ideas, and Economics. I attended the lectures of, and wrote essays for, 'young Mr Keynes'. (Dr Keynes was the Cambridge Registrary.)

Mr Keynes explained the Law of Diminishing Returns, and illustrated it by its effects on a woman dusting a room. For the first three minutes she dusts the tops of tables and other exposed surfaces; she gets off a lot of dust in the first three minutes. Then she dusts the mantelpiece and objects like chair legs; she gets much less dust off in the second three minutes. Then she gets down and dusts under the cupboard, under bookshelves and in the finicky places. She gets very little dust, proportionately for her time.

I have never spent more than three minutes in dusting a room since, because of the Law of Diminishing Returns! Young Mr Keynes (J. M. Keynes) must have influenced a lot of Newnhamites!

M. Deanesly (1909)

THE SUFFRAGE MARCH

Freshers came up a day or two before the experienced second- and third-years, and we were given a talk by the Vice-Principal of our Hall – in my case, Miss A. B. Collier. Amongst other things that she told us, I remember a caution against cigarette-smoking – it was not considered good for the young of either sex to smoke – not quite a prohibition but very close to it.

Of outside events, the one I remember most clearly was the great Suffrage march through London in the summer of 1910 or 1911.* We belonged to the non-militant movement, not the W.S.P.U., and our colours were discreet, red and white. I was one of those allowed to carry one of the poles of the Cambridge banner, and I well remember seeing men take off their hats in salute to the towers of Cambridge as we walked along the Embankment. At intervals in the procession bands played Dr Ethel Smyth's March composed especially for the occasion.

My subject was Classics, and the College lectures that I remember most vividly were those of Miss Louise Matthaei, Miss Bagge and, of course, Miss Jane Harrison. The last was a most dramatic figure. In one's first term to be introduced – after dinner – to lectures on Orphic elements in Greek religion was quite an experience. I wrote down notes and hoped that by the end of my third year I would understand them. Often a visible effect would be produced when a glittering shawl, worn by Miss Harrison round her shoulders and shrugged off at an exciting moment of recital, would fall in shimmering folds about her feet. But the most

* There were impressive Suffrage marches in both these summers. Mrs Garrett Anderson and Lady Strachey led large groups of academic women, dubbed 'Portias'; they were followed in one of the processions by a male contingent from the University of Cambridge.

dramatic effect that I remember was the time when an unearthly noise filled the room at the end of a lecture. A young man had entered the back of the room unnoticed and was demonstrating, according to Miss Harrison's instructions, what was meant by a bull-roarer.

Mr A. B. Cook's sculpture lectures in the Fitzwilliam Museum stand out in my memory, as do those of Professor Jackson, the modern Socrates. Gilbert Murray's occasional lectures were considered a treat. Francis Cornford was a well-known figure as he strode the Cambridge streets, and of course we knew his wife's poetry. The book describing the Versailles adventure by Miss Moberly and Miss Jourdain was published during my time at Newnham. It was a subject for discussion at our tea-parties.

M. E. Holland (1909)

*

THE RISE OF COMMITTEES

1911: Michaelmas Term. In this term the first students' committee came into being. It is intended to form a link between the staff and the students, and is composed of two representatives from each Hall, i.e. the senior student and one other member. A representative library committee has also been formed, composed of students taking the various subjects.

In the Political Society the Liberals were in power, Miss Jebb being the Prime Minister. Among the measures introduced were a Labour Disputes Bill, a Licensing Bill, and a Bill for the formation of labour colonies. On November 13th a debate was held to discuss the proposed Adult Suffrage Bill.

Extract from the North Hall Diary

*

THE HERETICS

We could invite men to join a tea-party in our pleasant bed-sitters only if we provided a chaperon. (We could give them tea in Hall unchaperoned.) My sister Evelyn, at the time secretary to the head of the Medical Schools, Professor (later Sir) German Sims-Woodhead, used to accept the role of chaperon. But another single woman, often invited to fill it, one day astonished hostess and guests, when the men visitors had left, by exclaiming, 'I had no idea that Newnham had advanced so far that *now* you can have men without a chaperon!'

When we went to such an event as the annual concert at St John's, we could have a male escort. But the Vice-Principal of my own Hall (Sidgwick) was almost reduced to tears when our head student – one of the most discreet girls in Cambridge – attended an afternoon football match with a male student – unchaperoned! This same don once had a curious conversation with my sister, as to why girls need go to dances. My sister mildly suggested that they might learn something about life. 'But what could they learn about life at a dance, Miss Fox, that they couldn't learn just as well from a good book?' From which it will be seen that she really *was* prehistoric, though charming – there was no other like her in Cambridge. When we went to the meetings of such a dangerous debating society as 'The Cambridge Heretics' (Girton girls were not allowed to join it; N.B. no one had to *be* a heretic to join) we were shepherded by a don. It met at the top of a house in Trumpington Street, the bottom floor housing a fish-business. For long after, the smell of fish recalled The Heretics. Amongst the special speakers I heard there were Rupert Brooke, G. K. Chesterton (at an 'open' meeting: that is, open to student non-members. He was replying to George Bernard Shaw whom I had just missed), Professor Edward Bullough, a very distinguished linguist, Frank Harris – the most repulsive speaker I heard at The Heretics – and C. F. Angus, a Classical lecturer. I must record that one of our most vociferous members was a Roman Catholic from Montenegro. C. F. Angus was a Christian and gave us what was practically a sermon. He was listened to with profound attention, and there was no heckling in the discussion. Whereas another Christian speaker who addressed us in a patronising tone was given a nasty heckling later. Our President was C. K. Ogden, later a well-known writer on philosophy, while still in his twenties.

No smoking was allowed in those days. I well remember one of the two distinguished Butler sisters – I cannot recall whether it was the one who later became the Mistress of Girton – coming in to me one day in a state of worry and exclaiming: 'I *must* have a cigarette!' So we committed the unheard-of crime of going out to the field just beyond Newnham grounds, and, seated with our backs to the hedge, indulging in a cigarette!

One or two incidents at the Medical Schools, in my sister's time, may be of some interest. Some experiments were being made, in connection with bubonic plague, on guinea-pigs completely isolated by tanks of water across which the carrier-fleas could not possibly jump. The Professor went away for a few days while his experiment matured.

Rumours of its nature leaked out in the town, and such fears of a possible outbreak of the plague arose that the guinea-pigs had to be killed and burned – to the great chagrin of the Professor on his return! He knew, of course, that his precautions had been perfect. He also, at one time, tried an experiment on himself at the Medical Laboratories. To test the effect of alcohol on the heart, he put himself to bed in the basement, and took varying doses of alcohol, having his heart's reaction tested. He was somewhat nettled that he was later twitted by his friends on the good time he had been having – he being a well-known teetotaller.

G. F. Fox (1911)

*

£5 PER TERM

Three of us went up together for the entrance examination, thrilled by the golden half-sovereigns (the first we had ever possessed) given us by our Headmistress K. H. Masson (Newnham, 1893) to buy something for our rooms – pictures, though Miss Masson had envisaged armchairs. The latter we got from students going down – half a crown each, I believe! We also had to supply bookcases, covers and cushions for our divans. I turned out the washstand with its china and so had more space in my small first-year room. Great was our delight when four of us moved to top floor Pfeiffer, with its informal access, via bathroom and roof, to the main building of Old Hall.

Our modesty in those days was excessive: I was in bed and did not admit the games captain when she visited me, so I lost the chance of captaining the Freshers' Team. We played hockey or lacrosse most days, or I walked across the fields to Grantchester, occasionally passing en route Rupert Brooke, 'young Apollo, golden-haired'. We often punted to the Orchard, or canoed to Byron's Pool to swim. Our activities were simple. Matthew's was the rendezvous for morning coffee or buying luscious cakes. Cocoa-parties with keen discussions were held almost every night when Silent Hours ended at 10 p.m. and sometimes concluded with a rowdy game around Hall when a distracted V.-P. would protest that we were shaking the whole building. One Rag Week, undergraduates raided Newnham and stormed the gates – in vain, but some actually penetrated to the garden and were ignominiously routed by stern dons. For any man to seek in the Library for his friends was unheard-of. The only time the sacred silence was broken was when I burst into laughter reading some French play. Luckily the Library was deserted and I came to my senses to find that everyone was in Hall and I had missed dinner.

About eight of us founded S.P.I.F. ('Society for the Protection of Innocent Freshers'), but except as a social literary circle it was not really necessary as we soon had good relations with all second- and third-years. Unless we were lucky in getting Miss Paues or a young married friend as chaperon we accepted no invitations to men's rooms – other chaperons seemed to cast a blight. We seldom spoke to men; even at lectures we were segregated. One Old Student still blushes to think of the cold looks she received her first term when she rolled up from the station in a hansom with the man she subsequently married. They never met in term-time again, even though they travelled together.

There were many College societies. Some of us were puzzled when there was trouble over an invitation sent by the Literary Society to John Galsworthy. 'He should never have been asked,' said Authority, and the meeting was relegated to a small lecture room.

We appreciated G. C. Macaulay's lectures – though he usually preferred to speak with his back turned. Two of the 'Babies' (May and June?) of 'Elizabeth in her German Garden' attended these, severely chaperoned and wearing picture hats and stylish dresses. 'Q', later Sir Arthur Quiller-Couch, gave a series of lectures, packed to the window-sills. He held discussion classes for a privileged few, and I shudder to think of my rudeness in referring to 'armchair critics' in a paper on 'The Alleged Obscurity of Robert Browning'; but Q was tolerant.

Clothes were perforce simple: my allowance for dress, books, fares, entertainment was £5 per term, yet I seemed to hold my own; I learnt later that my friends had up to £20. However everything was cheap by present-day standards: sugar twopence a pound, laundry ten shillings a term including stockings, tennis skirts, blouses, etc. An off-the-peg 'costume' was twenty-five shillings, a really nice one, £4; we envied the student in a lovely green suit made by her uncle's London tailor, six guineas! I managed to sport a round black hat from Paris with two ostrich feathers like question marks, and for a bet cycled to the station in Cambridge blue silk stockings. A £20 legacy gave me a month in Paris.

All good things come to an end. I remember the text 'Little children help one another' round the room where we took Mays and Finals, with banging workmen outside and a leaking glass roof which dropped tear-drops on my Anglo-Saxon paper. Between papers we were nourished by first-years on cucumber sandwiches in the sunken garden. Our year was unlucky as there was an outbreak of gastric influenza: one took an aegrotat, another did her papers in bed, I struggled on only to get a Third instead of the hoped-for First.

So we went down, with many happy memories, not least of our tutors – Miss Paues, Miss Collier, Miss Strachey (French proses), Miss Clough – and our Principal, Miss Stephen. The latter occasionally honoured us with an invitation, but seldom remembered names: meeting a crowd of Old Students up for a weekend she gently reminded us 'Oughtn't you to be in bed? Examinations tomorrow!'

W. Gascoigne (1911)

A REMNANT PARTY

A 'remnant' party was held on Thursday, December 7th, 1911, in Miss Robertson's room. After the minutes of the last meeting had been read and confirmed, soap bubble blowing and smelling competitions were held. Intervals of cocoa drinking were enlivened by the whole party playing popular tunes on combs, and when opportunities occurred, the third years living in Top Floor Pfeiffer were serenaded. After a hearty vote of thanks to Miss Robertson for the loan of her room, the meeting was adjourned.

Extract from the minutes of the 'Society for the Protection of Innocent Freshers' (see p. 90)

THE GIRTON MATCH

11 February 1912

I have got my braid [team colours]! Isn't it too lovely for words? And we have played the Girton match and won it – altogether a joyful state of affairs.

At the beginning of the week it was still freezing hard, and on Monday I skated all the afternoon. This week I have been doing ¾ hour's work before breakfast, as Nancy invited me to her sitting room, where there is a fire. As it was the week of the Girton match, all the team and possible members of it, had to be in bed by 10.30, or soon after, so getting up at 6.45 was possible, and means that it is fairly easy to do 8 hours' work a day – but it's no good if people come and stay late at cocoas. I can't do with much less than 8 hours' sleep, unfortunately – at least, not for many days on end – and it's no good getting tired. On Tuesday the thaw came. I had a coffee, and then we played, sang and mended.

On Wednesday there was a T.P. – perfectly miserable – ground a slough of despond – team out of condition – altogether horrible. I spent most of my time in falling down, and getting covered with mud, and thought I had done for my chances of the team.

On Friday the team list was put up, and my name was down to play. In the evening there was an exceedingly interesting meeting about the Workers' Education Association. Do you know about it? It is the poor people who can't give the years and money for college, but who are so keen that they pledge themselves to take a three years' course in economics, history or literature (these are the favourite subjects), and they do the most splendid work, under the most impossible conditions. It's too long to say much about now, but it's just the sort of thing I should love to help with if I could some time.

I came back from the meeting, and then worked till the college captain came in at 9.55 to see that I was ready for bed. (We have to be in bed by 10 the night before a match.) She was so nice, and finally told me I had won my braid. You can imagine my joy and excitement. I was absolutely mad with joy. I rushed up and told Barbara, who was awfully pleased too. Going to bed early proved useless, as I was much too excited to sleep till 12 o'clock or so!

The next morning I went and got my braid. It is gold, and looks lovely on the blue skirt. Vera Edminson sewed it on for me. (You always have your braid sewn on by a friend the first time.) It was a gorgeous day, warm and sunshiny.

At 1.45 the team started to drive to Girton in a brake. We took the cup with us. Everyone was so nice. Really all the team people are some of the very nicest in College, and it is so jolly to get this chance of meeting them.

The match began. I was nervous at first, but as soon as I began to play I felt all right. There were heaps of Newnham people there, and a continuous roar of 'Newnham' and 'Girton' was kept up along the side lines. It *was* an exciting match. We got three goals to their one, in the first half; but in the second, they got two more, and for what seemed an age we were three all, with the ball up and down the field in the most even way. Finally, just before time, we scored again. I *was* so thankful, for it was simply agonising before! All the people who were watching dashed back to carry the news home. We stayed for tea with the teams. Then we drove off. Girton cheered us, and we them. The drive home was lovely, and we were all tremendously happy. As we got near Newnham we saw a black mass at each side of the archway, and when the horses stopped, the most terrific noise began. People rang fire bells and bicycle bells, and banged dinner gongs, and coal shovels, and anything else they could lay hands on, and cheered and shouted! The whole team fled across the garden, but we were followed by the rest into Clough dining hall, and when the captain put the cup back in its old place (this is the fourth year in succession that we have held it), the noise began again. They cheered the team, the captain, and the cup, and continued to do so at every opportunity the rest of the day! There was a team dinner, with the cup in the centre of the team table, and a bunch of violets at each place. Miss Clough made such a neat little speech. She said: 'I do not think there is any need for me to make any remarks. *There* is the cup. *There* is the team. Let us drink to their healths!' At which, of course, there was much clapping. The captain made a nice speech in answer, and said every member of the team had played up splendidly. After that the rest of the Hall simply rose up and shouted 'for they are jolly good fellows,' and cheered until the team got up and marched off for dessert. After that there was a splendid concert. A Cambridge lady, with a lovely voice, sang charmingly. Then we danced, ending up with team lancers, after which we put the cup in the middle of the floor, and the team danced round it, and the rest of the people round the team. They all sang 'for they are jolly good fellows.' When we were too exhausted to dance any longer, there was a final burst of cheering all round, and then we attempted to go to bed – but I doubt if anyone managed it – we were much too excited. I went to D.'s room, and finally got to bed about 12.30! It was a day to remember, and I did feel so happy to think that I was a member of that joyful, victorious team!

M. M. McArthur (1911)

Extract from a letter home, reprinted from *That Friend of Mine* by Josephine Kellett

ALL HALLOWS' E'EN, 1912

A sharpshooting frivolous debate was held in Miss Foster's room on All Hallows' E'en. Before the debate a motion was brought forward and carried that a new Minutes book should be bought, in which should also be entered photographs, poems etc.

Refreshments were dispensed, and the debate opened with the following motion:

That each Hall should have a cat
Proposer Miss Wild
Opposer Miss Foster

The honourable proposer was greeted with cheers, but after her opening 'Madam' was called to order for eating during her speech. She then put it to the House that it would be a pity to be deprived of the cat's melody, as one would get too much slumber, and one's energies during the day would be too great.

The Honourable Opposer laid stress on the fact that one would never know that one's eatables were one's own. Footmarks would be found on the butter and on one's best notebooks.

Miss Waller-Stevens suggested that mice also walk over butter. Cats eat mice who eat butter.

Miss Foster contended that the cat eats both the mouse and the butter, because he takes butter to make the mouse go down. (Cheers.) The motion was lost.

Other motions were drawn in the following order:

That those who can force a shrinking student to speak for two minutes in their presence or to stand silent, are inhuman barbarians
Proposer Miss Reyner
Opposer Miss Carter

Miss Jepps and Miss Deakin also spoke. The motion was lost.

A fresher who crawls is preferable to a fresher who bumps
Proposer Miss Sewell
Opposer Miss Mason

The Honourable Proposer's speech consisted mainly of applause and encouraging suggestions from other members of the House.

Miss Waller-Stevens and Miss Gascoigne also spoke, and as the latter was the only one who stood up for the Bumper, the motion was won.

A College wall-paper and an ordinary carpet is preferable to an ordinary paper and a College carpet
Proposer Miss White
Opposer Miss Fox

The question was complicated by the various interpretations of the description 'ordinary'. The Honourable Opposer had to be called to order for sucking barley sugar during her speech. She dwelt on the joy of studying the flickering shadows on a nice paper when one has a large fire in one's room.

Miss Jepps suggested that in the case of a large fire, it would be more sensible to call up the Brigade (Loud cheers). The motion was lost.

Extract from the minutes of the 'Society for the Protection of Innocent Freshers' (see p. 90)

*

LIFE IN PEILE HALL

When I entered Newnham in 1912, Peile Hall had been opened for about a year and lacked the mellow appearance and traditions of the other Halls. I had entered as a post-graduate student and came up with the freshers, knowing nobody. My home was over 6,000 miles away and I was both homesick and lonely. I wondered why so many of my contemporaries seemed to know one another and it was not until I realised that they had been up together for an entrance examination that the reason for my seeming isolation became clear. The research which I proposed to do was to be carried out in the Botany School in Downing Street and this too added to my feeling of detachment. However, new students were not allowed to feel lonely for long. Each night after dinner students collected large mugs of milk later to be taken to cocoa-parties. Sometimes it was necessary to ask one's hostess to leave some milk in the mug for there were occasions when one was bidden to two, three or even four similar parties on one night and it was considered bad form to refuse an invitation. One was not expected to stay more than about ten minutes at each party, but as a way of getting to know one's fellow-students it served its purpose well. Before long I was completely at home and happy in the friendships that are fostered by life in College.

Before coming to Cambridge I had spent over four years at the South African College in Cape Town where men and women mingled freely both in the lecture rooms and outside. True, a chaperon was considered necessary at dances and other formal social events, but in general the sexes conversed freely whenever they met. Therefore it came as a considerable shock to discover that in Cambridge this freedom did not exist. In the Botany School where I was one of three women doing research, we were isolated in a small laboratory by ourselves. Then, fortunately, the proprieties being observed, segregation of the sexes ceased and round the tea-table and elsewhere one met one's male coworkers on terms of equality. One day soon after my arrival and before I realised the necessity of owning a bicycle, I came out of the front door of the School with one of the male students on his way to lunch in Caius College. Quite naturally we fell into conversation and walked together as far as the junction of Silver Street. There we said goodbye and I proceeded on my way to be overtaken shortly by a fellow-Newnhamite. She remarked casually that it was a good thing no don had seen me with my recent companion for walking in the street with a man, except in the case of a father or a brother, was strictly forbidden. That was my introduction to the taboos that surrounded female students in those far-off days.

Another irksome rule was that insisting that if one went out after dinner, one had to be back by eleven o'clock. On only one occasion in the year was this rule waived for the ordinary student. That was the occasion of the Greek Play, performed by members of the University in the theatre in St Andrew's Street. Fortunately in the case of the post-graduate student if one went out with a don possessing a key to the main gate, one was exempt from this rule. I was a member of the Marshall Ward Society which held its meetings in the rooms of its members, meetings at which discussions were often long and heated, and it was often after eleven before the meeting ended. Fortunately Miss Saunders was also a member and, as a don, she had a key. Looking back over the years, these restrictions were minor blemishes in a happy and carefree life. The authorities were broad-minded enough to allow me to take part in botanical excursions organised by the Botany School, excursions on which, on occasions, I was the only female present.

Having been admitted as a fourth-year student, I had the privilege of having breakfast and lunch at the High Table. Apart from the undoubted advantage of having a supply of warm food if one happened to be late for a meal, one met informally the dons attached to the Hall. Miss J. P. Strachey was in charge of the Hall and took a personal interest in all the students under her. She had not the gift of making easy contact with students but her innate kindliness and interest in the well-being of us all made her a much liked and respected head. She was known to us as 'The Streak', a name acquired no doubt on account of her tall, spare figure. She had not the tough independence of outlook which made Miss B. A. Clough such an outstanding head of Clough Hall. For example, when a student made an unusual request Miss Strachey did not find it easy to come to an immediate and independent decision. Instead she would ask for time to think over the problem. We all knew that what she wanted was time to consult Miss Stephen, the Principal at that time, or Mrs Sidgwick, an ex-Principal. Being in charge of a Hall was not an easy task for one with her retiring disposition, and she often found difficulties where a person like Miss Clough, with an easy approach to students and a decisive mind, would never have had these moments of indecision.

The most cheerful person at the High Table was Jane Harrison who was always the centre of animated conversation. Her striking appearance and often unorthodox clothing, added to her reputation as a scholar, made her one of Newnham's outstanding characters of that period. At lunch soon after my arrival she and I were standing together at a side table helping ourselves to food. To my amazement I saw her add to a plate which already had a helping of soup, some hard stewed prunes and the light brown liquid which accompanied them. For good measure some meat from another dish was added. As she sat down at table with this extraordinary mixture she remarked, with obvious satisfaction, that this was an interesting combination and we should try it.

As a Botanist I soon met Rebecca Saunders who at that time was a don in Sidgwick. She was not my supervisor as that task had been entrusted to Mr R. P. Gregory of the Botany School. She was known affectionately to all Science students as 'Becky'. She had striking features which became evident as soon as one was able to take one's eyes off her clothes. In those days the attire of men and women was sharply contrasted and no woman ever wore trousers. Miss Saunders' daytime clothing was a tailor-made costume, most uncompromisingly male in all but its skirt which was long and covered her ankles. A stiff white collar and tie added to the masculinity of her appearance. This was emphasised by her hair which, although not short, appeared to be so at first sight. She wore it brushed tightly back and secured in a small knot at the back. Her hats were as masculine as her dress and it was only many years later that I realised that she was capable of wearing an indisputably feminine hat. The occasion was a garden party given in honour of the British Association, visiting South Africa. In Cape Town on an extremely wet winter's day, she appeared at the party in a straw hat covered with artificial flowers. Her concern over the fate of these flowers was touching and we did our best to see that they were protected from the rain which marred that particular function.

Debates, both serious and otherwise, took place in Clough Hall. Among the outstanding debaters were L. F. Nettlefold and L. A. Wright. I remember a hilarious debate on 'Ragtime tends to insanity', in which

Leila Wright convulsed the Hall with her amusing remarks and demonstrations.

Among my fellow-Botanists was Ruth Holden from the United States of America. She came up in 1913 and later became a Fellow of Newnham College. Her somewhat forbidding appearance failed to hide a most lovable and interesting character, one with no time at all for orthodox ladylike behaviour. She hated sewing, mending garments in particular. Thus when holes appeared in her stockings, they were classified into those that could be worn with shoes and those which could be worn only with boots. One night when she was staying in Clough Hall after other students had gone down, she was wearing stockings of the 'boots only' variety. Sitting in front of her fire with slippers on her feet, she heard suspicious noises on the ground floor. Seizing a poker, she set forth to investigate. At the foot of the stairs she met Miss Clough and realised that it was she who had been responsible for the sounds that had brought her down. Apologising for her appearance brandishing a poker, she was about to go back to her room when she realised that if she turned round, the unfortunate state of her stockings would be revealed. So, keeping Miss Clough engaged in conversation, she proceeded to back up the stairs until she was round a corner and could safely say goodnight.

In those days research workers were allowed to remain in Hall a week after the end of term, and Ruth Holden and I often availed ourselves of this privilege. As we were frequently the only students in our respective Halls, noises seemed to echo in the empty passages. At such times ghost stories were not quite suitable for late-night reading. I well remember an occasion when I had been reading such stories until close on midnight. I was compelled to sing in my bath so as to convince myself that no supernatural beings roamed those long empty corridors, waiting to waylay me on the way back to the bedroom.

M. R. Levyns (Michell, 1912)

WHAT A CHANGE THERE WAS!

We were a small year who came up to Clough Hall in 1913, and most of us were from grammar or high schools, with much the same background. We revelled in our study-bedrooms, with coal fires, fortunately laid for us, though we had to light them ourselves which was not always easy!

There was no central heating, and Cambridge can be very cold, but once the fire got going what a cosy room it was!

As I was reading for the Natural Sciences Tripos, I had to be up for the whole of the Long Vacation Term – a thoroughly enjoyable time. There were botany and geology excursions, and long afternoons in a canoe or punt on the upper river. But these were interrupted by the declaration of war, which came as a shock to us.

When we returned in October, what a change there was! Most of the men had suddenly disappeared, except for foreigners and medical students. Instead of young demonstrators, we had senior members of the University. Soon, food became short, and one had to decide whether to be a vegetarian at lunch or at dinner. Evening milk, instead of appearing automatically, had to be ordered in advance. Very soon, the casualty lists began to contain the names of our contemporaries. In College itself, life went on much as usual, though we attended Red Cross lectures, and, when we had qualified for our certificates, some of us spent afternoons helping at the Wordsworth Grove Red Cross Hospital, where Miss G. L. Elles was Commandant.

In 1916, a party of us acted as 'guinea-pigs', trying out if women, especially university women, could be employed on the land in vacations. We were the earliest college to go down for the summer vacation, and we went to the Wingland Co-partnership Farm, at Sutton Bridge on the Lincolnshire–Norfolk boundary, to help with fruit-picking, mainly strawberries. The season was a late one, so we did farm work of all kinds, especially hay-making, until the strawberries were ripe. As a number of local women were always employed, it was not certain how we would 'mix', but all went well. We lived in the village hall a mile or so away, and cycled to our work. We slept on straw mattresses, and Miss A. E. Linsell came with us as chaperon-cook-housekeeper, so we had no worries about food, though we helped with chores. It was a happy time, though we found that land work used unaccustomed muscles. We were amused to be interviewed by the picture papers (*Daily Mirror* and *Daily Sketch*), and for a day or two we were news. But soon it became a commonplace for university women and others to spend their vacations working on the land. If we completed 100 hours' work, we were given our Land Army armlets, and were very proud of them. This was our last Newnham activity, for it was after the end of our three years, and I remember that the Tripos results came out while we were there.

M. E. Alcock (1913)

*

1914

'PALEY'S GHOST'

I came from Western Australia, then a very unimportant and little-known country, and found among other harassments that I had to take a 'Qualifying Exam' and a 'Little-go' – complete mysteries to a colonial cousin.

Paley's *Evidences of Christianity* was one set book, so having procured the tome I 'swotted' madly and arrived for the exam still clutching the volume. To my astonishment everyone else was wandering round the beautiful lawns and gardens with a slim little blue book in their hands. I knew no one else there but finally screwed up courage to ask what it was, and discovered that I was probably the only prospective student in the last fifty years to study Paley. Everyone else did 'Paley's Ghost', where all possible questions – and answers – were tabulated.

My next memory is not so harrowing, though I blushed on the occasion. Sir Arthur Quiller-Couch hurried down from some military occupation to give a Shakespearian lecture. It was not actually on our course, but he was too fine a scholar to be missed and we women went in force, though instead of notebooks we took our current warwork – knitting. Besides the hundreds of women there were about six men, some foreigners, some discharged casualties. We understood our lecturer had a strong dislike for female students, so awaited his entrace with interest.

He strode in, ran his eye over the audience till he reached the back row and began, 'Gentlemen...' The insult was too much, and we gave him a little rhythmic clapping. When we stopped he continued, 'As I was saying, *Gentlemen*, I am lecturing on a Shakespearian character. She made no impertinent clamour with her hands, she did not click small pieces of metal continuously; *she* indulged in womanly occupations, Hermione, the perfect woman!'

Two other short memories concern sport. We had a well-organised fire-drill, as the College lay in the path Zeppelins would take trying to reach London, and my job was to count College personnel into the cellars. A raid warning came though one night, and I found my cellar-tally one short. I scoured the rooms of Sidgwick Hall to no avail, but on the top floor noted that the trap-door to the roof was open. Racing up I found the lacrosse captain scanning the heavens. 'If those blighters drop a bomb on the oval and spoil it for tomorrow's match...' she snorted. I bustled her down, pointing out that if she stayed there and they did, *she* would not be interested in the match.

A last memory is of a cricket match in the Long Vac. Numbers of the men's colleges were being used as convalescent hospitals, and we were asked if we would play a match against some of the inmates. Rather patronisingly we agreed. I never discovered how many actually played because they arrived en masse and while two would come in to bat two others, with good legs, came too, to run for them, while their supporters lined the boundaries and demoralised us with comments: 'She can't catch that. There, I said she wouldn't'; 'I bet she makes a duck'; and so on. We became more and more helpless. They licked us hollow, but our shame was mitigated slightly when we were told that their 'team' included about fifteen county players.

O. J. M. Cusack (Drummond, 1914)

*

A RIPPING TIME

'Well, I am practically settled now and having a ripping time, the days are simply flying past and I have been here a week today.'

'I am getting on rippingly – I can see that this is an extremely nice place – We have such heaps to occupy ourselves with, I never have a minute to spare.'

The above quotations are from letters written to my family in my very first weeks at Newnham. The 'extremely nice place' stayed extremely nice for the following years; my diaries* and letters are a long record of a wonderful, carefree life of work and play. Owing to the war, our undergraduate days were necessarily not quite normal, but all the essentials were there. Belgians were always with us – my account book has a recurring item, 'Belgian family 2s 6d' – a Belgian Minister of State came and lectured to us – there were frequent money-raising efforts for Belgian refugees. The First Eastern General Hospital on the Backs, with its open wards and its nurses blue with cold, reminded us constantly of what was happening in France. In the spring of 1915, I read in one of my specially enthusiastic letters, the King reviewed troops on Parker's Piece and 'I saw him quite close'. During that first year many young men were waiting for their commissions, but they speedily vanished.

We were spoiled in many ways: real coal fires in our rooms, a can of hot water brought in by a maid every morning, etc. Life grew faster and fuller – one regrettable quotation from my diary reads 'did not go

* See pp. 113ff.

to any lectures, as I hadn't time'. We obeyed the 'house rules' but on March 5th, 1917 I read, 'College Meeting in the evening. Our Petition granted and all the idiotic chap. (chaperon) rules are extinct.'

Then came the last weeks. We sat in the Guildhall and gazed at the Tripos papers – we were given special Trip lunches and waited on by kindly dons. We gave each other Trip teas. And our last memory – on the last night we organised a roof climb, beginning on the roof of the Library. No one fell off.

Goodbyes to everybody, including our special dons; goodbye to

Ignatius Smith and Jemima Betts*
Two strange creatures kept as pets.

Arrangements for telegrams with good or bad news of Tripos results – and finally the train steams out of that rather awful station which is a long, long way from Newnham.

How dull it was to pause, to make an end.

N. McC. Smith (1914)

* Porter and portress.

*

'B.A. IS HERE'

In our day the only male who could be entertained without a chaperon in one's room was a brother, and we were called upon to remember (by Miss [B. A.] Clough I think) that 'the brother of one is not the brother of all'. No friends must be entertained at the same time as a brother.

Peile Hall had a bathroom under the staircase and practically at the front door. A notice appeared on the board signed by Miss Strachey: 'Will students kindly confine their baths to the bathroom and not let them intrude into the hall?' There was a story, I won't vouch for its truth, that one student of Clough Hall, having tried to get into a second-floor bathroom several times one morning, got exasperated and knocked and said, 'If you don't hurry out of this bathroom I'll tell B.A.' A voice replied, 'B.A. is here.'

M. Butterworth (Drury, 1914)

*

1915

THE GARDENS AND THE HALLS

I have always considered it undesirable to turn into a ghost before it becomes necessary in the course of nature. Yet it is an imminent risk which anyone takes who sets out, as I did, not forty, but fifty years on, to revisit the lost Elysium of youth, and he need not complain if he finds himself strangely regarded in haunts that to him are dear and familiar.

In the main, change cannot be dodged. Newnham itself, on three sides of its most lovely garden where the nightingales could keep even us awake on a summer night, has tucked its own new horrors away in one corner; not much in evidence, but there all the same. The ground-floor passage, however, has in places been reroaded, like a new bypass, and I had the humiliating experience of actually losing my way. I had to stop a child, who had apparently forgotten to put on her skirt, and ask how to get to the Great Hall. Parts of the ground-floor passage were ever dark and eerie, especially in blackout times. The stretch through Kennedy Buildings was always known to be haunted, and was never nice on a dark night alone; but I would not have believed I could ever fail to navigate any part of it.

I went up in 1915 and sat my Tripos in 1918, so the First World War is the inescapable background of all memories. The preponderance of women in the classrooms made the salutation of 'Gentlemen' more ridiculous than ever. But the colleges housed soldiers doing courses, studying this and that, marching and counter-marching through the streets and the countryside. Working in the Library at Newnham you could hear them going by, singing the haunting songs of those years, which still have the power to twist the heart. 'There's a long, long trail awinding' always brings back that scene. Two war memories stand out. Coming out of the cool cavern of the Guildhall, where we were sitting the Tripos in June of 1918, into the blazing heat of the market place and falling upon the newsboys to get the early papers and know if Amiens still held out against the German advance; and standing breathless in the still sunlight of early morning to catch in the far distance the sound of the guns in France.

I had one unnerving experience. I was going home to Newnham along Silver Street. I was halfway along on the one narrow footpath, just where the cliff-like walls are highest and blindest, when what appeared to be the whole British Army marched in at the other end in column of four. Well, I suppose I was fair game and there was no escape. I had to run the gauntlet as best I could, to whistles and cat-calls and 'Who's your lady friend?', 'Who were you with last night?', till I nearly died of embarrassment and of being conspicuous, which in my young days you ought not to be. In my old age, I can be glad I gave them that much fun.

Our own war activities inside the College were many and various. Looking back, they were rather pathetic, but we were dreadfully in earnest. The blackout was strict on account of the Zeppelins. One had actually been brought down not so very far away, somewhere in the Fens. So we had our air-raid warnings and our fire-drills. The College fire brigade had always been an élite body and now came into its own in the national effort. There was fierce competition between the units, as to which could rig its apparatus most quickly and first give the order to 'Turn on!' Not of course that we ever had 'Turned on'. Normally over the years this order had been followed by 'Turn off. Break up.' And then the performance was repeated in reverse. But then there never had been a fire, beyond the odd chimney. Indeed, there was an apocryphal story of a housekeeper who begged one Vice-Principal not to call out the young ladies, for she and the housemaids could very well cope without all that fuss. But now it was decided to put it all to the test and particularly the ancient hoses. So the little observatory in the centre of the garden was declared to be on fire, and each Hall, in wild competition, ran out its apparatus and the order to 'Turn on' was ecstatically obeyed. The result was like the fountains in an Italian garden. The water never reached the huge brass nozzles that had long been so lovingly polished, but the hoses themselves spouted fiercely in every direction. Four brigades were soaked, and the exercise expired in laughter and ultimately a new set of hoses.

The days were so packed with doing and being that, looking back now, it is hard to realise that it only lasted three years. Our work and our play, our joys and our sorrows, lectures and tutorials, societies, debates and play-acting, hockey and lacrosse, cricket and tennis, swimming and boating (some of us fell in and some did not) filled every moment of time. Quite often we did not get enough to eat, but that was cheerfully accepted, and we somehow managed to have our winter cocoa-parties and our summer teas in the garden. Our multitudinous bicycles carried us in every direction over the Fenland, and we walked inevitably across the fields to Grantchester.

Which brings me to the point where Rupert Brooke can no longer be passed over. Nowadays opinions about him differ wildly. Everyone has his own, and I do not intend to give mine. But one thing must be said:

Rupert Brooke expressed, as no one else has ever done, the mood and the atmosphere of those days. It was ignorant, if you like, for realisation of what modern war is came late to this nation. The strange exaltation, the burning patriotism, the enormous upsurge of the early days, were crystallised in his verse. This should be recorded, because Brooke only wrote what everybody was feeling. He made his own generation articulate. This, I believe, was the root of his popularity and his cult. Disillusionment came later, but he cannot be blamed for that, nor did he survive to experience it.

I had the happiness of going back as a post-graduate, to keep term in the summer of 1919, and so in the end I saw it all as it ought to be. Cambridge in May and June is in truth the Earthly Paradise. 'What do they know of England, who only England know?' It was through the eyes of a South African, who had come home to serve, that the realisation of its full glory was given to me. Coming from the high and barren veldt, he looked upon the procession of our changing seasons as on a miracle. The bursting trees, the blossom and the flowers were a ceaseless revelation. It was a curious experience to see anyone so overpowered by what we all can so easily take for granted. He did not quarrel with the way the English talk about the weather, for he could talk of nothing else. And so, with the colleges once more packed with those who had come home, we danced our way into the peace, through May Week and the bumpers and the college balls, under the flowering trees and the midnight nightingales. And when I went back this year Newnham was as beautiful as ever, and prosperous and well found, with extra modern luxuries. We were made most welcome, and given a superb meal in the Great Hall, more than we could eat for once, and the only difficulty was in recognising our old friends. Clutching a glass of sherry in my hand, I began to search the reception room. I came face to face with a bosom pal with whom I have never lost touch, and we both looked hard at one another and then passed on. And then, at the same moment, we both turned and looked back. Well, after all fifty years is a long time. But we soon made up for that

> Walking about the gardens and the halls
> Of Camelot, as in the days that were.

M. E. Waterhouse (Woods, 1915)

*

PROPRIETY BEFORE PUNCTUALITY

It was represented to the Principal that when several undergraduates were going from one University lecture to another immediately following, it was difficult on occasions to avoid walking with a male undergraduate. Her reply was that the Newnham student should either leave the first lecture early or arrive late at the second lecture!

O. W. Pound (1914)

*

A SHORT ACQUAINTANCESHIP

We were told that Helen Gladstone would be talking one evening in Old Hall about the early days when A. J. Clough was Principal, so we crowded into the dining-hall and were delighted by her stories. Especially by the one about an invitation for the women to go skating which Miss Clough declined, appalled at the possibility this conjured up in her mind of men and women falling in a heap, skirts flying and legs sprawling in all directions.

I had the honour to captain a hockey team in my second year, in a match betwen 'Probable Wives and Possible Spinsters'. As captain of the Possible Spinsters I was careful to ask only the prettiest girls to play for my side, and we disguised ourselves so successfully that we were told our own mothers wouldn't have recognised us. It was a jolly match. I got a black eye. I forget who won.

In my final term a young Spaniard timidly approached me after a German lecture and asked if he might escort me home. 'When can we meet again?' he asked. 'You can call for tea by accident if we arrange which day,' I forbiddingly replied, 'and we can introduce you to the Vice-Principal.' 'When can we meet again?' he asked. 'We can have a Tennis Tea Party without any tennis if you bring a man and I bring a girl and we book a quarter of the summer-house,' I replied. 'When can we meet again?' he asked. 'After Trip my mother is coming up and can act as chaperon if you ask the same man and girl to join us for supper in your rooms,' I replied, 'Where are your rooms?' 'In Grantchester,' he said, 'the Old Vicarage, Rupert Brooke's old rooms.'

I left Newnham next day and never saw him again.

M. Dawes (1913)

*

1916

THE UNEXPECTED

There is no objection to giving tea in a common room to old gentlemen who may pay unexpected visits.

Extract from the minutes of the Students' Representative Council, 23 November 1916

*

A THREE YEARS' FAST

Thersites, No. 50, 11 November 1916.

'Tis but a three years' fast;
The mind shall banquet, though the body pine.

The quotation confronted me on the cover of my first number of *Thersites*: a warning and a promise. At a distance of more than fifty years, which predominates, the dark strand or the bright?

There is no denying the literalness of the *fast*. Inevitable, of course. The U-boat war was at its height. The Government had classified us as sedentary females, lowest in the ration scale. Patriotism brought a letter-balance to the breakfast table for the scrupulous weighing of each slice of bread. Our meat ration, it was rumoured, went to the maids, to persuade them not to go off and make munitions. But need the damsons in the pudding have been preserved in vinegar? Need the vegetable concoctions have been quite so revolting? C.T.A. stood for College Tummy Ache, a very prevalent ailment.

But we were a hardy generation, adding voluntary endurance tests (disguised as privileges or spiced with disobedience) to those we could not avoid. We were not allowed to sleep out in our hammocks in the garden, but we *were* allowed to sleep on the roof – not with any College bedding, of course, but with such private rugs and cushions as we could muster to mitigate the hardness. How we scorned the one Sybarite who had equipped herself with a camp-bed! We must have become inured to cold. It was not until after tea that conversations broke off with: 'Well, I must go and fight my liar.' The Spooner habit was still rampant but here the transposition was apt enough: it *was* a fight to get one's meagre evening fire to burn. Earlier in the day there were lectures, or a session in the Library cocooned in a rug, with all the books one could possibly need piled up within hand's reach.

The allowance of bath water was four inches. Perhaps it was this that made river-bathing before breakfast on a May morning not only tolerable but delicious – indeed, irresistible, since it was a forbidden pleasure. Newnham had a bathing place of its very own – a sluggish backwater which we shared with fallen leaves. It was not exhilarating but it had its uses. When I had joined my companion in crime, anyone who might be abroad in the early-morning stillness would have assumed that we were heading for that decorous bourne. Having undressed in its cubicles, we scaled the high wooden fence that sealed the stagnant pool from the outside world. Then, with uplifted hearts, we dropped into the sparkling freshness of the live river. The current carried us down between banks fragrant with hawthorn and golden kingcups. The world seemed new-created and, for half an hour, life, which we took so seriously, was fun.

In those days, whatever our shape, we wore a corset armoured with whalebone (supposed to be pliant; but, rather than bend, it would often break and inflict a cruel jab). There was also a pitiless steel busk that dug into our flesh whenever *we* bent. The social structure of the College was rather like that corset – needlessly uncomfortable if not actually cruel. The gap between the generations was unbridgeable. Authority, fossilised from the age of forty, was there to dispense instruction and to see that we obeyed the rules, many of which carried the ultimate penalty of being sent down. In a respectable physical crisis such as the flu epidemic of 1918, Authority might show a softer side, coming to our bedside with Arthur Waley's translation of Chinese poems, to read aloud. One could consult Authority about the syllabus, but would it have occurred to any of us to seek its aid about a psychological or moral problem? Nearer to us in age there was a less formidable Minor Authority, a small group of young women, aged about thirty, who were known as the 'Baby Dons'. They were likeable, well disposed and mildly progressive. But they too remained aloof and they seemed to have little influence on the administration of the College and on its atmosphere.

Symbiosis with the Baby Dons was, on the whole, easier than with our fellow-students. To add an extra dimension to the artificiality of social life in a unisexual group, great gulfs, visible and palpable, were firmly established between third-years, second-years and freshers. Oh, those frightening first evenings at College when your room was invaded by strapping young toughs or imperious young goddesses, who would not go away until they had wrung from you a faint undertaking to play hockey or enrol in the fire brigade or join a circle studying some alien and rebarbative subject!

Then there was the intimidating etiquette that encrusted almost every detail of student life. All this had to be learned. Take beverages: a condescending second-year could invite a gratified first-year to cocoa; but if an exalted third-year proffered a cup across the gulf between eighteen and twenty, it had to contain coffee and the invitation must be for after lunch on Sunday. Is it more blessed to give than to receive? Not always. At the beginning of my third year I knew nothing of the mysteries of coffee-making except that there were mysteries (for Nescafé had still to be invented). I gladly accepted the suggestion of a contemporary that we should give our coffee parties together. But the hostess-smile froze on my face when I saw my partner simply pour boiling water on a spoonful of coffee placed in each cup. The coffee, of course, immediately rose to the surface. Dissimulating their dismay, hostesses and guests continued to make stilted conversation. The coffee had now settled on each upper lip but nobody dared to laugh, or swear or apologise. Even tea in Hall had its pitfalls. A kindly third-year, meeting a belated first-year by the tray, pointed to the hotter of the two large tea-pots saying: 'I think *that's* the fresher tea'; and the fresher blushed crimson, in the conviction of having blundered into yet another solecism.

The most pernicious artificiality was the 'propping' system (short for 'proposing'). Presumably some bright mind had originated this as a joke; but it lingered on, to cause constraint, embarrassment and exhibitionism. 'May I prop?' meant 'Shall we call each other by our Christian names?' The formality was observed even between first-years. Any first-year might prop any other first-year but only a second-year or, in rare cases, a third-year might prop a fresher. The up-and-coming freshers then had a delightful time name-dropping, while the down-and-going freshers, drooping unpropped, suffered corresponding dejection.

The incredible 'chap' rules, resented in theory, hardly affected us in practice. After all, in wartime what men were there in Cambridge? Yet it was tiresome that, except in Gilbert and Sullivan week, Newnham girls could not go to an evening theatre performance or concert without roping in a reluctant don as duenna. And it was humiliating that a sister was not considered an adequate chaperon for her brother, so that, when her dear one came on leave, she could not invite a fellow-student to tea with him without inviting a don as well.

When after the Armistice the men's colleges began to fill up again with undergraduates home from the war, it was really too late for my contemporaries to savour the return to normality in the University. By now the relentless approach of Tripos was blotting out every other prospect. To quote the cover of *Thersites* again (my last number this time):

> But I can hear the stricken Trippers praying
> With whitened lips, 'Would that we too were Maying.'*

However, there was one cold spring afternoon when the companion of my bathing escapades persuaded me to accompany her to Jesus College to take tea with her second cousin, newly up. The V.-P.'s consent had been obtained; the chaperon, provided by the young man, would meet us at the festive board; everything seemed to be in order. But it wasn't. There was the host, there was a roaring fire, there was a table loaded with luscious food; but where was the chaperon? It seemed that the lady invited by our host had had to cancel the engagement and a telephone message to Newnham, asking my friend to bring a substitute, had evidently miscarried. What was to be done? My companion had no doubts. We must depart at once. Polite dismay on the part of the second cousin. A stifled groan of disappointment on my part. Not one crumb of chocolate cake, not one browse along the book-shelves, not even time to stretch my chilly hands to the glowing fire?

'Well then, I'll take you both out to tea at Matthew's.'

My friend shook her head. That too was forbidden. Couldn't we risk it? Impossible. The V.-P. was sure to enquire whether the chaperon had turned up. Crestfallen, the poor young man ushered us out of his perilous domain.

'Well, anyway we'll go to Matthew's on our own and have muffins and cream buns and marzipan fruits, shall we?'

'Yes! Have you any money?'

'No. Haven't you?'

'No.'

Then a long cold walk back to Newnham, where, of course, tea in Hall was over. So, once more the body pined.

And what of the mind at the end of three years? Undoubtedly it had grown a little, in one direction. But a good degree was not the 'open-sesame' I had expected it to be. I left Newnham knowing, temporarily, quite a lot about one subject and thinking I knew everything. No wonder the world at large had a prejudice against uppish young women graduates! Cut down to size I began to acquire the additional knowledge which enabled me to earn my living more or (sometimes) less comfortably.

* 'Mays' was then the name for pre-Tripos examinations.

Not, to be sure, in any *congenial* way – that would have required personality as well as, or instead of, qualifications.

But in one respect my gratitude as an old girl is wholehearted and unstinted. To Newnham I owe friendships that have lasted more than half a century; friendships that continue to open doors and enrich my life.

E. M. Riley (1916)

*

THE RAINBOW IS DISCOVERED

I came to Newnham in the spring of 1916, arriving at Sidgwick Hall, where I had come to finish Little-go, in a hansom cab. I think that few freshers could have been more green and gullible! Yet I enjoyed every scrap of it immensely. To me Little-go was a great help as it gave me both an introduction to Cambridge and Newnham and also to several people who remained my friends throughout the whole of my time there.

As I had not been at a boarding-school I was at first, in October 1916, very homesick – I have dazed recollections of 'Auctions' where I bought a lampshade, cushions, a kettle and many other completely unnecessary objects, in a whirl of enthusiasm. In those days we *did* have cocoa-parties, and second- and third-years 'propped' to freshers when they wished to; until that delirious moment arrived we were all most correctly 'Miss' to each other. Some of the 'highlights' of life were being 'propped' to by some star far beyond one's orbit! My first Sunday was a very homesick affair until Kathleen McArthur took me to a C.U. meeting in the evening and treated me with normal friendliness. Kathleen was captain of both the fire brigade and the hockey team, and it was an education in itself to see her fly down the field with the ball. Of course I joined the fire brigade, and have vivid recollections of early morning 'alarms' involving lightning calculations as to the locality of the fire and the duties of the number in the team that I happened to be. They were great days!

I read History and found the work exciting and stimulating. Among many others I was inspired by Dr Glover, Dr Cunningham, Dr Coulton, Dr Previté-Orton, and, later, Dr Lapsley, who lectured to us in Trinity dining-hall while rats came out and gnawed remains left upon the floor! But the lectures were amazing, and bred in me a tremendous desire for research which I have never been able to satisfy. In our third year we went to Lowes Dickinson for Political Science B and, though much was above my head, I was able to hold my own with the help of dear Isabella Rea (now Lady Herbert). In addition we had of course Miss Firth, 'The Firkin', our indefatigable coach, and the inimitable Jane Harrison. The first lecture that I went to in Newnham was one with slides, given by Jane Harrison in one of the rooms in the old Coaching Room Passage [now demolished]. It was on archaeology, and archaeology claimed me as her own for ever. I still go to view digs in which my great-nephew is working and wish I could take an active part in them myself.

Games, bicycle rides and the river took up much of our time, apart from work and, as it was the custom in Clough to 'High' students for dinner as they came in, woe betide any unlucky sinner who stayed late on the river, and appeared unchanged and dishevelled and had to engage in polite conversation with the dons, conscious of burning cheeks and muddy shoes! Miss Firth roomed in Clough and, as she was a vegetarian, our dinner often resounded with the vehement cracking of nuts; Clough wouldn't have been Clough without it!

B. A. [Clough] was Vice-Principal of my Hall all the time I was up and though I was far too shy to know her well I was always grateful for the numerous kindnesses she showed. Never shall I forget her speeches at debate, always with such subtle humour (and she always voted 'neutral'). As I intended to teach until I could become a missionary (among other societies I joined the S.V.M.U.), I asked B.A. for a reference. I still have it in her well-known writing, and I was intensely pleased by one remark that she put in it: 'Miss Merryweather shows great capacity for growth.' It was not until considerably later that I realised what a two-edged remark it was! I can imagine B.A.'s whimsical lift of an eyebrow as she penned the sentence, welcomed with delight by callow youth, but indicating great immaturity.

I was at Newnham for the Armistice of 1918. As almost the whole College had just had a bad flu epidemic the whole affair seemed rather like a nightmare dream. All of us who were working in the old University Library were called to the market place to hear the announcement of peace; bells rang and everybody seemed to go mad. As I went back to Newnham I saw a taxi, full of men undergraduates or cadets, tear down King's Parade to the *Cambridge Magazine* shop where they began to smash all they could to pieces and ransack it. I suppose because it was reputed to be pacifist in sympathies.

There was the freezing winter of early 1917 when for weeks on end we were able to skate on Coe Fen. Ice-rinks were almost unknown in those days and many could not skate but, as I had lived in the country and we had a pond at the bottom of our garden, I had learnt to skate when young and it was a great moment when Olive Pound, a second-year, much admired from a distance, asked me to 'go round' with her as I was one of the few who could stagger along.

Many will speak of the beauty of Evensong in King's College Chapel, with all the candles lit, and the mystery that was in some ways more felt when all was dark and subdued than now when, even though one admires the grandeur of the Rubens reredos, all is so light and clear. It has all been most artistically and exquisitely restored, but in some ways one misses the dimness.

Then there was the Tripos; in those days we all set off on bicycles, plus cushions, for the Guildhall, each one, on the first day, clutching a sprig of rosemary given to us by B.A. When the daily ordeal was over it was followed by Trip teas in the garden provided by those who were not victims. There were also the joys of the Long Vacation Term when time was almost entirely our own and the sun always seemed to shine; the moon was always full, and there was something ecstatic about the warmth and magic of August evenings on the river, the moon shining in a glowing sunset sky and the air full of laughter and gaiety, not the sound of radios and transistors. That magic, that happiness, that beauty, were the things that made Cambridge mean so much; those things and the thrill of acquiring knowledge were what really mattered. 'The rainbow is discovered.'

Sister Phyllis, C.S.M.V. (E. P. Merryweather, 1916)

TOUJOURS ANGLO-SAXON

23 January 1917: Took good old 'Prospérité' to the Hopp,* she swallowed it all. True and untrue. Played a fives foursome in the afternoon with Molly, K and our Cole. One part of the court was appallingly slippery, but it was great fun, and we laughed till we were so weak we had to lean against the wall. Janet heard us from the hospital – sent a message to say how cheered she was.

24 January 1917: Cold and snowy – spent the morning at University Library, which is beautifully warm. Danced reels after lunch to get warm,

* 'Prospérité' was an essay and 'the Hopp' was Mlle Hopp, the College's Assistant Lecturer in French.

then worked for an hour. Rela came to see me [from Girton] after tea, strictly against rules, for we have mumps and they have measles. K, C and I went to cocoa with Pyke and L. Smith – great fun. We fear we stayed too long, but we hope not.

26 January 1917: Worked before breakfast. 9–10 lecture. 10–1 *Hamlet* – finished more or less. 2 played a fives foursome with K.M.M. and M.R. Work 3–4 – *Hamlet.* 4.30–5.30 Anglo-Saxon. 5.30–7 Shakespeare coaching. After dinner worked again – toujours Anglo-Saxon. Then had half an hour off, then worked again 10.30–11.30. Bed, with the Anglo-Saxon books at my side.

29 January 1917: Arose at 7 and skated until breakfast. Came home with a lovely appetite – after great fun. Worked most virtuously all morning, although lots were on the ice. Skated 2–4.30; we are much better and hope soon to be brilliant. Went to tea with L afterwards, ate many toasted muffins. Went to Poli business meeting after dinner, then had a bath, then worked for a little while – good old *Beowulf* again.

3 February 1917: After lunch took our thermos and went down to the ice. Skated till 4, tea'd, skated again. At 5 C and I were skating quite well – the moon was out and it was great fun. Debate after dinner re punishment, was very bored. Danced a little afterwards, including a very rowdy set of lancers.

5 February 1917: Overslept! First time for ages. K and A brought me some breakfast. At 11 Lizzie and I were so cold that we went skating! Very wicked. Skated again later on. At High Streak [Miss Strachey] said 'And how are your studies getting on?' I – guilty conscience – had a horrified face – then all realized she meant skating studies – much mirth.

21 February 1917: Overslept – till 9 o'clock. University Library till 11.30, then breakfasted at Matthews. Chelsea and a bun. 12, Q – very good but a little sloshy – he inclines that way. He also fishes most disgustingly. Worked all afternoon, to make up for the morning. Had a rehearsal after dinner; at 10 K and I went to see A and L – got some refreshment.

5 March 1917: College Meeting in the evening – our petition is granted and nearly all the idiotic chap. rules are extinct. The Steve [Miss Stephen] was really very sensible and likeable. D makes me sick. We had L and M to cocoa.

9 March 1917: Snowed hard in the morning – match postponed. Stopped at 2 so we played – sliding about all the time on the slippery snow. Again sojourned in the Library with Chaucer but gave it up fairly soon, as my brain went on strike. After many efforts, have propped Cairns.

1917

15 March 1917: Packed in spasms after dinner, had an impromptu cocoa at 10. Have propped Pyke (quel courage).
1 May 1917: Slept out – lovely moon.
21 May 1917: Trip begins. First paper Shakespeare, very nice. Second 'outlines' – loathly. A barrel organ played in the afternoon. Trip tea with A and L.
22 May 1917: Spent the day at the Guildhall. Both papers nasty. Trip tea with M.W.
23 May 1917: Both beasts. Anglo-Saxon – which I thought would perhaps pull me up a little – very nasty.
24 May 1917: French begins – Translation very horrid. Tea with J and C.
25 May 1917: No so bad. Tea with P and E. Went on the river for supper.
26 May 1917: Last day of Trip – in the morning a nice paper, in the afternoon a 'berute'.
30 May 1917: Went to breakfast at the Orchard with L and K. Bathed on the way down. At 6.30 fourteen of us started out in punts and canoes for a river supper-party – J.T.'s twenty-first birthday. Arrived home 9.45, but nothing was said.
2 June 1917: Arose early and went to try canoeists. Z.V. fell in – we just missed seeing her. Darned, read etc. all forenoon. Played as a sub v. the Wounded Soldiers at cricket – made 21 and was caught. Rag debate in the evening – quite fun – I opened my lips once and a half. K, C and I ate scraps later.
13 June 1917: Trip result came. Third.
14 June 1917: Boiling hot. Trip result wrong. Really Second. Would that the progression would continue.
15, 16, 17 June 1917: Ditto.

N. McC. Smith (1914). Extracts from a diary

COUNTING ON THE SHEEP

1917: May Term. Vegetables are still being grown in the war-garden, and at the beginning of term we were anxiously awaiting the arrival of sheep upon the lawns. It has been found more practicable however to let the grass grow up for hay.

Extract from the North Hall Diary

*

1917

A RESTLESS GENERATION

The Newnham students of my generation were, I believe, more ready than some of their successors today to accept and be thankful for the unchanging delights of a student's life in Cambridge. And yet, they were, like the present generation, critical, restless, and very conscious of being 'the moderns' and of their difference from their parents (even when the parents themselves, like the mother in *You Never Can Tell*, could claim to have been 'advanced before you were born').

We knew that we were living in a changing world and we had inherited from the progressive tradition of our founders the hope that future changes would be for the better, a hope reinforced by the teaching of Shaw and Wells, and in our own time by the light-hearted mockery of Strachey's *Eminent Victorians* (1919) and by rumours, based I believe on simplified versions of Freud, of the liberation which the new psychology would bring to the human spirit. But by 1917, when the men's colleges were almost empty of our contemporaries, the terrible background of the war was unforgettable, even for those who escaped personal bereavement. (The youngest-looking of the Newnham students reading my subject was a war widow.) The knowledge of the price that was being paid, above all by young men of our own age, deepened our reaction against the present and brought, at times, fear as well as hope for the future.

In my own, necessarily personal and limited, memories of academic work and social life in Newnham and Cambridge, I find always the same consciousness of change and the same mixture of hope and sadness. The academic side of my Cambridge experience brought me, then and later, much happiness. The Modern Languages Tripos had just been through one of the earliest of its periodic reforms. We were not compelled to learn Mediaeval French, and were encouraged by the new literary syllabus to study the 'background' of European history and ideas. Even today I feel a thrill of pleasure when I look at the Modern Languages shelves in the Newnham Library, where the complete works of Dante, Montaigne, Descartes, Voltaire, waited to be explored for the first time.

If my enjoyment of my work came largely from entirely unsupervised reading, this was mainly because, in the war years, and for some time after, there was very little teaching to be had. The few University lectures which I attended seemed to me less interesting than the published work of some of the lecturers, and in my first year the atmosphere was saddened by pathetically small audiences, mainly of women. ('Mesdemoiselles, Monsieur...' one lecturer began with an attempt at humour.) For Part I French there were College language classes, and in my second year Miss Strachey lectured in Newnham on nineteenth-century French literature. From her I learnt, once and for all, that good literature is different from bad, and that the difference really matters. And from the two French *lectrices* who corrected my essays and the prose classes of the alarming and highly intelligent Monsieur de Glehn, I received some admirable training in logic and the literary use of language. But in Italian, my second language, I had no teaching, either from College or University, for weeks on end; and in my literary work for Part II I never wrote a paper or essay of any kind, except on one occasion when a University lecturer suggested that some of us might like to write answers to some questions and discuss them with him at his house. My enjoyment of browsing freely in libraries was no doubt increased by the lack of formal instruction, but I feel now, looking back, how greatly I would have profited by a small fraction of the guidance and training offered by Cambridge supervisors in the nineteen-seventies.

In the closing years of the war social and domestic life within the College differed from life in pre-1914 Newnham, both because of the inevitable and very real privations and discomforts of wartime housekeeping, and because student criticism was turning, more I think than in any previous generation, against some sides of the College tradition itself and of the views of its senior members.

It would be easy and wearisome to pile up instances of icy rooms and inadequate meals. I remember very clearly a lecture delivered in Clough dining-hall by a visiting lecturer whom I knew. The three-course dinner, served at the High Table as well as to the students below, consisted of thin soup, crushed lentils and ground rice; and the lecturer said to me afterwards that it had been quite a good dinner, but that he could not distinguish the third course from the second. I remember also the chill of the unheated Hall during the lecture, and that the members of the audience in the front rows were muffled in fur coats. In my first year, before the introduction of compulsory food rationing, the government's plan for 'voluntary rationing' was scrupulously followed in the catering arrangements and urged on the students as a patriotic duty. I remember that the number of spoonfuls of porridge which we could conscientiously eat was worked out in decimals on the hall notice-boards.

These conditions and the emotional tension of the war added to the sense of strain between dons and students, although there was much admiration and affection for individual Fellows, and an enduring respect for a tradition of integrity and disinterestedness which the students were aware of, without, I think, fully understanding it. Their criticisms of the authorities took many different forms and varied greatly in intellectual and emotional seriousness. As the war drew to a close, the increasing pacifism of some of the most intelligent and sensitive students was sharply opposed to the equally intense patriotism of many dons in a painful conflict of opinion, fully conscious and adult on both sides. On the other hand, a wave of mild anti-feminism, partly inspired by a sane reaction against the extreme feminist position, was much less deeply felt. When the Newnham Debating Society not only discussed but passed the motion 'That Woman's sphere is the home', the votes of the majority were motivated more by a youthful desire to startle their elders than by a serious examination of the problems of marriage and a career.

There was also much discussion by the students of surprisingly sweeping changes to be made in the whole administration of the College. Student self-government was advocated, and freedom from what a writer in *Thersites* whom I quote from memory called 'the oligarchy of the experienced'. 'Self-government' was never very clearly defined, and I believe that my contemporaries differed from today's extremists because they did not in their hearts believe that their more far-reaching demands would ever have much effect. There was, however, one misguided attempt by the students, after a mass meeting in Clough dining-hall, to intervene in a College appointment.

Other student demands of those days, in particular for some modification in the fantastically out-of-date chaperon rules, were sensible and very moderate, and most of these were met by the action of the authorities before I left Newnham. A new staff–student committee, on which I served for a time, met in a relaxed and quite friendly atmosphere to discuss grievances, though the division of opinion between traditionalists and moderate reformers sometimes seemed very wide. We were discussing whether a Newnham student could be allowed to take an afternoon walk with an undergraduate, and a senior member said, 'Well...yes...if she is engaged to him.' To which a friend of mine on the committee replied that it seemed a heavy price to pay for a walk. Minor changes were also taking place in the social customs of the students themselves. In my first year second- and third-years still 'propped' to freshers, but, if I remember rightly, the expression had died out by my last year.

As long as the war lasted the abnormal condition of the University, more than College restrictions or even our official exclusion from membership, had made it hard for a woman student to think of herself as sharing fully in the social and intellectual life of Cambridge. But now Cambridge gradually returned to normal, and by 1919 or 1920 the men's colleges were again full. I remember a light-hearted occasion in my last year when I presided over a joint debate in Newnham with members of Trinity Hall. This was the first mixed debate ever held in the College, and I think, looking back, that it was not very well managed by the student hostesses. The Newnham tradition in those days was that debates were held in Clough dining-hall and that all members of the College, whether or not they had any interest in speaking, were encouraged to attend in evening dress. Trinity Hall had the more sensible arrangement of restricting membership to active debaters, and their small group of representatives were terrified when they saw the crowded audience. One of their speakers almost refused to perform, but their more confident and practised leader began cheerfully, 'Madam, I feel like a lion in a den of Daniels...' and the debate proceeded to its close, with no lack of speeches, serious and flippant. I am ashamed to say that I have forgotten what motion we were debating.

In 1918, even before the Armistice, there were meetings of The Heretics society, attended by senior and junior members of different colleges, with discussions which I have perhaps idealised in memory, in a room on an upper floor in Petty Cury. I remember especially one evening (it may have been after a discussion on the nature of poetry led by the forgotten poet, John Drinkwater) when I walked back to Newnham in unusually brilliant moonlight, thinking of the age-old imagery of the word 'enlightenment', and realising dimly what the intellectual tradition of Cambridge might have to give to those who learnt to understand it.

M. G. Wallas (1917)

ARMISTICE DAY SIEGE

Of my three years at Newnham, two years and half a term were spent in wartime conditions, until the Armistice came early in our third year. Recollections of World War I are obviously mingled to some extent with those of World War II, yet my College life is still very clear in my mind even after half a century.

College food, affected by wartime shortages, was very poor, consisting largely of semolina in various forms, and strange unidentifiable vegetarian dishes, of which the most revolting was the one known to us as a 'mess of lentil pottage'. The Principal, Miss Stephen, courageously set us a noble example, encouraging us to force it down our reluctant throats. At the end of our first term our families remarked on our buxom appearance, due to the rich midnight brews of sweet milky cocoa, boiled on the coal fires in our room, for wartime coal rationing could be got over either by sharing fires, or by lighting them on alternate days only. The more enterprising (or greedy) boiled up concoctions of jam, made with our pooled sugar rations, blackberries gathered on cycle rides to the Gogs, and sour windfalls scrounged from derelict orchards. Occasionally the odd hip or haw, likewise brought from the Gogs to decorate our rooms, would unaccountably get into the jam.

The only male undergraduates around were those classified as C 3, physically unfit for the Services, and a number of dark-skinned gentlemen whom we designated the 'Indian Princes', and whose presence at Quiller-Couch's lectures at any rate justified his famous opening greeting of 'Good morning, Gentlemen', which filled us with hilarity when, as often happened, his audience consisted solely of Newnhamites and Girtonians, for he persistently refused to make any concession to femininity. Alas, our dearest and most popular 'Prince', an obese gentleman with a round smiling pudding-face, snuffed out like a candle in that terrible Spanish flu epidemic at the end of the war, sorely lamented by all.

The war atmosphere, with its massacres on the Somme and its long casualty lists, clouded the background of our College life. A few students departed to run canteens or drive generals' cars. Our brothers were being killed, maimed, taken prisoner. Yet, for youth is resilient, we led happy and full lives. To a brash girl from the industrial North, Cambridge seemed like Paradise, the dons and Fellows like goddesses. Our lives were centred much more on the flourishing societies within Newnham than, as now, on the University. The Raleigh, the Debating Society, the more important Political, with its rarer and more formal meetings, were all going strong, and had been active since at least before 1889, as I discovered to my surprise from reading Catherine D. Holt's *Letters from Newnham.* I remember a meeting of the 'Poli', with May Graham Wallas as President, seated very grandly in the presidential chair up on the dais in Clough Hall, when a solemn and lengthy debate took place on 'The Endowment of Motherhood'. May's parents were invited guests in the audience, and great hilarity was caused when Graham Wallas, the famous Political Scientist, rose to his feet at the end, and with a meaningful glance at his presiding daughter, remarked that it would be much more to the point if *fatherhood* were endowed.

We joined, of course, such University societies as were still functioning in wartime, notably the C.U. Musical Society, with its strong choral section, conducted by Cyril Rootham, the Organist of St John's College, and including such distinguished musicians as Edward Dent – frequently reproved by Rootham for his chattering! Our rehearsals took place in a back room of the Cavendish. An anecdote concerning Rootham, probably apocryphal, was whispered around. Asked why the 'h' in his name was not pronounced, he remonstrated in reply, 'But you don't pronounce the 'h' in Beethoven.'

In the Lent Term came the money-making week for the Christian Union. Two of us in Peile set ourselves up as a laundry, with suitably ornamental advertisement on the notice-board. To our horror, our first commision was to launder a delicate cobwebby corsage of coffee-coloured chiffon and lace, belonging to one of the 'goddesses', Jane Norton, a fourth-year (who later attained great distinction in the bibliographical world, editing the superb three-volume 1956 edition of Gibbon's letters, and cataloguing the Pepys Library at Magdalene). We spent hours sweating over the fragile confection with its plunging neckline, impressed by her reference to it as a 'bloose' whereas we had been vulgarly calling it a 'blowse'.

I wonder if the Astronomical Society still exists. We had learnt our constellations at school, in spite of the smoky fog of the West Riding atmosphere, so that when on arrival at Newnham I ascertained the existence of an Astronomical Society, and found that in order to become a member one had to pass a test on the names of the principal stars listed on the membership card, I presented myself nervously at the door of the Secretary in Sidgwick. Inviting me in, she opened her bureau, took out a bundle of the cards and handed them to me, remarking laconically, 'You'd better take over.' Thus I found myself, willy-nilly, the new Secretary – or, more accurately, I *was* the Astronomical Society, for there was never another member during my three years. The great advantage of this was that I gained sole and undisputed possession of the key of the observatory on the hockey field. Dropping out of a ground-floor window at dead of night (after suitable conspiratorial arrangements with the occupant of the room to let me in again in the small hours) I taught myself in an amateurish way to open up the shutter of the observatory roof, work the ratchet which swung it round and focus the telescope lens so as to observe the moon. Enthusiasm for these unlawful nocturnal expeditions waxed and waned, like the object of my observations, and was finally quenched by the damp bone-chilling night mists rising from the Fens.

In those days Newnham possessed a private bathing place, a leafy but muddy fenced-in backwater off the Grantchester Meadows. We cycled there at 8 a.m. through lanes gloriously scented by overhanging lilacs, and greatly daring (for those days) emulated the example of one of the most attractive of the Fellows by bathing in the nude.

Unquestionably the most striking and quietly forceful character in the College was B. A. Clough, then V.-P. in Clough, but shortly to become Principal. Affectionately dubbed 'B.A.', she was, with her all-pervasive presence, deep chuckle, twinkling eyes and shrewdly humorous features, the delight and object of affection of many generations of students, being the embodiment of the living tradition begun so gloriously by her aunt, Anne Jemima Clough. In the Holt letters it is recounted that in 1889 B.A. broke up a students' party which was going on too late. In 1919, a whole thirty years later, she was still 'night prowling', for at a time when 'Lights Out' was at 11 p.m., I received a tap on my door at midnight because B.A. had seen my reading-lamp shining through the fanlight.

The College made its contribution to warwork in the shape of the parties of students who went to work on the land during the vacations, mostly to pick strawberries, apples and potatoes. The first was back-breaking; the second, exhilarating when, perched on a swaying ladder in the tree-top one filled hanging baskets with rosy red Quarantines; and the third was devastating, for the potatoes were turned up by horse-plough and invariably, before we had picked up our stint of so many yards, Charlie the horse was round the oblong, snorting, whinnying and champing over our lowered heads. We bathed communally in the large farm onion-tank, and slept in canvas cubicles erected in the barn.

Life changed for us early in our third year with the sudden and unexpected (by us) announcement of the Armistice on November 11th, 1918. Town and Gown went mad and everything became chaotic, with a bewildering mixture of joy for the end of the slaughter and grief for the countless ghosts of the lost generations, whose silent presence pervaded the clanging uproar. (Out of seventy undergraduates who came up to John's in 1913 only four returned to resume their interrupted University career, of whom two were my brother and my future husband. The fourth member of this sad little group died almost immediately in the flu epidemic.)

As one man we downed pens and books and rushed down town to mingle with the milling yelling crowds. The big bell of Great St Mary's was tolling away, and there was a strong rumour that it was a Newnhamite who had climbed the tower and was pulling the bell-rope. Returning to Peile for lunch we found that one of our group had shown great initiative in importing a bottle of champagne for the third-year table, to the dismay of the dons, for it must be remembered that in those days students were not allowed alcohol in College. But of course on such a day 'anything went'.

The great event of the day however took place in the evening, when the undergraduates of Ridley Hall climbed the walls and invaded the College. The windows of Clough dining-hall were rapidly opened by the besieged so as to allow the besiegers to climb in, and at once mixed dancing, then unknown in the College, was initiated. There were two pianos in the Hall, a grand at the dais end and an upright at the bottom end, and although B.A. rushed frantically up and down trying to push the men out, she was quite helpless because as soon as she succeeded in stopping the music at one end, the pianist at the other started up. Finally the men made their exit through the windows and everyone joined in lighting up a huge bonfire on the Clough lawn. The unforgettable sight of the equally unforgettable evening was of B.A., distracted and with hair in wisps, dramatically lit up by the leaping flames, struggling to wrest a Clough dining-chair from the grasp of a young man who was about to put it on the fire.

It was difficult to concentrate on work for the rest of the term for, starved of social life for four years, we naturally embarked gaily on a rapturous round of thé-dansants, Victory Balls in the Guildhall and all the social and University activities which were revived with the return of the men. It took some time for the various restrictions in the way of rations, lighting and fuel to be lifted. At the very end of the Armistice term my brother, released from an East German prison-camp, came up to Cambridge to make the necessary arrangements for the resumption of his interrupted University career, and was allowed to come and dine in Peile. The long trek through the Stygian gloom of the labyrinthine corridors between Pfeiffer and Peile and the sudden plunge into the female chatter in Hall appeared to terrify him more than his years of incarceration!

The Lent Term was notable for even more feverish bursts of activity, for a three-week period of severe frost coincided with the arrival of the Navy! A number of young naval officers were sent on a special course to

Armistice night, 1918: B. A. Clough tries to rescue the dining-hall chairs (drawn by D. M. Field (Ellis))

the still under-occupied Cambridge colleges, and their strong arms supported us in intensive bouts of skating on the frozen fens. Better still, they brought their motor-bicycles with them, so every Sunday, out on the road to Ely (then an undiscovered country because beyond the range of our bicycle rides) the Newnham occupant of the side-car would exchange places with the driver, and hoisting her skirts to mount astride the saddle, would learn to manipulate the beast, directed by the nervous owner, and rejoicing meanwhile in the unaccustomed freedom of being out of range of donnish eyes.

During our last term, notwithstanding Triposes looming ahead, and the desire to spend as much time as possible in and on the Cam, student protest (yes, half a century ago!) began to rear its head. We formed a 'Grievance Committee', whose aim was to urge the College authorities towards a relaxation of the chaperon and smoking rules which, in the climate of increasing freedom induced by the importance of women's contribution to the war effort, began to seem out of harmony with the times. A Suffrage Society was formed, deputations were sent by it to take part in London meetings, and old Newnhamites who were working actively for Women's Suffrage, such as Mrs Oliver Strachey, came down to address us. Gradually small gains were achieved in the matter of the smoking and chaperon rules; in connection with the former it was rumoured, to everybody's delight, that B.A. herself used to take a cab out to a certain spot on the Grantchester Road, and enjoy a quiet cigarette in the fields. With regard to the chaperon rules, two sisters in College, hoping to shame the authorities into compliance, inveigled their mother, a widow, into renting a house just behind Peile in Grange Road, where they proceeded to hold frequent parties for their young men, and made sure that the Principal heard about it.

One of the most attractive features of College life in my time, which I believe is not allowed nowadays, was the 'sleeping-out' in the open air. Every dry night in the summer term processions of students could be seen carrying a load of rugs and eiderdowns, heading either upwards to the lead flats on the roof, or downwards through the windows to occupy the hammocks slung between the trees in the garden near the raised Sidgwick Memorial. This was of course against the regulations, but was winked at, provided that the hammock occupiers got themselves in again at dewy dawn before the College was well astir. Possibly the reason this custom lapsed was that at some point those rows of trees were replaced, and young saplings obviously could not take the weight of hammocks.

The post-war climate of greater freedom only crept on us of course very gradually, for our mildly rebellious leanings were considerably damped by the news that a fourth-year student, noted for her brilliant auburn hair and exotic appearance, had been sent down only a couple of days before the end of term (for riding pillion down Sidgwick Avenue on a young man's motor-bicycle) and thus deprived of the May Balls, revived then for the first time after the war years. A few of us, determined to finish up in a blaze of glory, and exalted in spirit by attendance at our first May Races, were unwise enough to attend six May Balls on six nights running, and to eat six successive punt breakfasts in a chilly dew on the Cam. Complete physical wrecks, we crept away sadly to our respective homes, thus ending the most tragic but most exhilarating three years of our youth.

D. C. Booth (Lawe, 1916)

'POISONOUS PLACE'

I am a Scot. I was born in Aberdeen and, as far as I know, am of Aberdeenshire descent for the past three or four centuries. I was already a graduate of Aberdeen University when at the age of twenty-one I came into residence as a student at Newnham in October 1917. My secondary schools had been the Dundee High School and the Aberdeen High School for Girls, both day-schools. Before October 1917 I had not seen Cambridge or indeed much of England at all. In those days the internal combustion engine was much less ubiquitous and the population less mobile. I remained as a student at Newnham until June 1920.

The only manuscript in my possession that is contemporary with my residence at Newnham is a diary kept by my father and which I first read in 1950; this consists of an intermittent account of my activities from birth onwards, of which the two last entries are as follows:

11 March 1918 (My second daughter) went up to Old Hall, Newnham College in the autumn (of 1917). (The Professor of Greek at Aberdeen University) objected strongly to Newnham as a 'poisonous place' It is interesting to note that the poison has already begun to work. (My daughter) is attending with great enjoyment the meetings of the Cambridge University Socialist Society... At Christmas she surprised us all by coming home with her hair cut short... Her most intimate friend at Newnham seems to be Miss Alice Selby, a fourth-year student and a very advanced person.

21 November 1918 On the declaration of the Armistice there were great doings at Cambridge and (my daughter) took part in the defence against an attack by the cadets on the premises of the *Cambridge Magazine*. She is still an Anarchist, Socialist, Bolshevist.

These entries require a little annotation. They are I think more damaging to myself than to Newnham. Can I have been so raw and crude? I think of myself as a shy and timid person, who never in her life took part in, although she may have witnessed, a riot. I was wandering about Cambridge on Armistice Day and saw the devastation that had been wrought on the premises of the *Cambridge Magazine* by cadets and others. These premises were in King's Parade about opposite to King's. The *Cambridge Magazine* was, I think, founded and edited by Charles K. Ogden, that eccentric all-but-genius who originated Basic English, and it published during the First World War excerpts from the foreign press. Although I may on arrival at Newnham have wanted to be 'an Anarchist, Socialist, Bolshevist' at one and the same time, later on, while still at Newnham, I remember trying hard to sort out the various -isms. My Aberdeen Professor, who was so completely out of love with Newnham, was an ardent champion of Mr (later Sir) William Ridgeway, at that time Disney Professor of Archaeology at Cambridge, whose views on the origin of Greek tragedy differed from those held by Miss Jane Harrison, who was then on the staff of Newnham. It is difficult now to imagine the rancour which then existed among male Classicists of varying schools of thought; part of the mediaeval *odium theologicum* seems to have descended to these Classicists. The Aberdeen Professor was not a Socialist, but then, as I soon found out, neither were most Newnhamites, staff or students. He may have objected to the spirit of toleration which I found to be a leading characteristic of Newnham. I well remember how every shade of opinion and belief was permitted and even fostered in Newnham. In miniature it had most of the elements of a true democracy. My Newnhamite friend, Alice Selby, had previously read English for three years and had been placed in Class I. That autumn she was reading Anthropology with Dr A. C. Haddon, then Reader in Ethnology at Cambridge, whom she greatly admired and used to visit at his house in Cranmer Road. At the end of 1917 she left Newnham. Of all contemporary students she made the deepest impression on me, and was to my thinking a real original. She took me in hand. She not only encouraged me to join the Cambridge University Socialist Society, but also did her best to make me appreciate the old saw: 'There is a time and place for everything.'

1918

Before I arrived at Newnham I had had no experience either of a boarding-school or of a residential university; Aberdeen University was at that time non-residential. From the first, my impressions of life at Newnham were enthusiastically favourable, and any criticisms that I have to make minor and unimportant. I remember being overwhelmed on arrival by the English 'public-school' atmosphere. I do not mean to suggest that there were at that time no public schools in Scotland: there were at least six, founded in the nineteenth century on the English model, and I already knew this. I do not think that at Newnham I ever succeeded in absorbing the ethos of the 'stiff upper lip' or the mystical efficacy of team-games. The former cult often seemed to me inhumane, nor could I understand why some Newnhamites should attach so much importance to getting into teams. Very soon, however, I began to realize the rich variety of individual differences underlying this seeming uniformity. It helped, too, to be a Scot: I might have been at the wrong schools, but this had occurred in Scotland. In a general atmosphere that was warm and welcoming the occasional rebuff was easily accepted.

It is, I think, indisputable that towards the end of 1917 Cambridge was a disturbed and turbulent place. In addition to the wordy war that is often waged in academic circles, there were the strains and stresses of real war. I recollect that in 1917 or 1918, George Bernard Shaw, when invited to address the Cambridge University Socialist Society, sent in reply a postcard declining the invitation on the ground that he should not be asked to visit Cambridge when he could speak in such comparatively tranquil centres as Petrograd. I was in Oxford throughout 1922, and was told that things had not been so stormy there during the war. The most plausible explanation of the difference that I then heard was that Oxford had not been so highly polarized as Cambridge, certain leading persons in key places having been more extreme in their political views at Cambridge than at Oxford. Bertrand Russell was one of the foremost of these. In 1917 he was no longer in Cambridge, but Cambridge seemed to me full of the reverberations that he had left behind. I think that I came at that time as close to a religious conversion as ever before or since. I had not previously heard of Bertrand Russell; then quite suddenly he was everywhere and nowhere, and (as to his more important writings) incomprehensible. At the opposite pole were a group of Bertrand Russell's opponents.

At Aberdeen University I had been accustomed to the hooliganism that occurs at graduation ceremonies and rectorial elections, but this was a new and more sophisticated kind of hooliganism. There were at the men's colleges only a small number of undergraduates, mainly those rejected for military service. These were slowly reinforced by men who were discharged from the fighting forces as unfit for further military service, some of them sadly disabled. The men's colleges were mainly filled by cadets in training for the fighting forces; these found in Cambridge a wide assortment of political views, some of which displeased them. A favourite form of 'rough justice' was ducking in the Cam. I recollect a gathering of Socialists at the Friends' Meeting House in Jesus Lane, at which I looked in when returning to Newnham by a roundabout way, after dining at the institution which is now called Hughes Hall. The cadets had arrived. After some speechifying by Socialists in a mounting uproar, there was glass-breaking followed by ducking. I did not stay for the ducking, being unescorted and supposed to go straight back to Newnham. I remember another occasion when Norman Angell, author of *The Great Illusion*, was saved from a mob of angry young men by being rushed into the fire-station by other young men. Then there was the wrecking of the *Cambridge Magazine* premises on Armistice Day, which I have already mentioned.

In those days I was a member of the Cambridge University Socialist Society. At first it was predominantly Marxist and run by the two Dutt brothers, who lived in Cambridge and whose mother was a charming and friendly Swede, an accredited 'town' chaperon of Newnham. The younger brother, Rajani Palme Dutt, a brilliant Oxford Classicist, later took an active part in founding the Communist Party of Great Britain. I remember him in 1918 as a tall hypnotic figure expounding Marxism, and drawing an impressive parallel between what the Bolsheviks had had to do in Petrograd in October (Julian Calendar) of the previous year and what Augustus had had to do at the foundation of the Roman Empire. In October 1919, with a change of President, the Society became much pinker, less exotic and conspiratorial perhaps, but still very interesting. In 1918 I might have become an insignificant member of the Communist Party of Great Britain, had this institution existed. I gather, however, that after prolonged and complicated negotiations it only came into existence in August 1920, and by that time I had become rather pink myself. By 1921 Bertrand Russell's *The Practice and Theory of Bolshevism* (published in November 1920) cured me for good and all of wanting to join a Communist Party anywhere.

The Newnham of 1917 was smaller than it is now and housed about 250, comprising both staff and students. In my time the usual practice was for a student to have a bed-sitting-room only. There were besides some sets of two rooms; in the east wing of Old, before its remodelling, there were I think two of these sets and one extra-large bed-sitting-room. On the top floor of the Pfeiffer Building, in a much coveted position, there were four bed-sitting-rooms occupied by third-year students of Old.

In June 1920 I left Newnham and had to face the harsh world outside without the help of the Women's Appointments Board, which was not then established. The fight for status for the women's colleges and for degrees had begun but had not yet had time to get seriously under way. I did not take a titular B.A. when these were granted [1921], but proceeded after 1948 straight to the M.A., one of a proud minority, wearing the M.A. hood with an undergraduate gown. As I look back after fifty years, my residence at Newnham seems to have been the most important part of my life. Why do I value it so much? Here are a few of the things that I would celebrate.

I salute the pervading and diversified beauty. For three years I bicycled nearly every day over the Silver Street bridge, with its view, as yet unobstructed by the Fisher Building, along the Backs from Queens', simple, homely, and to me most lovable of all the Cambridge colleges, to the grander colleges beyond. Though my glances were unheeding, some of that beauty must have become lodged in my brain.

I salute the much-enduring and manifold kindness. I cannot forget the cordiality with which in 1917 I was received at Newnham, or the hospitality which I met with elsewhere in Cambridge.

I salute the quest for compelling if elusive truth. According to Professor Housman there should be constant striving at universities 'to set back the frontier of darkness'. I am not clever enough to have taken part, but at Newnham more than at any other place I learnt to respect those who are.

I salute the shifting yet stable blend of the old and the new. In 1955 I knelt in the Senate House before the Vice-Chancellor while he uttered something which sounded like: 'Auctoritate mihi commissa admitto te ad titulum Magistri in Artibus designati ... in nomine Patris et Filii et Spiritus Sancti.' It was a form of words, altered it may be and abbreviated, which had been used by friars about seven and a half centuries before. In 1970 I read of an exhibition, held in the same Senate House, of rocks collected on the moon by astronauts the previous year.

Finally, I salute the underlying if modified freedom. During my residence at Newnham I came nearer than I have ever done to living in an

Open Society. Searching for a suitable epigram with which to end these rambling memories, I have found these words of Tacitus in *The Oxford Dictionary of Quotations*: 'Rara temporum felicitate ubi sentire quae velis et quae sentias dicere licet.' (*Histories*, I. 1)

K. B. MacP. Cope (Wattie, 1917)

*

FROM THE CHINESE: E.M.M., J.B.

For a whole year we sat at meals together
Not often at breakfast, but always at lunch:
Their faces were cheerful even in the East wind,
Their laughter was gay and reminded me of my own youth.
Now they tell me they are going away.
One of them wore a white coat embroidered with red,
The other had a blue coat made of silk:
I suppose they will go and live in other places
And I shall never know how they are dressed.
Someone asked me to write something about them,
I can only think of dull and foolish things,
I can only think that they will soon be gone.
I shall stay here with the plates and the cups,
The sun will shine on the wall opposite,
Everything will look as usual.

J. P. Strachey (1895). From *Thersites*, 5 June 1918

AN ISOLATED COMMUNITY

Looking back, I think that my chief recollection of this time is the fact that the College was then very much a community and, in some cases, an isolated community. It was also a very much livelier place than it is now. I call it a community for a variety of reasons.

The students were grouped in a kind of hierarchy, and the entertainment arrangements were such that every student had at least one meal or other entertainment with every member of the Hall. The convention was that all third-years invited all freshers to coffee which was regarded as the lowest form of entertainment; all second-years invited them to cocoa or coffee, and invited third-years I think to coffee; freshers invited each other to cocoa, and I suppose might have invited their seniors to cocoa at the end of the year. Cocoa was an informal entertainment with talk going on far into the night while coffee was shorter and more formal. The dons living in the Hall also formed part of the entertainment cycle. They were asked to coffee by third-years and by their own students in other years, and they in turn had their own coffee parties – though never cocoa-parties!

There were a considerable number of meetings in Clough Hall, the main College Hall. A notice would go up saying that the C.H. freshers were to clear the Hall of chairs, which was done very rapidly by shoving the tables to the back of the room and slinging the chairs into line. The Senior Student called meetings on anything that seemed interesting, and the Principal had some impressive meetings. I remember the meeting on the evening of the Armistice when May Graham Wallas read Pericles' funeral oration. The Hall was also used for the two debating societies – the main Debating Society which covered all subjects, and the Political Debating Society known as 'Poli'. These were often lively and attended by 100 or so students. Again, the dons took part in these. The younger dons were in demand as speakers and the older ones emerged on occasions. (There was the memorable debate in an end-of-term spirit on the motion 'That the White Queen was a nobler type of woman than the Red'. Miss Strachey defended the White Queen, looking as vague and wispy as the White Queen in the *Alice in Wonderland* drawings of the time.)

College societies flourished and dons often took a lively part in these. It was an experience to go to the Literary Society, presided over by Jane Harrison, sunk in a large and rather dilapidated armchair and breathing fire. Entry was by an audition in which one read unseen poetry, bits of plays or novels. I myself started a Dramatic Society which rather boldly put on *Androcles and the Lion* for its first play. The enormous dark blue curtains which we used in Clough Hall may still exist, unless they were made into blackout curtains! We had an annual pantomime with skits on College or University life in which the senior dons were always disappointed not to be guyed in some way or other. Ignatius, the porter, also appeared in every pantomime in one of his mythical roles. The Raleigh Society is of course the only one of these College societies which remains.* Otherwise, in a curious way the College

* See note, p. 43.

resembled a men's college with its own societies much more closely than today, when the women's colleges are socially dependent on the men's.

Our relations with other colleges were of course much more limited. I never remember going to Girton during the three years I was up at Cambridge and though some girls had brothers, cousins and boy-friends in men's colleges, others might spend their whole time without being entertained there. This was partly because of the bother of complying with the chaperon rules.

Nevertheless, we participated in University societies. I call to mind memorable meetings of The Heretics club held in a tiny crowded room in K.P., when Lytton Strachey and others of his group were the speakers. During my time there was also the first joint meeting of the Newnham Debating Society and a men's college – in this case Christ's. J. B. Priestley was the President of the Christ's society and Ada Harrison, who afterwards wrote essays and travel books, was President of Newnham. Christ's later returned to debate in the College Hall.

The custom by which woman students sat in the front rows of lectures and had separate benches in the labs. also kept us apart. After the war, when the University was crowded with returning soldiers, women were of course resented. As they walked down the steps of the big lecture theatres to their places in the front row, every man behind them clumped and stamped in time with each of their steps. I remember on one occasion leaving my dissecting scissors behind when I came to work in the Anatomy Lab. Though surrounded by men who all had extra pairs of scissors, I felt it necessary to bicycle back to Newnham to get my own!

The man business did not loom so much in our lives as people think. This was partly because it was assumed in those days that one would not marry until College was over, or before the age of twenty-two or twenty-three. It was also because we many of us had the sense that we were a special dedicated group who would not marry because we had more exciting things to do. There was even a sense that a girl who got engaged was almost letting the side down. But the chaperon rules were of course resented, even by those who did not want to break them! It was impossible to go into a college room without a chaperon or to have a young man into one's own room if one was alone. It was necessary to have a chaperon in some part of the theatre if one went there. When I asked Miss Clough what help it would be to have a female don sitting in the stalls when we could only afford gallery or pit seats, she replied, 'There might be some unpleasantness, Miss Richards. I do not think I need say more!' (This, in her deep sepulchral voice, was truly alarming.) When we performed *Belinda* by A. A. Milne, girls of course took the men's parts. Miss Clough, then Principal, decreed that only brothers or fiancés could attend because it was not suitable for any other men to see women in men's clothes! As President of the Dramatic Society, I put up a notice saying that no tickets would be issued to men who were not brothers or fiancés, and gave the reason. Miss Clough who saw that I was writing with my tongue in my cheek summoned me to one of her disciplinary breakfasts, when one was invited at eight o'clock to a very superb breakfast, served by a maid, in the Principal's flat. After breakfast she boomed her disapproval.

Nevertheless, in spite of this there were passionate love affairs and of course engagements. I think we thought of these, as I said, as taking time off from the real business of life. It must be remembered too that Newnham did not invent the chaperon rules. One's own parents had very much the same ideas and behaved in the same way.

Those in authority in Newnham or the University were in some ways closer to us than now, and in some ways much more distant. They were closer because they entertained more and because the more lively of the Newnham dons joined in societies and other activities. Miss Clough, when she was a Tutor of Clough Hall, used to stand on the dais and call six or eight students at random to sit at High Table. This was thought to be alarming, but actually most students enjoyed it. Miss Clough's own conversation was racy – delivered in the booming voice. She would often open the conversation with an account of the book she was reading. I remember her saying, 'I am reading a splendid book on missionary work in the Gobi desert. There is very little missionary and a lot of Gobi in it.' I can remember also interesting talks with Miss Firth, the History lecturer; Enid Welsford; Elsie Butler, and many others. On the other hand, contact with dons was for intellectual stimulus and never for advice on private life. I do not believe any student would have told a don about her love affairs, her mother's divorce or the problems of her wardrobe, as is sometimes done today.

Curious how large the river looms in my memories. There was a cult of expert punting, canoeing and rowing and one had to pass tests in these before going on the river at all. Boats were cheap and one wrote essays in them – lay in them and talked in them – rose early on Sunday and dashed up the Granta in a rob-roy – bathed near Byron's Pool and breakfasted at the Orchard on boiled eggs and bread and butter – often alone!

Dancing, too, was a constant occupation: thé-dansants – college dances – society dances, as well as May Week.

A. I. Richards (1918)

*

A FAMILY

This week-end (10–13 October 1969) four old Newnhamites celebrate together the Golden Jubilee of the friendship which began with our meeting at Newnham fifty years ago. This was at Old Hall, and covers the years from 1918 to 1922. Two of us studied Mathematics, one English and History, and one Economics and French. We have tried to jot down some of our memories of those years at Cambridge after World War I: some will apply to anyone up during those years and some will necessarily be more personal as we formed a fairly tightly-knit little group, a 'family' within the community during most of our College days. Here are some of our recollections:

On one occasion two of us and two undergrads went on a punt excursion chaperoned by an attractive young Newnham don. After a picnic at Byron's Pool it grew later than we intended and the young don remembered she had a coaching in College imminent, so at the nearest point she jumped to the bank and raced for home while we finished the trip unchaperoned. During our time chaperoning and other restrictions were reduced, chiefly owing to a series of vociferous and well-supported student meetings.

For several weeks before Trip we rose early for revision, fortifying ourselves with black coffee, and in order to make this more effective we gave up all coffee for a period beforehand. During Trip, the victims who had two papers were entertained to lunch in College Hall and waited on by the dons. Trip teas after exams were held in rooms or garden (those summers always seemed fine and hot). Formal invitations were issued by friends or seniors or anyone not involved in exams. Enormous quantities of cream-cakes, a post-war novelty, and ice-cream (out of thermos flasks) were consumed, and the feast was much appreciated.

Shortages of fuel and food were obvious in those years, and were coped with in various ways. We remember especially how we did so as a quartette. The only means of heating were coal fires, and coal was scarce and rationed. On the amount allowed it was impossible to have a daily fire all day in one's room. Our plan was to club together and have one fire all day from early to late in one room, and we were able to have one other fire between us for evenings or if any of us had visitors. Even so, owing to strikes and other shortages, we frequently worked in unheated rooms in sleeping bags and all our outdoor warm clothes. Food was not very inviting and not too plentiful. We had a 'housekeeper' for the week (turn and turn about) who had to supply bread, butter, coffee, cocoa, cheese, etc., and it was quite usual to come straight up from Hall dinner and start on the loaf and butter.

Outside activities now, we gather, are much encouraged among the students, but were frowned on by authority in our day. One of us had been asked to run the 3rd Cambridge Guide Comapny, meeting in Malting Lane, but the Principal gave her a lengthy lecture to the effect that she was wasting the golden opportunities of College life and should not undertake any outside social work whilst up. Nevertheless all four of us eventually became involved, and ran a Guide company and Brownie pack and numerous camps (in the vacation), one of which was a joint camp with a company run by the College Bursar Mrs Lacy. It was a great pride to us when the *Guide Gazette* published our Tripos Results: one Wrangler and three Second Classes.

Work – not mentioned yet – was a very large part of our lives and was seriously treated with long scheduled hours of study. Perhaps our three or four years at Newnham did not contribute anything startling to the College tradition, but fifty years of firm friendship has been a rich inheritance.

R. D. Morton Evans (1918), G. E. Pearse (1918), K. C. Prior (1919) and S. E. B. Smale (1918)

YEARS OF RENAISSANCE

The early twenties were years of renaissance. The war was not long over and Cambridge was still on a wave of exhilaration. A tribe of giants occupied the high places in the undergraduate world and lorded it over those fresh from school. Some had been up before the war and had come back to finish, others were new to Cambridge but had war service behind them. Added to these and distributed among the colleges were batches of young naval officers, who had gone to sea before their time and were now filling gaps in their education. Many people, of course, were hiding personal wartime losses and tragedies; but the general feeling was one of enthusiasm and high spirits, and an impatience with old pre-war regulations.

In the twenties the most popular and widespread amusement everywhere was dancing – in London, Rome, Paris and every city and town. Hotels, small and large, all had thé-dansants and dinner-dances. At the Great Exhibition at Wembley in 1924 we invariably finished a visit to the other amusements on one of the dance-floors. At Cambridge there were regular weekly dance clubs which were a great attraction. On a higher plane there were the music societies, the Union and College debating societies, including Newnham's, which were all busily patronised; and others, religious and unreligious, such as the S.C.M. and The Heretics, where every side of life was talked over. I can picture at this last Lytton Strachey, folded up in a chair beside Jane Harrison, while the subject of 'Art and Indecency' was discussed. Jane Harrison remarked that indecency made her feel very sad.

An afternoon diversion, to which like many other girls I was escorted once a week by a boy-friend, was the cinema, followed by tea, usually at the Dorothy Café in Sidney Street. It was here on one occasion that I was profoundly shocked by the entrance of a group of Australian soldiers with stitched faces and bandaged eyes, led in by brightly chattering nurses. My escort who was an ex-serviceman himself didn't seem much moved and said they were probably having plastic surgery at Addenbrooke's.

These were the days of silent movies, which lent themselves to vocal comment and wit by the undergraduate audience. We considered it very funny, for instance, when we were shown Moses contemplating the Tablets of the Ten Commandments and a voice called out, 'Only four of these to be attempted.'

I suppose there have always been students' rags at all universities and Cambridge had a good many. There was the regular Guy Fawkes bonfire night, when it had become the custom to march on Newnham. The rags were more or less harmless, as they were not inspired by grievances or violent intentions like the student 'demos' or marches of the present day. They were mostly humorous, like the Pavement Club meeting when 'members' all sat in the roadway and pavements of King's Parade one morning, and certainly diverted the traffic; or the take-over of the market place by a large body of self-styled Egyptologists for excavation purposes, when the underground Gents' entrance made a splendid tomb of Tutankhamen (much in the news in the nineteen-twenties). The inconvenience was chiefly to the Police who, as usual, were not amused and lost one or two helmets – these being precious trophies in undergraduates' rooms.

The theatre at Cambridge, apart from the Gilbert and Sullivan seasons, was not an important feature of our amusements. Far more vital were the productions of the dramatic societies and, of course, what someone called the 'Folies Bergères', i.e. Sheppard's Greek Plays. There were theatrical productions at Newnham too. The first one I saw there was an Arthur Milne play with Alice Hopkinson (newly engaged to Lawrence Bragg) as a beautiful heroine, supported by Ella Harley-Jones in a ginger wig as a neat little midshipman. Among the stars at the A.D.C. Steven Runciman and Dennis Arundel in their time played many parts – including a terrifying self-destroying Oedipus by the latter – and Sinclair Baddeley was a principal in the famous *Aladdin* pantomime of 1923, singing of 'The dear old Union Jack' and 'Daffodil time in New Zealand'; while at the Footlights Revue Cecil Beaton fascinated us as the dizziest blond of all time. (Girls had not yet been invited to help out; Oxford were well ahead in this.) But most memorable of all dramas in the twenties were Sheppard's Greek Play productions – among them a quite wonderful *Agamemnon*, with Adrian Bishop (Aegisthus), Paul Paget, George Rylands and, as it seemed to me then and as I still think, the most superb Clytemnestra – I wish I could remember who played her. I know he's not Prime Minister, but I feel he must be Somebody now.

Newnham itself was as gay as the rest of the University. Everyone there had lived through the war and suffered hardships and shortages, and in most cases some bereavement; and all were ready for the new world. I had already stayed in Newnham for my entrance examination, in Sidgwick, and though I had been allotted a rather unattractive north-facing room, I liked their small, friendly dining-hall, and their soothing grey-green breakfast china. When I later came into residence in Clough, the Hall seemed too big and bright, with its lofty ornamented ceiling and its glossy white balconies, and the noise of so many knives and forks on the crimson-flowered china quite intimidating. But of course we loved it in the end; and I think affectionately of the nut-cracking echoes of our two dear vegetarian dons presiding at their tables – one the charming Miss Paues, over life-size, with her genial smile, and the other, on the same diet, little Miss Firth, more serious but friendly, and sizes smaller! Most of the students' rooms then were distempered in white or pale neutral shades – but, in one or two, William Morris wall-papers had been preserved, and we all disliked them intensely. Patterns generally were out of fashion, and these we considered dreadfully unattractive and 'busy' – particularly one in dark greens and blues in a high-ceilinged ground-floor room coldly overlooking the front courtyard. We pleaded for the poor occupant that she might have it distempered, but Miss Steele Smith

('Minna') looked at us benignly through her thick spectacles (and is it my imagination or *did* she wear a white fleecy shawl?) and said, 'One day you and your children will greatly admire William Morris wallpaper. We must save it for them.' She was always full of wisdom. I hope she can see us now choosing William Morris for our drawing-rooms.

Our dons in those days wore a variety of suits and dresses, but their skirts were always long. Miss Elles I can see in brown tweeds, and Miss Thomas ('Tommy') in a manly grey tailored suit with stiff collar and tie, as worn, I think, by the generation before her. Miss Jane Harrison, who was still in residence when I came up, though I believe no longer in office, was a picturesque figure in a wide flowery straw hat; and one of her companions had made a concession to the new fashion for jumpers (designed to go over the skirt) instead of blouses, by wearing her blouse outside, but retaining the tapes tied round its middle – a feature of our school blouses deemed necessary to keep them neatly inside the waistband. All of us of course wore hats when we went out. Indeed at home our mothers sometimes put on hats for their own lunch parties. In the summer most girls wore white stockings and shoes, and their skirts were usually calf-length. White or coloured silk stockings and satin shoes were worn with dance frocks – sometimes, rather becomingly, with satin ribbons crossed round the ankles. A smart little arty-crafty shop in King's Parade did a brisk trade in rather lumpy hand-woven linen jumpers and skirts with patterned edges and fringes – I can picture Camilla Wedgwood in a woven lavender blue, and Ruth Singer, with her dark curls and pink cheeks, in dazzling orange – 'The young', as the arty-craftswoman remarked to her, 'can wear *anything*.' Both of them had their hair in short thick bobs. This fashion swept through the College in our first year; and the little hairdresser in Regent Street must have made a fortune shearing off our manes.

Handwoven bed covers and peasant pottery adorned our rooms, and many people pinned up the Rhyme Sheets published by the Poetry Bookshop – and removed the 'Piper of Dreams' and the Margaret Tarrants they had nostalgically brought with them from their nurseries.

Hospitality within the College mainly took the form of tea-parties, and these could be of considerable size if three girls combined as hostesses. I think we were allowed three or four male guests apiece. Unlike cocktail parties (which were only in their infancy in the outside world and had not yet reached us) where the main activity is conversation, a tea-party involved playing games such as 'Beaver' which necessitated shouting;

in my first year this was unfortunate as my room was the otherwise desirable one above the Clough Combination Room. Afterwards I moved above it again to the top floor, to the nicest of all rooms, with its tiny separate bedroom and a lovely view over the lawns and treetops. Among ourselves, parties in the evening took the form of gatherings for coffee immediately after Hall, which were reasonably short; or later, when most people had put in an hour or two of concentrated work, the most fattening of all things, cocoa-parties with cakes, which could go on to any hour of the night, as in this relaxing atmosphere everything under the sun was discussed and beliefs and theories revealed – a most necessary and valuable thing in a young person's life and an opportunity that living in a community easily provides.

In the winter a small but important thing in our daily routine was the fire-lighter – a little bundle of wood-shavings and sticks impregnated with paraffin, without which it was hardly possible to kindle our coal fires. A stalwart ex-naval rating named Mr Bowen was a familiar sight in the Clough corridors, pushing along his trolley laden with coal for our scuttles. He was very good-tempered and did his best for us even when he thought we'd really had more than our allowance. At an early hour of the morning, as in any ordinary household of the time, the maids would come into our rooms, their hair rather attractively tied in coloured handkerchiefs, and kneel at the fireplace with a clatter of fire-irons to clear out the ashes and re-lay our fires. On being asked by a newcomer if she would kindly put a light to the fire one of the maids replied, 'Oh no, Miss, these are damp sticks. You have to buy fire-lighters.' A Scots fellow-student once lent me a pencil in a moment of need, and when I said, extravagantly, she was most kind and how could I repay her, she replied that she would like two fire-lighters. And she called for them next morning. I well remember that one of our friends kept her fire-lighters in her 'coffin' [storage chest] alongside her supply of cake and biscuits. We attributed this undesirable arrangement to the fact that she was a product of a school reputed to sacrifice gracious living to great scholarship. Another of her schoolfellows would regularly empty her rubber hot water bottle into her tea kettle.

The maids in their kerchiefs and cotton frocks appeared again at morning prayers in Hall (thinly attended by students), and later in the day in black afternoon frocks with white lawn caps and aprons. A very dignified head parlour-maid, tall Gertrude, was not to be seen until lunch-time when she was in charge of affairs. Her cap, flat but frilly-edged, was of generous size and obviously modelled on the Vice-Chancellor's. Each Hall had its army of maids, handyman and housekeeper; and at the main gateway, in his little office, was a Mr Smith, called by us, rightly or wrongly, Ignatius, said to have been appointed to his job of, among other things, checking in latecomers, on the strength of his guaranteed misogyny. It was he, they say, who was asked by a visitor what the young ladies did all day and replied gloomily, 'They eats and eats, with intervals for meals.' It is a fact, I believe, that one of these young ladies when her long-suffering Tutor enquired when did she actually do her work said, 'Oh I manage to fit it in somehow.'

We did indeed fit in a great deal of work, in our rooms, in the Library, in the garden (if you were a hammock-owner you rushed out on arrival in the May Term to pin your name on to a desirable tree), and of course at lectures. I remember with great pleasure going to early lectures on Lucretius by Mr Angus at Trinity Hall, which involved a bicycle ride along the Backs, very quiet in those days and very lovely on a summer morning, and over the bridge in Garret Hostel Lane. His lectures were stimulating and amusing, and incidentally accustomed us to the useful English word *functional* which a few years later was rediscovered and used *ad nauseam* by the architectural world. Professor Ridgeway was one of the most striking and original characters of the time. With him we sat at a table in the 'Ark' while he pushed round Greek coins to us, barking out 'What do you make of that?' He was almost completely blind then but could feel the coins and he knew where we were sitting and who we were. There were only six of us: R. W. Hutchinson, Seltman, Harden, J. H. Iliffe, an American whose name escapes me, and myself. The first two, I think, were post-graduates. The same group was invited to tea one Sunday at Ridgeway's house at Fen Ditton, and the occasion was one of some embarrassment to me. The maid showed me into the drawing-room where Lady Ridgeway, whom I'd never met, and a crowd of ladies kindly entertained me, and it was some time before it dawned on one of them that I belonged to the party in the study upstairs, and they all rippled with laughter as the maid was summoned to take me away.

Sheppard's Homeric lectures at King's were enormously popular, and gate-crashing friends often came in with me to witness them. His views on the unity of the Homeric poems were fascinating, his humour unconventional, and his reading and gestures highly dramatic as he perched perilously on the edge of the desk or the back of a chair, waving his arms or winding his gown round him, while his voice dropped to a whisper in some heart-rending passage. A group of his friends, including the Lucases and George Rylands (his yellow hair set off by the cobalt blue shirt he always wore), would file in and sit in the front row. In return Sheppard, Mrs Lucas and Rylands would attend Lucas's lectures on Greek drama, less sensational but quite moving. In spite of these attractions, I know that if I could relive any lectures I would choose the quiet pleasure of A. B. Cook's on the Greek Melic poets, in the old chapel at Queens' one hot May Term. As one came in from the sunlit court the little chapel had that delicious smell of damp stone and ancient wood like a country church, and the sunlight filtered in from the high windows. You couldn't have a better background for A. B. Cook's reading of Sappho's lovely 'Apple-gatherers'. I often think of it and can still see it, although my life since that time has had little to do with the Classics. Whatever today's architects may give us in the way of see-through glass panels and cantilevered concrete, they can never invent a more perfect lecture room than the old chapel. Alas, I see, from the outside, that it has been remodelled into a modern library. I daren't go in.

It can be well understood that in between these events one needed a pause for earthly refreshment; and the Whim, which I see still exists, was a favourite meeting place for coffee. In those days it was decorated in the latest tea-shop colours – orange and black and purple.

As I look back on our activities the wonder grows how we did fit it all in, and the answer is, of course, *the bicycle*, which made everything possible, night and day. Some undergraduates did own cars but I think the use of them was restricted, and even the higher ranks seemed to do without them. Believe it or not they actually walked. Many is the time we have seen A. B. Cook, flat-footed but well-beloved, making his way up Sidgwick Avenue from Queens' or the Ark to his home in Cranmer Road. Girton, of course, from its far-flung outpost had its own cabs. When I first visited it, during the Great War, these were horse-cabs which took parties down to the Girton 'Waiting Rooms' in St Edward's Passage where the students had their lunches and waited between lectures. As for the rest of us, we pushed our bicycles into the railings that surrounded King's and most other college entrances in those days – very handsome railings they were, too, apart from making excellent bicycle stalls. One almost regrets them.

I must add a footnote to my memories of the twenties. This summer (1969), after a long interval, I revisited Cambridge with my family and found it as beautiful as ever – my only regret being that the central shrine had lost its immense and dignified quietude and had become a show place, with tables of the money-changers displaying postcards, tourists shuffling up and down, and guides telling their parties who had designed the new trendy altar-cloth and chandeliers. A little dejected by this and an overdose of scarlet geraniums in college gardens and on windowledges everywhere, we finished our morning with a glance into Newnham, approaching up Newnham Walk and through the Clough Gates. I have never before seen it all looking so lovely, serene and still – the lawns well cared for, and the borders filled with flowers like a real country garden. No geraniums, no tourists. I *was* proud of it. φιλοκαλοῦμεν μετ' εὐτελείας indeed, if we can interpret εὐτέλεια as an absence of pomp and extravagance. The producer must be a genius and, I hope, well satisfied.

D. L. Halliday (Hatswell, 1920)

*

SMOKING

Smoking It was agreed that the rule limiting smoking to after lunch should be deleted. It was asked that smoking in the garden should not be made too obvious.

Extract from the minutes of the Joint Committee of Staff and Students, 29 April 1920

A CORNER ROOM IN OLD HALL

I came to Newnham in 1920, and I think I was the last person to get in without a competitive entrance exam. I had been promised a place in 1919 on the strength of my results in the Cambridge Senior Local Examination. Then I think the authorities were rather short of places and, as I should only have been just eighteen in 1919, they asked me to wait a year and come up in 1920. Under those circumstances, they didn't like to ask me to take the competitive entrance, having promised me a place. All my contemporaries in 1920 had had to take this competitive entrance, as was pointed out to me by Miss Cook, who was my first Director of Studies (she afterwards went to St Hugh's).

I was in Old Hall with Miss Collier as our Tutor. She was so very kind and good to all of us; I think everybody liked her very much indeed. Miss Clough was Principal: naturally one didn't get to know her very well, but certainly I had the most immense admiration for her. I was very lucky in my room. Both my second and third year I was in what was known as West Wing of Old on the first floor, a corner room right at the end. It was quite a big room, not classed as a big room but quite a good size, with two windows looking out on to the garden. Outside one of the windows was the most gorgeous poplar tree; I always regarded it as my tree and got very attached to it. Since then it has come down, although there is a new one to take its place. We had very pleasant furniture: we had a bed, of course, and a table, two upright chairs, an armchair, a writing desk with good drawers where one could keep some of one's clothes, a small hanging cupboard behind a curtain in one corner and a wash-stand behind another screen in another corner, and an oak chest in which we kept anything we felt like – a nice large oak chest which held a great many of one's belongings. Then we had open fireplaces and we were provided with a smallish scuttle of coal every day in the winter. It didn't keep one's fire burning all day: I remember going out and buying a couple of fire bricks to put in the side of my grate because I had rather a large grate. I also remember buying logs and stacking them under my bed. But if one didn't light one's fire until certainly after lunch, or even the early evening, it kept going until one wanted to go to bed, and one of my great joys I remember was stirring up the logs last thing at night so as to get a flicker of light, turning out the main light and going to sleep with the flicker of the firelight.

We had a very kind maid in our branch of Old. She wasn't supposed to make our beds: she was supposed to clean the rooms, and we were supposed to make our own beds and tidy up generally. But if one overslept or got late and rushed out leaving the place in chaos, probably with dirty cups and unmade bed and clothes lying about, she was very good and used to clean up and tidy up for one. We had a very ingenious form of lamp, I remember. It had the bulb hung from a shaped frame, and you could either hang it on the wall on a hook so that it was above your writing desk or you could stand it up on the table and use it as a table lamp.*

The food was not good, it was badly cooked. I believe that in Clough it wasn't so bad because they had the kitchens next door, but for the other Halls it used to be brought over in trolleys quite a long time before the meal was going to be served, and kept hot, which meant that if it was something that could dry up it did dry up. At any rate it was rather overcooked and not very nice and very often there was not enough. I suppose they didn't want to bring over more than they were sure was

* These lamps were made to a design by Mrs Sidgwick and were known as 'the Newnham twist'.

going to be eaten, but if you came in a bit late for lunch for any reason you might find that there was practically nothing left to eat at all. Hall in the evening was not very attractive, and early. I remember that we used to have the most appalling meals for ourselves at about ten o'clock at night – why we didn't ruin our digestions I cannot imagine. We ate things like new bread spread thickly with butter and tinned crab; it makes me shudder to think of now, but we all survived it quite happily. We very often were really extremely hungry by that time of night and needed something to keep us going.

It was during my time at Newnham, that the gates were broken down, and I remember that evening very well indeed. I think we must have been working in the Library or something, because I know some of us were coming back to get to Old at the time that the crowd had arrived outside and had smashed in the gates. We wanted to get through the archway to get back to Old, and I remember Miss Clough standing in the gateway, the archway, facing the gates with the howling mob just outside, and she waved us through quickly into Old. Then we went upstairs to some of the students' rooms in Pfeiffer and looked down directly on to the mob. I remember very well that there were a couple of Proctors with their Bulldogs between the gates and the crowd, and while we were there a lot of policemen, about fifteen or so, were loosed through the gate out into the crowd too. I remember even at that moment, crisis though it was, thinking that they looked exactly like the policemen in *The Pirates of Penzance* as they trotted out through the gate.

The University had a lot of ballroom-dancing clubs in those days; I remember three of them: there was the Quinquaginta, there was the Vingt-et-un and there was the Cambridge University Dance Club. You were invited by a man who was a member; only men were members, but they used to invite partners from the women's colleges, and one was allowed to go once a week. They all met once a week and different people went to different clubs; I remember I patronised the Quinquaginta – I used to get invited there as a rule. Apart from that, one wasn't allowed out much in the evening. You had to be in for Hall and were not allowed out again after Hall without special permission; and if you were going to a dance club once a week you were lucky if you got permission to go out again in the same week, and only for something like a concert or a really good play – something of that sort.

Everyone seemed to go on the river a tremendous lot. At week-ends the river between Silver Street and Grantchester was absolutely alive with punts, largely being manoeuvred by young men who didn't know much about punting, so there were frequent collisions and shrieks and people falling overboard. At Newnham we were not allowed to punt or canoe until we had passed a test, which I think was very sensible – we would have been a menace otherwise; but for some reason which I never fathomed we were not allowed to try and punt or canoe until we could scull. We used to be taken out in double scullers and made both to scull and cox these wretched boats. Well, it didn't worry me because I had had several holidays on the Thames and could handle a boat quite reasonably well; but for poor young women who had never seen boats before, they got most terribly tied up: particularly, I think, with the coxing when they had to give directions to their crews. I have recollections of the most extraordinary manoeuvres on the Mill Pool by the Silver Street bridge before breakfast, trying to get people through this wretched test; and seeing whether one could surreptitiously, while one was sculling, do a little to help one's cox, so that even if she gave completely the wrong directions one could still make the boat go in the right direction to help her pass her test! Once one had passed one's test it was great fun, we all used to go on the river a lot; I remember I managed to become what they called a star punter, which meant I had to help other people, I had to train other people; it also meant I was allowed to punt a canoe, which really was the greatest fun even if rather wet – I never fell in but I very nearly did several times.

In those days the only swimming baths were all in the stretch between Silver Street and Grantchester. There was the University bathing place and then there were the two town bathing places, one for women and one for men, and there was the old Newnham Bath. I know we used to use the women's town bathing place a good deal. Sometimes we used to try and use the Newnham Bath, but this was just after the first war and I think they hadn't been able to get it cleaned out at all during the war, so that it was terribly silted up with mud; and what we used to do very often was to use the undressing facilities in the Newnham Bath, then climb round and out, and bathe in the main stream just outside, where the bank was nice and steep and one could dive in off the edge, and it was great fun. I have recollections of an inter-Hall swimming competition taking place in the Newnham Baths, muddy and all as they were. I was never at all a good swimmer, but I think Old was very short of swimmers because I remember I was pressed into service to do one length in the relay race, and we just ploughed up and down in thick, thick muddy water.

I think in those days there weren't these Rag Weeks which universities seem to go in for now. I remember a good many rags by the University, but I think they always took place on a Saturday morning just for that day. Two in particular I remember. One was the opening of Tutankhamen's tomb, when I think some medical students went up to London and managed to borrow (or perhaps we should say steal) the figure which was the mascot of one of the London University colleges. I think his name was Phineas and he stood outside a tobacconist's shop when they weren't using him as a mascot. At any rate, they brought this figure down to Cambridge so that he should act as Tutankhamen. I remember the tomb was in the market place, and there was a wonderful arrangement by which hawsers were rigged up from a top window down to the tomb in the market square, and down these hawsers slid angels complete with wings and harps – it looked absolute suicide but they seemed to arrive quite safely the other end. That was most amusing. The other one I remember particularly well was the Pavement Club rag. Somebody discovered that if you sat on the kerb with your feet in the gutter you weren't breaking any law, that was quite legal, so they decided they would all do this; and the whole of King's Parade was full of people sitting on the kerb with their feet in the gutter, knitting scarves in Pavement Club colours, I remember, and playing cards and everything you could think of. Needless to say it held up the traffic completely while this was going on, which was not quite so legal perhaps as just sitting on the kerb; but the traffic was mostly bicycles in those days.

K. D. McKeag (Vicars, 1920). Extracts from a tape recording

INSURANCE AGAINST PROCTORIAL RISK

On Saturday, November 13th, a joint debate was held at Emmanuel College. The evening opened with private business, special applause greeting the suggestion that Newnham on attaining membership of the University should be admitted to the Emmanuel College Society for Insurance against Proctorial Risk.

The House then proceeded to debate 'That the banquet of the Modern Press has become too generous for the public digestion'.

From *Thersites*, 2 December 1920

1921

THE BREAKING OF THE GATES

Despite the 1914–18 war and the realisation it brought of women's ability to cope with a variety of unladylike activities, a good deal of the attitude of the past still lingered on in the printed rules which governed our comings and goings, particularly where men were concerned. One which caused us much amusement said, 'Students may not be alone with a man either in a canoe or in a room, unless the man is either a fiancé or a brother. Students will inform their Tutor immediately upon arrival, how many brothers they have in residence'.

After a few days in residence we were asked by some of the seniors to meet them by the upper river at the strange hour of 7 a.m. The object of this was to discover which freshers, if any, were likely to be good oarswomen: the reason for the early hour was then revealed. It appeared that one of the many ways in which Newnhamites in the past had been the cause of hilarity to others and shame to themselves, was by conducting this test at a reasonable hour on the lower river, near the college boat houses. Owing to inexperience in such matters, some had, as a preliminary, seated themselves back to back in a boat: a situation so awful that, ever since, the time and place had been chosen with a view to privacy. Since anyone could see at a glance that I was unlikely to be much use in a boat, I was soon dismissed and bicycled back to breakfast rather hungrier than usual, having enjoyed the early morning freshness of Cambridge in October. As Father's one condition about my coming to Newnham was that I should not play hockey, of which he disapproved professionally, rowing was a second athletic possibility out of the way. I had no desire to play hockey of which I knew nothing, or lacrosse which at school had been so popular.

I now solved the exercise problem in a manner which nearly led to disaster at the outset. Having discovered a riding stable in the village at Newnham, I decided to hire a horse for an hour whenever opportunity offered, and to balance my accounts by paying for it with the money Father gave me for the expenses of laundry. Not knowing much about the layout of either the village or the College, I turned down a promising-looking country lane, leading eventually to an iron gateway on to a field. The moment we were through the open gate one glance revealed my mistake, the left-hand portion of the field being full of maidens wielding hockey sticks. My decision to withdraw came too late: once the horse felt the grass underfoot he refused to compromise. I was afraid to make us still more conspicuous by arguing, and there was no time for the difficult operation of descending from a side-saddle. There remained only the unsuitable alternative of cantering across the College playing field, keeping as far to the right as possible and hoping that no one but the hockey team would see me. The feeling of being involved in criminal activity was increased as we reached the limits of the field, and clattered on to the gravel path leading round by Old Hall and out through the Clough Gates.

I knew nothing of Tutors apart from the formal five minutes I had spent on arrival with the Tutor of Sidgwick Hall, Miss E. M. Chrystal. She had been welcoming, but I had been overawed by her official position and mature age. (She was I believe at this time thirty and as new to Newnham as I was.) I reproached myself with being every kind of a fool and decided that, unless by a miracle my idiocy had passed unnoticed, my career at Newnham was already over. Nothing was said that night and I began to feel hope rising, until at breakfast I received word that Miss Chrystal would like to see me in her room. So this was it. How could any College Tutor tolerate the continued presence of a fresher so devoid of sense, I asked myself gloomily, as I gulped down the last of my coffee and prepared for execution. I knocked and a deceptively pleasant voice said 'Come in.' Miss Chrystal continued to sit; I remained standing. Her remarks were as follows: 'Miss Roberts, I happened to be in Old Hall as you went past yesterday afternoon. I am sure you will agree that we cannot encourage cavalry on a large scale in the grounds of the College: so perhaps in future you will make other arrangements. That is all.' I never have been quite sure whether I did, or did not, detect a twinkle.

The Director of Studies in Modern Languages turned out to be Miss J. P. Strachey. Tall and thin like her brother Lytton, shy in manner with a humorous, quizzical and wholly endearing personality, she was greatly appreciated by her pupils to whom she was affectionately known as 'Streak'. There was about her a refreshing element of the unexpected that showed itself on such occasions as when, for instance, addressing a large gathering of Newnham students, she announced to our surprise and delight that 'the proper study for womankind is man'.

In the summer of 1921 the question again arose as to whether women were to continue to be awarded titular degrees, which they received through the post, or should be allowed to receive them from the Vice-Chancellor, in the Senate House, as did male graduands. The question, being of interest to all members of the University, was to be open to non-resident voters. This spread a very wide net, since anyone who could call himself an M.A. of Cambridge was included. Bearing in mind that any male student who acquired a B.A. degree automatically assumed the dignity of M.A. by the simple process of allowing five years to elapse and paying the requisite fee, it is easy to picture the number of gentlemen of all ages who took this opportunity of visiting their old colleges and exercising their right to vote on this burning question. The impression that remains with me – allowing of course for distortions of memory over so long a period – is that they came in their hundreds, from all corners of the United Kingdom: those aided by sticks and crutches being animated by a passion of anti-feminism in proportion to their years. Since the resident vote was for the most part in favour of the motion that women should be given degrees in the obvious and sensible way, the victory of the 'antis' must have been achieved by the invading army of angry old gentlemen – for the women were defeated.

When this was announced outside the Senate House, one of these elderly warriors so far forgot himself as to utter inflammatory words urging the young men to proceed to Newnham College – with what precise object he did not specify. Not unnaturally, given the circumstances and the highly emotional state of so many excited young men, this was followed by action that was as discreditable as it was uncharacteristic. Filled with explosive energy and devoid of any idea as to what to do with it, they surged up Newnham Walk in the direction of what was then the main entrance. Here unfortunately they came upon one of the long-handled, four-wheeled trolleys used by the porters for distributing coal. This they seized, and used as a battering-ram to smash down the Clough Memorial Gates.

Those of us who were in residence at the time did not of course have any clear idea of the sequence of events during the remainder of that day, though we heard later, on all sides, that Miss Clough faced the situation and young men with great dignity and calm, and the University took prompt and drastic action. It could hardly be expected that we, the Newnhamites of the day, should not enjoy to the full such a uniquely dramatic situation. College temporarily resembled a beleaguered fortress which we were forbidden to leave. As darkness fell we gathered in rooms looking out over the garden, where Junior Proctors and Police scuttled from bush to bush, while the Senior Proctor came and went inside the College with impressive speed and awful solemnity.

Next day the University was steeped in gloom and guilt, to an extent I imagine seen neither before nor since. Apart from the official and collective apology of the University, Miss Clough was inundated with contrite statements from every conceivable group of undergraduates, athletic and otherwise. Certainly the captain of the University rugger team rose to unprecedented heights of oratory in his plea for contributions to the fund to make good the damage and wipe out the stain.

So the gates were repaired and the hubbub died down – but the women of Newnham and Girton had to wait another twenty-six years before the Senate decreed in 1947 that they be given in person the degrees they had earned. In 1948 Queen Elizabeth – as she then was – came as the first woman to receive an Honorary Degree. Despite private anxieties concerning the King's health, she managed to distil an atmosphere of serenity that affected everyone in the Senate House. We all felt grateful to Her Majesty who then, as now, seemed able by her mere presence to banish fuss and tension. Shortly afterwards I made the necessary arrangements, just in time to take my M.A. before my daughter Rosalind took her B.A. degree – in the Senate House.

M. E. Henn (Roberts, 1920)

*

'IN AND OUT THE WINDOWS'

The Principal commented on the growing practice of using Ground Floor windows as entrances and exits. She pointed out that the practice badly damaged the flower-beds below the windows, and injured the brickwork of the window sills, which was soft. She urged that students should be discouraged from using Ground Floor Windows as thoroughfares...It was decided that the Senior Student should put notices in the Halls, dissuading people from getting in and out of windows without due reason.

Extract from the minutes of the Joint Committee of Staff and Students, 1 November 1921

*

A YOUNG RESEARCH FELLOW

When I was a young Research Fellow I lived in 27 Grange Road. It was reopened (it always was College property, I understand) at this time, and four of us went into it. B.A. was Principal and she was responsible for it; and she had put in two terrifying housekeepers. One was a middle-aged woman who'd been Matron of a boys' school, and was very much on her dignity; the other was well over seventy and a woman of very uncertain temper. The latter took a very great dislike to me – no shame to her – and a very great liking to Maud Brindley, another Research Fellow. She used to wake up Maud Brindley of a morning with a sort of song; I was not quite sure I wasn't glad I was in her bad books! Everything that went wrong in the house was put down to me. One day Maud Brindley filled her rather antique kettle at the bath and blacked it. In came one or other of the housekeepers, I forget which: 'Oh look at that dirty Miss Welsford, she's blacked the bath!' Maud told me this with shrieks of laughter, and never confessed. My bedroom was only curtained off from my sitting-room, and the housekeeper who hated me used to take it out of me by going and doing my sitting-room while I was still in bed and indulging in a very loud soliloquy on the subject of my character, and mainly of its very obvious defects. It really was rather a dreadful life, and if one told B.A. she just laughed.

This accounts for a sad episode, though it's rather funny really. In those days there were three ventilators, at each side of and over Kennedy front door: they weren't glass then, they were open. Well, one day I went out to dinner in a long evening dress, and when I came back to 27 Grange Road, some ass had made the Yale lock so that no key would open it. I was too terrified of the housekeepers to ring the bell – I just was too terrified. So I thought, 'What do I do now?' I went across to Kennedy and at Kennedy I saw bicycles ranged against the wall. I was young and active in those days, and though I'd got a long evening dress I climbed up on to the saddle of one of the bicycles and hauled myself up on to the spikes, and there like an ancient martyr I sat on the spikes. And then I found how difficult it is when you're sitting on spikes to turn round and get down the other side. While I was pondering on this difficulty some students came by, so I crouched very, very quietly and hoped they hadn't seen. I was a Research Fellow, you see. They had, obviously from what happened later; but I hoped they hadn't. I managed to get down, and I went and knocked up Miss Pybus, she was always ready to help you in that sort of thing: we laughed a great deal and then she put me on her sofa. All would have been well if a maid hadn't come in to do her room. I did give her a turn, and she went out shrieking, and it all came to B.A. B.A. of course had me in, and she said, 'If Research Fellows behave like this, what can we expect of the students?' That was that. However, a rumour then started round the College that Kennedy Passage was either haunted, or that there was a lunatic who mopped and mowed from the top of the spikes. By that time Edith Chrystal was

Junior Bursar, and she, thinking to stop any of this sort of nonsense, very foolishly glassed in the two side ventilators. So I said to her, 'Edith, it's no good, that: because I tried to get through those and I stuck in the middle.' She was awfully angry with me. And that's how they all came to be glassed.

When I first became a don Ruth Cohen and Elsie Duncan-Jones together were absolute life-savers to me. There was a hideous scheme at that time that the dons had to head dinner-tables and make conversation to students; and it was awful if you had been supervising practically to the dinner-gong – you had no conversation to make. Ruth and Elsie used to come and sit next to me, and I must record my gratitude!

At that time Miss Strachey was Principal. She was a wonderful Principal in many ways. At the end of B.A.'s three years it was an enormous joy that, with absolute acclamation, every single one of the Fellows voted for Miss Strachey. We would have voted for her long before, but she just wouldn't take it on. Anybody who knew any of the Strachey family will know how they talk, and in her way of talking Miss Strachey was just like them. The first thing that happened to me when I arrived (and pretty advanced in years – I was over thirty, as I had already been supervising for years) was that I dropped my College keys in the passage. Miss Strachey picked them up later and without a word handed them to me. They weren't labelled, and I said, 'How in the world did you know they were mine, Miss Strachey?' And she said, 'Elementary knowledge of psychology!'

Later, when I was President of the Women's Research Club, the Club was addressed by an old lady who was a student of a notable Early Father whose great study was the Trinity; and Streak asked me round to her flat after the old lady's paper to have a smoke. I think she did this out of sheer mischief because she knew my views were not hers; she was a renowned humanist (though she had a great love of the Establishment: Archbishops and such were much appreciated by her) and I was an orthodox Anglican. 'Well, what did you think of the meeting?' she asked. I said I thought it was very interesting, and that I thought the speaker was very scholarly, but that I couldn't help being rather astonished that she managed – considering her subject – to refrain from any mention of the Trinity throughout the course of the paper. Streak said, 'Yes – I'm so disappointed; I thought she'd be talking about the Trinity. The Holy Ghost – so amusing, I always think!'

Miss Strachey was there for just the first year of the Second World War, before she retired and Dame Myra took her place. It used to be my miserable task, once a week at least, to go all around looking for lights to make sure the blackout was done properly. And one time the Principal's blackout wasn't done properly, and I knocked at her door to tell her her lights were showing. I had a ridiculous costume – my old ski-ing costume with a silly sort of ski-ing cap on my head; and she said, 'Good heavens – the Police!'

In Dame Myra's time we had an enormous kind of official air-raid practice, all over the College. One of the officials came up to me and she said to me, 'Now, Miss Welsford, I want you to imagine that there's a fire already burning in Clough Hall, and it is rapidly approaching the Combination Room. What would you do?' And thinking no harm – in fact, I think it was a very good idea – I said, 'Save the Turner!' She was furious. I should have said 'Pull down all the curtains', you see.

E. E. H. Welsford (1911). Extracts from a tape recording

WITH REST AND REFRESHMENT

I went up to Newnham in 1922. Freshers used to go up a week-end before the rest of the Hall. I was shy, and very homesick, and I felt that the extra hour provided by the end of the Daylight Saving period was the last straw. Never was a longer evening so unwelcome! An odd thing was that the one or two people with whom one first 'chummed up' were people to whom one practically never spoke again after settling down. I am sure other freshers beside myself had this experience.

It was very cold in the morning. Coal was rationed. We used to bank up our fires with slack on going to bed, and an astonishing blaze would arise in the small hours – until finally a *real* fire put a stop to this practice. My rather restless nature, on mornings when one had no lectures, prompted the following Triolet, which appeared in *Thersites* in March 1923:

I find that I can't work the whole morning through,
With rest and refreshment I work so much better.
Although I have plenty of reading to do
I find that I can't work the whole morning through;
So I stop for some cake, or a biscuit or two,
Or to see if the postman has brought me a letter –
I find that I can't work the whole morning through,
With rest and refreshment I work so much better.

I. M. Shewell-Cooper (1922)

THE ART OF THEORISING

One was living at a tremendous pace. There was first the intense excitement of the work itself. We were blessed with some distinguished lecturers on the Modern Languages side in those days and they opened up a new approach to knowledge. The lively debates which had accompanied meals at home had sharpened my wits to hold my own with my father, but the charm of his mind was its extraordinary youthfulness. He never subjected his heroes to the indignity of a critical analysis, and he had adopted without questioning the outlook and opinions of the late-Victorian writers on whose works he had been brought up. These he would defend with enthusiastic loyalty from the united attacks of the family. Stimulating as it was, this sort of intellectual exercise had tended to generate more heat than light, while at school I had always felt too weary and too hard-driven to try to think things out for myself. I had, in fact, never consciously thought; I had merely had a few ideas, a good many opinions and a whole farrago of likes and dislikes.

Listening to the University lecturers and in discussion with my tutor I now began to see how differently the products of other minds ought to be approached. In the first place it did not matter, at any rate at the outset, whether I liked or disliked the work I was studying. The essential thing was to understand it, and this was only possible if it was approached with humility and respect; if one could, as it were, lay one's mind alongside that of the author, see through his eyes what he was trying to achieve, and then judge him by the extent to which he fell short of it. The whole cargo of one's own performance and prejudices had to go overboard, and their place was taken by a few hard-won fundamental principles on which a new scale of values was gradually built up. This careful reflective building-up from first principles was new to me, and I can still remember the occasion when I first arrived, slowly adding step by step in a chain of argument, at a conclusion I had not anticipated but which was demonstrably logical. I jumped up from the wicker armchair in which I had been sitting before the fire in my room, saying to myself in great excitement, 'Why, I have been *thinking*!' I have long forgotten the conclusion so painstakingly reached, but I can still recall the thrill of the achievement. This, I felt, was the proper way of looking at life. I would give my mind a thorough spring-cleaning. Throw away the accumulated rubbish, and rebuild all my opinions on a foundation of reason and logic.

The spring-cleaning which extended over the next year or so had some odd results. I very nearly managed to throw out the baby with the bath water. Arguing from first principles requires the ballast of experience and knowledge of the world. At nineteen, the ship is top heavy with theory. The art of theorising seemed astonishingly easy once one had got the knack of it. I built up theories on every topic which came before me. Some of them were so beautiful I fell in love with them and would pursue them, of an evening round the fire, to the last, fine-drawn conclusion in long discussions with my contemporaries, most of whom were going through the same phase. We would often have been hard put to it to say what we, as individuals, really thought about the points we argued so hotly. Had we done so we could I think sometimes have been surprised, and ashamed, to find how widely our innermost private thoughts differed from the line of pure principle that we were advancing. We believed that we were in pursuit of 'truth', but we did not at that stage realise that tradition, emotion and plain blind instinct all have a place in this conception. So we went on gloriously, convinced that no generation had ever thought so clearly and logically about the universe before, and that, inspired by this new spirit, human affairs would never again sink beneath the waves of traditional prejudice.

Most lectures took place in the morning, in the Arts School and in different colleges, and we hastened from one to another in the traditional fashion, on bicycles, our notebooks in the basket on the handlebars, and in winter a muffler round our necks by way of outdoor clothing. Women students did not at that time wear gowns, but were quiet, not to say mouselike, in their dress. Not so the men. It was the era of 'Oxford bags', and their wearers paraded in all the prettiest pastel shades, from soft rose pink to pale pea green, their trailing draperies set off with all the blazonry of the college blazer above. The sight of all this finery awakened in me a longing to wear pretty colours too, and I set off my khaki flannel suit with a muffler in pigeon's-neck colours knitted by Mother. This would fly out bravely behind, until one day the end caught on a bicycle going in the opposite direction with the most disastrously undignified results.

The morning ended with lunch in Hall, rather a scrambled affair, eaten with the mind already on the afternoon's occupation. In my case the afternoon was dedicated, simply and crudely, to exercise in the open air. I had detested organised games at school but I had learnt to recognise my own overriding need for physical exertion, and when I had arrived at College it had seemed natural to take part in organised games. I had just begun to find out how enjoyable lacrosse could be in my new adult status (and how much better I played it), when a badly sprained foot set me looking for a temporary alternative where running was not required, and some enthusiastic member of the Boat Club inveigled me on to the river in a tub. Had I known it, that was the point of no return. From then on I regularly spent my afternoons on the river, and found there a very sizeable share of my general enjoyment of life at Cambridge.

At that time the 'Jesus style', which involves shooting back the slide at the beginning of the stroke, was coming in. It later seemed to me doubtful whether this was the ideal style for a light crew in a very heavy boat, but our coach was a Jesus man. We shot our slides with the best and on one occasion two young women shot them right through the back skirts of their entangled gym tunics, rather than interrupt a burst which had been pronounced 'not too bad for once'. How much all this meant to us and how much earlier generations had missed I did not fully realise till many years later when, having come up to Cambridge for some College meeting, I found myself sitting at the High Table opposite Miss B. A. Clough who had been Principal of Newnham during my first year. There had been some small exhibition in connection with the meeting, and photographs of early Newnham students, in long skirts, leg-of-mutton sleeves and straw boaters were laid out in the Library. These had been Miss Clough's contemporaries and I asked her about College life in those far-off days. We were indulging in the pleasant game of comparing 'then' and 'now' ('now' being my own student years), when Miss Clough leant across the table and asked me with all seriousness, 'Did you fight much?' It took me a second or two to realise that this small, fragile, grey-haired lady meant precisely what she said. I was almost as surprised as if she had said something indecent. The pent-up energy and nervous irritation which had found this curious form of expression in Miss Clough's generation was sweated out in my day on the lower river.

As women students we were accepted, even if sometimes considered rather odd. We were treated courteously at lectures, by lecturer and audience alike. We could join most of the University societies. We were hardly conscious of such disabilities as still existed, and I know that I felt our position to be almost all that one could wish. It was not until later that I realised how hardly a position so favourable to the students might bear upon the women dons, many of whom were undertaking a lot of University work but were ineligible for any University appointments. But, whatever still remained to do to put the College in its entirety in its proper place in the University, at our level as students the anti-feminism with which earlier generations had had to contend had disappeared completely. My contemporaries were for the most part hardly aware that it had ever existed. In my second year the principal speaker at our annual Commemoration Dinner in the summer term was Susan Lawrence. She chose as her theme 'The kingdom of heaven is to the violent and the violent take it by force', and round this she wove a rousing, fighting speech of the kind which ten years earlier would have brought her audience shouting to their feet. We received it in silence, profoundly shocked. It seemed such dreadfully bad form.

In my third year I found myself skipper of the Newnham Boat Club, an office which I took very seriously. The Club, though small, was very keen, and we worked hard and spent all the time we could spare on the river. One obstacle to progress was our horrible tunics. In a boat they had always been ugly, inefficient and, on slides, verging on indecent, and by now they were old-fashioned as well. We all thought we looked much nicer and more suitably dressed in the shorts we wore on the Thames, and we determined to seek permission to wear them on the Cam. I wrote a note to Miss Strachey asking if I might come and talk over the request with her. She replied, fixing a time for our talk and suggesting that I might perhaps bring with me 'a pair of the garments in question'. I carefully selected from our stock of chocolate-coloured shorts the pair which fitted me best, put them on, with my overcoat on top, and called on Miss Strachey at the Principal's flat. We went into the drawing-room, and The Streak perched on the arm of a chair in her familiar bird-like attitude while I stood before her on the hearth rug. 'Yes', she said, 'very neat, quite unexceptionable. I really don't think anyone could take any objection to that – that is, from the front. Would you – ?'. I did a right-about-turn. 'Nor indeed from the rear. Now, you want of course to row in them. Do you think perhaps you could go through the motions so that I could see the effect?' So I gingerly boarded a footstool and rowed round Miss Strachey's drawing-room, on the polished parquet floor between the rugs, while she murmured, 'Yes, very suitable, really very suitable indeed', interspersed with little chuckles of amusement.

E. M. R. Russell-Smith (1922)

*

1923

FIRE-LIGHTERS AND PREMISCONCEPTIONS

Wednesday, 10 October 1923: Arrived Cambridge station, which was packed. After half an hour finally got a taxi to Newnham. Got a jolly nice room (in Clough), almost square, window west, and nice bureau and bookcase. Fire may be lit any time! Hung pictures and lit fire, both with much difficulty.

Thursday, 11 October 1923: Woke at 6.30. After I was called went and had a bath and was in time for breakfast, as nearly everyone was. Rearranged pictures finally, at least I think it's final. Went into town with Miss B. (another fresher)*...biking a fearful job there, especially in Silver Street and Petty Cury (in 1923!). N.B. Must I get a kettle? (The answer soon became obvious.)

Friday, 12 October 1923: After tea freshers' meeting with Miss T., senior student of the Hall; she explained the rules to us, also the constitution and the etiquette, which was v. useful, and all in the most charming way. Rearranged my room, putting bureau to other side, and rehung pictures.

Saturday, 13 October 1923: After dinner College Meeting. Miss Strachey gave a short speech, not bad; then Miss L., senior student, jawed: v. nervous but rather nice. After that dancing. Then cocoa with a few others with Miss L. and Miss T. Finally got to bed at nearly 12.30!

Tuesday, 16 October 1923: Up at 6.30 and down to the river to be coached for Div. II of the Boat Club. Great fun. Everything looked lovely from the river. After dinner Amalgamated Games meeting, very long and dull.

Wednesday, 17 October 1923: Auction in Peile. Couldn't stay very long, so got Miss B.K. (another fresher) to bid for a biscuit tin for me.

Friday 19 October 1923: After breakfast spent a fruitless $\frac{1}{2}$ hour in trying to light my fire, but the sticks were soaking so finally gave it up. After tea, lecture on Pascal. Pouring when we came back. Finally lit fire with half of one of C's fire-lighters.

Saturday, 20 October 1923: Couldn't light fire again. Finally M.K. gave me some fire-lighters and it worked. Suggested a Clough Freshers' debate: 'That the greatest invention science has given us is the fire-lighter'.

Saturday, 27 October 1923: Sharp practice debating after dinner. The motions were:

* Some (bracketed) glosses have been inserted by the author at a later date.

That Newnham should wear uniform.

That early rising is immoral.

That woman's greatest asset is man's imagination.

That a powdered nose is better than a shiny one.

That the episode of the cherry tree is a blot on the greatness of George Washington.

Monday, 5 November 1923: Rag (about 10 p.m.). Dressed in pyjamas, tunics, and rugs, on top of other clothes, and stocking headgear and masks. Started at one end of the 2nd floor and processed in the dark with an effigy of Felix the Cat, with the musicians, of which I was one, playing the Chopin Funeral March on combs, with gong accompaniment. Got to the other end, and caused some amusement to the 2nd and 3rd years, when Steely [Miss Steele Smith] rushed after us and told us we were making rather a noise. I can quite believe her! So we had to desist. Processed in solemn silence to the common room and there burnt Felix. Then processed to cocoa in F's room.

Sunday, 4 May 1924: Inter-Hall Part-Singing Competition. We (Clough) drew first. Not as good as we have been. Peile sounded heavenly. Sidgwick not very good. Old not bad. We had to do 'Dame Hickory' again, and Peile 'Fear no more'. He said very nice things about us all, especially about Clough's conductor being a disciplinarian. He said Peile and we were practically equal, but we sang from memory, so won. Great jubilations! Blessings on E's head for suggesting our singing without copies! Celebration at supper: H. and S. and I bagged the menu and wrote out several copies appropriately; (hot milk pudding was 'Céréale accoutumée'). Steely showed her copy to Streak amid great stampings.

Saturday, 31 May 1924: Slept out on roof for sixth night this term. Had to come in at 3.15 because of rain. Fearful scrum, seven of us trying to get in via the cubby-hole and ladder at once, *with* bedding.

Saturday, 7 June 1924: B.A.'s portrait presented to College. We watched the proceedings from the gallery. At dinner H. drew a picture on the menu of B.A.'s portrait with a triolet underneath; which we sent up to High:

> It must be in Clough,
> We all of us says;
> There's quite room enough;
> It must be in Clough,
> Else we'll get in a huff

And fail in our Mays.
It must be in Clough,
We all of us says.

Dons and Lecturers [gleanings from different parts of the diary]
Went to Forbes on Wordsworth and Keats. Odd man, who said 'Pre-mis-con-ception' 15½ times in the hour. One side-piece of his spectacles tied on with green string. Very long words. 'This magnificent poem...' then, fumbling over the pages '...if only I can find the beastly thing!'

Richards was fine again, analysing the experience of reading a line of poetry with the aid of little diagrams. He is always very clear, in spite of being so subtle.

Q. very good again. (He addressed us as 'Gentlemen' as usual.) He said that 'Lady Clara Vere de Vere' was only 'When Adam delved and Eve span Who was then the gentleman?' transferred to the pianola.

Essays back from Leavis. He was very good, and most amusing about Forbes and Q. Told us to beware of Forbes's vocabulary, and said there really should be a less idiosyncratic course on the Romantic Revival. He scribbles the whole time.

C. was hopeless. I had to go because I've been only three times before. He said that 'and spread the truth from pole to pole' was by Wordsworth!

Miss Butler really is a dear. She ticked us off about cutting lectures and about E. borrowing notes promiscuously instead. Next year she says we are going to begin an absolutely pure system of working.

At High Table: Steely excruciatingly funny about her first public examination, when someone fainted and they all failed. And again at High: Steely very amusing as usual, and Shark [Miss Sharpley] suddenly exclaimed, 'I think our Tutor is quite a wag.'

M. A. Scott (1923). Extracts from a diary, 1923–5

MET BY MOONLIGHT

I was scuttling along Library Passage late one evening. Everything was silent – Newnham in those days was silent after 10 p.m. – and no one was in Library Passage. The moon was shining – there was no other light – and the statues outside the Library were dim white shapes. Suddenly I saw three enormous figures advancing towards me – three tall women in long flowing robes – approaching without a sound along the matting which covered the floor. For a moment I felt a frisson of fear – then they moved into the moonlight – still without speaking and with the same stately tread, and I recognised them, Miss Strachey, Miss Edith Sitwell and Miss Paues. I remembered then that I had heard and seen Miss Sitwell earlier in the evening when she gave a lecture in Clough Hall. She was dressed as usual in a magnificent robe of peacock brocade, and wore huge jewels on her dress and on her long fingers. Miss Strachey – equally tall – wore a long gown too, and Miss Paues with her golden hair piled high was like a stately Norse goddess. I don't think they even noticed me – but I can remember even now with pleasure the striking picture these three distinguished women made in the moonlight.

K. M. Drabble (Bloor, 1925)

*

'SHE SHIMMIES LIKE THE DEUCE'

Newnham in the nineteen-twenties, to one remembering over a distance of forty-odd years the smaller things of life, seems like part of another century, almost another world.

Dresses were loosely tubular, with a belt somewhere round the hips. Being small for my age and more or less flat up and down by nature, I managed quite nicely, but I realise now what some of my more amply proportioned friends must have gone through in their efforts to achieve the fashionable shape. When Margaret Morris visited the College to give a demonstration of her school of dancing, wearing a dress which revealed that she had both a waist and a bosom, we felt rather uncomfortable and avoided looking at her. To go about without stockings was unthinkable, even in summer in the garden. Two of my year took off their stockings once before going for an exercise run along Grange Road after dinner, and were sternly rebuked. We were forbidden to go to lectures, or into the town at all, without hats. We might go hatless for country walks or bicycle rides, but there was a definite demarcation point, somewhere near the Newnham end of the Silver Street bridge, at which the town was deemed to have begun, and there we must stop and cover ourselves decently before proceeding further.

Traffic consisted mainly of bicycles, with a few surviving tricycles on which the more elderly Cambridge ladies might be seen taking the air. During the whole of my three years there only one Newnham student had a car. She sometimes took parties of friends in it to Newmarket, where, it was darkly rumoured, they actually bet on the races. A fellow-student of mine, who learnt to ride a bicycle after coming up, never mastered the art of getting on and off unaided, but managed to cover long distances all the same. When, for example, she visited Girton, her friends at Newnham would put her on at the beginning of the journey, and her friends at Girton, warned beforehand to be on the look-out, would rush out and help her off. This was, of course, before the days of traffic lights. In fact, news of the installation of the first traffic lights at the top of Petty Cury made several Old Students feel that the world was coming to an end.

We were allowed to entertain men in the afternoon, in the garden or in our rooms, with the Tutor's permission, if suitably chaperoned. But all men, except brothers and fiancés, had to be out of College by half past six in the evening, when the dressing-bell rang. Two of my year invited to tea one Sunday two very shy and awkward first-year men from the neighbouring theological college. When the dressing-bell was heard, one of the hostesses said politely: 'I'm afraid you must go now – that bell means that all men must leave the College.' 'But,' said one of the guests in honest bewilderment, 'isn't that the bell we hear at half past seven every morning?'

Among the Newnham maids were some women of character who deserve to be remembered. In Old Hall we had Ida, whose standard reply to any sort of complaint was: 'If you never see anything worse than that, you won't see much!' I remember a polite remark about the weather (in mid-winter) being crushed by: 'If you'd done as much work as I have today, you wouldn't be cold, miss.' In Sidgwick Hall, they had a hymn every morning at pre-breakfast prayers and – though this I cannot vouch for personally, having it only on hearsay – it was said that the Advent hymn, 'O come, O come, Emmanuel', was sung there once a week all the year round because the maids liked it, in the hope of encouraging them to stay. There was in my time a weekly institution called 'Maids' Dancing', an hour after dinner during which the College freshers, bullied into it by their seniors, fox-trotted solemnly round College Hall with the College maids. Before starting on my first taste of this, I was warned: 'Be careful with the Principal's maid – she shimmies like the deuce!'

Four small but very vivid pictures of Cambridge are recalled to me by their smells. The first is the sweet-briar hedge in the College garden on a summer's night. I hope that no vandal has yet uprooted it or built over it. Next is the extraordinary honey-like sweetness of the early almond blossom on the Silver Street bridge; then the incense-laden coolness of Little St Mary's church, and finally – a sort of extended odour of sanctity – the savoury smell of the little cook-shop in Little St Mary's Lane, from which Sunday dinners were being collected as we came back from church. I remember especially, one bright frosty morning, a Dickensian old lady in bonnet and shawl carrying carefully away a large pudding in its basin and cloth.

One memory that is still, surprisingly, mint-fresh when so many important things have been forgotten, is a verse from the psalm which was read before breakfast by my Tutor (on whom be peace!) on my first day at Newnham: 'The lot is fallen to me in pleasant places; truly I have a goodly heritage.' It was one of those golden, fresh October mornings with which Cambridge is so generous, as though promising hopefully that winter will never come.

And connected with this memory, though removed in time, is the picture of Mrs Sidgwick, a very tiny old lady, slowly crossing the garden. She was wearing a stiff black silk dress and a square of white lace on her silver-white hair. It was my first glimpse of her – and the last.

S. Keith-Walters (Fawcitt, 1925)

SONGS FROM A PANTOMIME

Tune: 'To thy fraternal care' – Yeomen

The high and mighty powers
Have passed a stern decree
That during certain hours
Dead silence there must be.
They hope when noises cease
That we shall work in peace.

Chorus: They think we ought to work, From morn till afternoon,
From afternoon till night, From seven o'clock till two.
From two till evening meal:
From dim twilight to eleven at night
They think we ought to work.

Let those burn midnight oil
And waste their time on books
Who aren't afraid to spoil

Their temper or their looks.
But our philosophy
Is 'Live and let others be.'

Chorus: We do no stroke of work, etc.

Tune: 'He who shies' – Iolanthe

Risks you may run ere set of sun
Aren't so safe long after seven:
Be so kind to bear in mind
Gates are bolted at eleven.

Chorus: Whether your watch be fast or slow
Cut that last act and homeward go:
Tyres may be punctured now and then:
Safer to start at half past ten!

From the pantomime *Aladdin*, *Thersites*, Lent Term 1925

SUNDAY NIGHTS IN KENNEDY

In my student days, '23 to '26, we went to lectures in men's colleges, because there were very few lectures given in University buildings, apart from some of the Science ones. I remember one lovely lecture room in the corner of the second court of St John's, which had a roaring fire in winter; and then one would perhaps rush along to another lecture in Peterhouse, and so it went on. And in the summer, which always seemed to be hot and sunny, we wore summer frocks and white cotton stockings and white shoes, and hats, always hats. The theory was that it was not considered proper to cross over the Silver Street bridge without a hat. You could go down to the river and have your country walk without a hat, but you had to have hats when you went into town, including lectures. And when the women began to lecture in 1928, they lectured in hats. We didn't wear gowns, and Newnham and Girton decided between them, I think with the leadership of Girton, that the appropriate wear was a hat. So the Newnham Fellows had lecturing hats. Not too large, turned up in the brim, just neat and appropriate. The Don [Dr Elles] had a marvellous sort of russet-coloured felt hat that she plonked on her head; it had a brim which swept across her nose and the crown was almost non-existent.

There is one story which I think is rather nice about Rebecca Saunders. At the corner of Market Passage and Sidney St, there was a cheap draper's shop that sold all sorts of things. One day it had in the window a lot of hats, old-fashioned hats even in those days, and they were labelled 'Absolutely the limit, 1s 11d'. They were pepper-and-salt straws – the sailor type of things. One day at lunch, in came Miss Saunders wearing one of these hats. There was a hushed silence all through Clough dining-room. She stalked up to the High Table with this hat on with a chocolate-box ribbon around it. It was just her type of hat. Gertrude Elles, her junior, was another character in her own right, and the two of them were always absolutely at daggers drawn: whatever one said the other contradicted flatly. They were entirely different characters: Miss Saunders was rather precise and conventional in her way, whereas Miss Elles had a very lively, young mind and was always really ready to take up new ideas.

Our third year was the year of the General Strike. Before it became general, there was a miners' strike: I have vivid memories of sitting about in rugs, or perhaps several of us joining at one little fire in somebody's room, because of the lack of coal. I remember a whole group of us wrapped in rugs in Sidgwick Fic [Fiction Library], above the Tutor's room, and there were several Scots amongst us. Before long we took to dancing reels and the Highland fling, and up came Edith Chrystal in an absolute fury. Rugs were all right as a warmer, but Scottish dancing was *not* a warmer. When the strike became general, it was announced that the Triposes were to be postponed until after the end of the strike – indefinitely. People could either go home or stay in college as they pleased, and we were free if we stayed to carry on with our work or to help. Some took it very seriously: some delivered telegrams or drove cars. Some of the men drove trains. There was a wonderful story of one train that set off from Cambridge with five engine-drivers and two guards.

When I was a young Fellow I had a room at 27 Grange Road. When I went into my new room there were no curtains. I had: a large round Victorian table, a corner seat, two if not three settees, perhaps a bookcase, and very little else; and even my corner seat was taken from me after a few months, because the then Steward said that it was in the inventory for one of the other rooms. I made my own curtains; one took it for granted that that was the thing one did. That Steward was another wonderful character. After the amalgamation of the railways, after the 1914–18 war, for ages we had toilet paper or soap that said 'Great Northern' or 'Eastern', and I even had a basin with 'L.N.E.R.' on it.

I was the Secretary of the Governing Body as a young Fellow, for a very long time. My predecessor was Mrs Palmer, who was the Tutor of Peile Hall. She had more than a little Irish blood in her. Miss McKnight, the Principal's secretary, told me that when she used to go over the agenda with Mrs Palmer, she would remind her that she had to begin with the minutes and the business arising. 'Oh,' said Mrs Palmer, 'I always find that *so* tiresome.'

We had wonderful Sunday nights in Kennedy Buildings with Don Elles. Sunday nights, there was no coffee in the Combination Room, therefore immediately after supper on Sunday Miss Elles went to her room and she made excellent coffee, and she collected all the younger dons – Dorothy Garrod, McKnight, Ann Horton sometimes and Dorothy de Navarro. You took your mending and sat around the fire, and she told the most marvellous stories of her second sight, and how much was imagination and how much was real one never knew. But they were good stories. There was one she told about being at a Cambridge tea-party, sitting on the sofa with other Cambridge ladies; and she turned to one of them and said, 'And when is Professor So-and so's funeral?' The woman blinked and said, 'But – has he died?' She said, 'Oh – I don't know!' But true enough he had died. There were some stories that never finished; they began again the next Sunday, but were still never finished, so there were some we never knew the end of.

Then Miss Elles was very deaf. She had a radio which she played very loudly, and she always listened to the Derby. And sure enough, if you looked out of the window when Miss Elles was listening to the Derby, you saw five of our gardeners weeding the beds at the same place. She was a very stimulating teacher, and not only of members of the College – she was in great demand. She taught geological mapping in the Sedgwick: everybody went to that. She was marvellously clear and very, very fierce.

M. E. Grimshaw (1923). Extracts from a tape recording

THE NEWNHAM RIDDLE

My father frequently used to quote the riddle (current when he was an undergraduate):

'What is the difference between a Newnham woman and David's second wife?'

'One was Abishag the Shunamite – the other shabby hag the Newnhamite.'

R. L. Cohen (1926)

*

1926

WESLEY'S ELDER SISTER

I came up to Cambridge in 1926 on an Adult Scholarship of £200 given by the Extra-mural Board (Stuart House), but which included the Rigby Scholarship for Newnham. As the most 'in' student who was ever 'out', according to my friends, I saw a great deal of several worlds. I was twenty-nine and so could be trusted to be an out-student, and was asked to give up my room in College so that a younger student could be given a place. To this I agreed and was given a large bed-sitting-room in the Bursar's house near Grantchester Meadows.

I was to read for a degree but had not passed Previous,* so my first year was pretty hectic – working for Parts I and II, and trying to pick up the threads of an education I had missed since I was fifteen owing to ill health. I was the first woman student my Latin coach had ever had; I forget his name but he was an Esquire Bedell, and specialised in getting undergrads through the entrance examination after they had been received by their colleges, usually for proficiency in sport. I learnt to hate and then respect his terrible red pencil, but he drilled me into translating unseens accurately at one-third speed, enough to get me through instead of hopelessly thrashing about. (Horace I passed by learning Books 3 and 4 by heart from a crib.) French I could do, but Maths was again a problem. I finally passed at the fourth attempt by taking Science instead of the second paper, and being drilled by the third tutor to whom I was sent, who made me concentrate on the Geometry question, and then showed me how to set down the Arithmetic and Algebra questions and so gain two marks each, with the warning that on no account was I to try and work anything out! It was apparently due to my struggles that all adult students after me were excused all or part of Previous, as it was considered that I would have gained a First if I had not been so hampered.

Meanwhile I enjoyed myself immensely – I was adopted by some charming second-year students who were asked to look after me, I joined everything I could, including the political societies, one at a time, and the S.C.M., and made friends with several of the younger dons. I came up when the ruling was that girls from Girton and Newnham could visit men in their rooms if they had a suitable chaperon. I was accepted as such by the authorities and had a great time, my escorts

* See note, p. 14.

being rather older research students or theologians, indeed I got the name of 'Wesley's elder sister and Westcott's maiden aunt'.

As I was 'out', there were several disadvantages. I would be nicely settled down, reading hard, with a congenial companion, or in the middle of an interesting and world-important argument when, the hour approaching when everyone else had to be 'in', I had to seize my books and tear through the passages to the gate so as to get 'out', and so to my digs. Not so pleasant in wintertime. But it had its advantages, for I was able to stay on at the Festival Theatre to the end of the play while the others, standing ready at the back to the last possible moment, had to rush through the streets on their bicycles to get in before the gate closed for the night.

The Festival was my delight – an entirely new world of sound and action and colour. I had the same seat on the same night of the week for three years, and enjoyed every moment. The plays I saw were an education in themselves and influenced the direction of my mind for many years. Even after I retired, I lectured for Exeter on the Modern Theatre largely on what I had seen and discussed at Cambridge twenty years before. I was also lucky in that in my four years I saw two Greek Plays.

After taking English Part I (Old Regulations) I followed some of the papers for the old Part II into their new guise of Archaeology; and after that, still not knowing what to do with myself, I was given a fourth year and took the Board of Education Certificate in Drawing, attending the local Art School (where Arthur Bryant was briefly passing through as Head) for Life and Perspective, and getting my other knowledge at the Classical Museum, the Architecture School and the Anatomy School. I examined dissected limbs and spent hours drawing the demonstration skeleton and clothing him with muscle. Most of my Perspective problems were worked out at Newnham in one of the tutorial rooms near the gate, where I was allowed to leave my drawing set up with strings and T-squares for all the week-end.

Everyone was most helpful. At first it was not certain if my sight would stand the strain, and Miss Welsford read to me and we discussed the poets I had missed. I will always associate Pope with autumn leaves falling as she read to me in the dons' garden. I got extra coaching in *Beowulf* and permission to use the University Library even in my first year. Gradually I spent more and more time there and less and less attending lectures; indeed, the year I concentrated on Archaeology there were only three students for Professor Chadwick, Dame Bertha Philpotts, and Mr de Navarro to teach, and we were left to sink or swim on our own.

I got lost in Egyptology, and never recovered myself sufficiently to get back in time to study some aspects of the enormous syllabus that I really needed for my Tripos examination. What the modern student would have made of our three supervisors, I cannot think: three world authorities in their especial subjects, but highly individualistic, living in a rarefied atmosphere of the past. Dame Bertha could recreate the Viking Age but was a nervous lecturer, and her fingers were never still; de Navarro always referred us to page after page of reference books, mostly untranslated German, Italian or French, which we seemed to have no possibility of reading; and the Professor, who took us in his library, had a tiny voice despite his large bulk and persisted in turning his back on us and talking up the chimney.

At Newnham we were very particular about our 'river image'. The first week of the summer term, the first-years assembled before breakfast to be coached in the art of poling a punt or paddling a canoe, finally passing a test – 'Throw up in three'; 'Steer off the bottom'; 'Pull up in one'; proving we could swim. Then we were allowed on the river. We were very conscious that our general behaviour must be circumspect in contrast to those dreadful 'Townees'.

In my fourth year, while at the Art School, I worked with those 'Townees' and learnt how they regarded the University. Some contact between the two was already possible, principally through the churches, as several of the clergy had open house on Sunday afternoons to which both Town and Gown came. But when I was an Art student we organised our own 'Mays' dance between the girls of the Art School and the undergrads they knew. We hired a hall, the men decorated, the girls cut sandwiches and brewed and baked, and for a sum within our means, a happy time was had by all. We even hired punts and some of us finished up with breakfast on the river.

D. E. Whitford (1926)

*

A BAD EIGHT

We cycle down to the boathouse, four abreast, defying angry drivers who hoot at us – Bill with her trilby hat on top of her Eton crop, Mike enveloped in a long scarf some rugger friend has given her, Nora pedalling in her erratic way, two hard pushes then a free-wheel: 'It's the only way I can get this bike to go!' We bump down the narrow path to the boathouse and meet the cold wind coming off the river. Inside there is a smell of perspiring bodies, the First Eight changing. Underclothes, shorts, long brown stockings thrown everywhere and old shoes strewn on the floor. 'Ah, Newskin!' shouts Bill, sniffing aggressively. 'Someone is using Newskin on her blisters. Foul stuff!' In the middle of all this the captain of the Second Eight, a serious, bespectacled girl, is sitting with Steve Fairbairn's booklet in her hand, *Slowly Forward*, 365 maxims for coaches and oarsmen. She reads out, 'To quicken, shorten, then you will quicken and lengthen...' and looks up at us, puzzled. Bill leans over her shoulder and proclaims, 'Slow and easy, lazy and long!' At least we can accept *that* slogan. We change, and I go for the man to help us to get the boat out and feel foolish standing there calling for him, dressed in my masculine shorts with a sweater tied round my neck.

The boat is launched and all climb into it in their proper turn, grasp the oars and paddle out into midstream. It is a bad eight. Stroke is too slow and Cox too inexperienced to know how to quicken the pace. The two freshers in front of me are, for all their weight, mere passengers. In go their oars to the water and out they jerk without any force. The boat wobbles painfully on the 'paddle light'. Up past the Gasworks and the Concrete to the Long Reach we go, the water grey and ugly, broken up into choppy little waves by the wind between the leafless willows. I plunge my oar in at Bow to try to get a good puddle but it is no use – the boat is like a badly running car. 'Easy all!' bawls Cox and the boat turns at Ditton Corner, but too close to the bank one minute – 'Watch the bank, Bow! Easy, Two and Four! *Easy*!' – then too far out from the bank and a ghastly mess-up in midstream. Something is coming up the river, there is a not very distant swishing sound and then we see them, the pale blue oars batting the air like angels' wings, the Varsity Eight sliding by, superb, unperturbed, with an air of complete superiority. Fortunately the female eight has battled to the bank in time, and we sit watching the passage of the supermen in apathetic gloom until there is a shout from our male coach on the towpath: 'Come along! We'll bring her home now!' A friend passing him on a bicycle remarks with caustic wit: 'You look like an energetic Turk, John, exercising his harem!'

No one laughs, least of all the coach, but there is a burst of better rowing in the Long Reach and the lack of balance in Two and Three is not so noticeable. But the wind blows harder and I cannot get my oar clear from the water as I bring it back on the feather, and it dribbles along the surface. Then comes the crash! The Grind* has already left its mooring to cross the river at the Pike and Eel, and our eight does not stop but

* See note, p. 73.

comes round the edge of the Grind rather sharply. 'Easy there!' yells the startled Grind man. 'Easy all!' echoes Cox, unable to see what is in front of her. 'Hi, easy!' shouts everyone from bank and boat. I turn to see four oars making smartly for the small of my back and lean over to avoid them, shouting to Two who has not time to pull her oar in. Crack go the oars against each other, big splinters shoot up in the air and land on our boat. Number Two's oar is smashed off at the blade, and the other eight also goes on with crippled oars. Very pink in the face the female eight clears away from the Grind and rows homewards disgruntled.

But all is not over yet. Passing the house-boats there is another eight coming to meet us and Cox, over-anxious and worried by our lack of balance, goes too close to the bank in order to avoid another collision. I cannot get my oar in quickly enough, and it catches on a house-boat and neatly sweeps me off my sliding seat and into the Cam. The water is not as cold as I expect and I manage to scramble back into the boat again without upsetting it. Sweaters are handed to me and we keep up a smart pace from there to the landing stage. The captain comes up to me and asks if I am all right, and reminds me of the saying: 'Fall into the Cam and get a First in your Tripos', which is not much comfort to me in my soaked condition (and was, at any rate, proved untrue by later events). 'Quelle aventure!' remarks Bill laconically as we put our oars together up against a wall. Across the river the sunset has suddenly flared up golden against some dusty black clouds, and there are orange pools in the grey water. I wonder why I have taken up this sport rather than others that were open to me, but reflect that not all our outings are like this one and some reach great heights of efficiency and even, at times, express the poetry of motion.

A. D. Winchcombe (Whyte, 1928)

*

MRS WOOLF COMES TO DINE

I had in my first year a scholar's room on the ground floor of Clough Hall, near the Combination Room, very delightful. But it was papered with Morris's 'Daisy', one of his earliest patterns. I learnt from my elders and betters, the second- and third-year students, to make a hardship of this. In 1926 Morris papers were absolutely out of fashion. Ten years later, in his *Pioneers of the Modern Movement*, Pevsner was to praise the Morris 'Daisy' as 'strikingly fresh and "modern"'.

In my first year the only picture I possessed was a Medici reproduction of the portrait of Beatrice d'Este, a present from my Headmistress Mary Jackson. In my second year I daringly exchanged this for Van Gogh's 'Sunflowers' and felt very avant-garde: many students, I seem to remember, still favoured 'Peter Pan in Kensington Gardens'.

At the beginning of my third year I was invited by the literary editor of *The Granta*, T. H. White, to review books for him regularly – the first time, to my knowledge, that a woman student had been asked to write for *The Granta*. He wanted me to come to his rooms in Queens' every Tuesday to have tea and choose books. I told my Tutor, Miss Steele Smith, who at first was delighted. After consulting Miss Strachey, however, she told me that I mustn't go to Queens' every week, 'they wouldn't like having a woman student about the place'. The young man must come to Newnham. I went every week to Queens', I fear, notwithstanding. No evil consequences.

In June 1929 I was faced with the prospect of reciting in the Senate House the poem that had been awarded the Chancellor's Medal for English verse. Women had newly obtained the right to compete for University prizes, but as we were still not members of the University we could not wear academic dress. I put it about, naughtily, that I should appear in a flounced summer dress. Miss Steele Smith was alarmed and gave me a gentle talking-to. In fact I wore a black coat and hat and gave no offence. I. A. Richards told me privately that when the entries for the Chancellor's Medal were being considered the then Master of Magdalene, one of the judges, declared that he would vote for the most masculine-seeming poem, 'be it what it might'. (The entries were submitted pseudonymously and A. B. Ramsay chose to support the one from Newnham.)

I remember going to Miss Strachey to ask permission to produce a play in College. Miss Strachey acquiesced but said in tones of anguish (she knew she would have to be present), 'Keep it short: oh, *do* keep it short.' Miss Strachey sometimes forsook her exquisite remoteness to condescend to very minute personal counsels. I remember a composition of hers pinned up on the notice-board in Clough, which described in exact detail how to get out of one's bath in such a way as to leave the minimum amount of water on the floor. I suppose there had been complaints from the maids of messy bathrooms. It was more in character that Miss Steele Smith, Tutor of Clough, should put up a notice denouncing the practice of going down to breakfast without first stripping one's bed. It began memorably: 'Some ladies seem to creep out of their beds like bunnies out of their holes.' I know I was one of the 'bunny girls'.

1929

The visit of Miss Strachey's close friend, Virginia Woolf, in 1929 to read us a paper was a rather alarming occasion. As I remember it she was nearly an hour late; and dinner in Clough Hall, never a repast for gourmets, suffered considerably. Mrs Woolf also disconcerted us by bringing a husband and so upsetting our seating plan. After the paper there was coffee with Mrs Woolf in the Principal's rooms. Mrs Woolf was really very well disposed to us as a group of intellectual young women; but we found her formidable. All I remember of her talk is that she praised very highly a poem of Stella Gibbons's, 'The Hippogriff'. It was disquieting to learn later, when I was in Paris as a research student, that Mrs Woolf had brought out a book (*A Room of One's Own*) describing her Newnham dinner. Her purpose was, of course, to evoke pity for the poverty of the women's colleges: but at the time it made us, her hosts, decidedly uncomfortable.

The same Literary Society that invited Mrs Woolf had also the bad taste (was I responsible?) to invite on another occasion a poet, then of some repute, called Humbert Wolfe. We had undertaken to pay the speaker's fares: and he took a taxi, I think, all the way back to London.

Edith Sitwell was another distinguished speaker, aquiline and gorgeous in a stiff brocade dress.

E. E. Duncan-Jones (Phare, 1926)

A ROOM OF ONE'S OWN

When I think of Newnham I think of the golden maple tree that grew outside the window of my room in Clough. And I think of the silver birch that turned to gold in October, and the polished mahogany chestnuts that spilt out of their white kid cases in Sidgwick Avenue. But even more precious than anything outside the room was the room itself; to have a room of one's own – that was the supreme pleasure, the unspoilable joy of being at Newnham. To choose curtains and cushions, to buy flowers and books, gramophone records and fire-lighters (whose enchanting smell no longer, I suppose, haunts the corridors of Newnham) – these were all delightful activities, a first taste of freedom, a first taste too, perhaps, of ivory-tower-building; for the room, whether fire-lit and warm in the little hours, or sparkling with sun and frost after breakfast, or deliciously ominous on thundery afternoons in July, had a charm which only the most congenial of friends could rival.

Perhaps the same could be said of my other great discovery at Cambridge, and that was the river. I had never really known a river until I went to Cambridge; but I sought out the company of the Cam whenever I could. I was never very good at punting, always managing to get extraordinarily wet along one arm; but it was still bliss to take a punt down the Backs, shooting gently under the sun-dappled bridges, tying up where the willows dropped their tents of green, delighting in the juxtaposition of water and stone, the social scene and the book waiting to be read. Even better than this was a canoe on the upper river, on a morning in mid-week (can lectures have been cut, or was it during the Long Vac? I can't remember now) when the solitary stream beckoned one relentlessly on, and a portable gramophone in the bows played Bach over the glassy stretches, and the water-boatmen at Grantchester skimmed witlessly over the reflected chestnut trees. I remember the little pollarded willows, and the long meadows running with buttercups, and the human beings, viewed from below the river bank, looking like giants, full of drama and interest.

But I return once more to the room of my own. Because it was here, after, I think, the famous or infamous dinner, when prunes and custard were eaten and wine was not drunk, that Virginia Woolf stood and sat, and looked and spoke. She had come to address a Newnham society, and the post-address coffee and biscuits were distributed in my room, because it was a fairly large one. I think I had expected some profound, philosophic remarks, even after prunes and custard; but fixing me with that wonderful gaze, at once luminous and penetrating, what she actually said was, 'I'd no idea the young ladies of Newnham were so beautifully dressed.' The prig in me was chagrined, even if my vanity sat up and purred; but over the years what has persisted has been the quality of her look, which seemed to say so much more than the words that came with it. The look held a hint of a smile, a hint of compassion, but it was above all an absolutely ruthless look; my pretty frock was no proof against it.

U. K. N. Stevenson (Carter, 1926)

PLUM STONES RHYME, PEILE HALL

Teaching, typing, training, research;
Lewis's, laundry, left in the lurch;
Policewoman, prostitute, poetess, nun;
Suicide's really the only one.

Anon. *c.* 1929

*

1929

THE TABLE IN THE GALLERY

I have a photograph dated May 1929 of the executive committee of the Student Christian Movement meeting at 9.30 a.m. on the Granta in punt and canoe: an original and pleasant place for transacting business. I note that this small committee included the present Dean of Westminster, the Archbishop of Melbourne, the Bishop of Lichfield, two Honorary Canons, a future England cricketer, a lacrosse and a rowing Blue. Obviously a cradle for ecclesiastical dignitaries and athletes.

In the great freeze-up of February 1929 the Cambridge shops sold out of skates, and the lecture room took second place to the frozen fens and river. I remember, after a seminar at Miles Burkitt's house in Grantchester, setting off for Lingay armed with skates and lunch. After some exhilarating hours on the ice in the cold bright sunlight we returned to tea and crumpets by the fire. No crumpets since like Cambridge crumpets, oozing with butter.

At Newnham there was for me a special feeling associated with a hot bath and tea with spice buns after a hard game of lacrosse. There was an extraordinary glow of well-being and joie de vivre as one's limbs soaked in the hot water. Then College tea and buns. Perhaps they were yeast buns: I forget. But they were round and had currants, and sometimes we toasted them. This combination of games, bath and tea seemed to induce a maximum work-rate. I could retire to the Library and work with greater concentration than at any other time of the day.

On many nights there were numbers of notes to be delivered with some urgency in other Halls. Very vivid is my memory of tearing along the interminable passages from Sidgwick to Peile and back from Peile to Old. All was hushed and quiet and warm, except for one stretch between Clough and Peile which was always cold. It was an odd sensation, this dashing from end to end of the quiet College, lights above some doors, others in darkness. It was also odd how in these seemingly deserted corridors I so often rushed full tilt round a corner into the arms of Miss Strachey, tall and serene, walking with soundless footsteps. A hurried and embarrassed apology and we pursued our separate ways.

A warm still night in May and a quick change into a bathing suit under pyjamas with a light coat to cover all. A moonlight bathe with a friend in a channel of the river near the bathing sheds. The quiet walk back to College glowing with warmth, pyjama legs rolled up under coat, squeezed swimsuit in hand. Goodnight outside the gates, and so to bed.

When I had no early lecture it was my habit in the May Term to sit at the table in the gallery of the Library by the window overlooking Sidgwick Avenue. It was lighter there and cooler, but more distracting. The people walking down the Avenue caught one's eye. The sun seemed always to be shining, the cuckoo perpetually calling. It was too early for work. The day stretched before one, rich, promising, exciting. Limbs were full of energy and itching to be off somewhere. The mind followed the cuckoos to the willows by the Granta, followed the cyclists dashing down to lectures, followed the likely course of the day. How could one work at 9 a.m. on an April morning in Cambridge?

A. G. Storrs Fox (Philip, 1926)

*

'I DIDN'T LIKE NEWNHAM'

I didn't like Newnham.

I'm sure I was a rare bird in that respect. But then I was a rare bird, for those days, in another respect too. I was – shades of the long ago, of Harry Wharton and all that – a Scholarship Girl. I came from a working-class home in a not-quite-slum of south-east London.

The reason I was unhappy and a misfit wasn't due to any snobbery. Good heavens, no. In fact I remember once spending a baffling ten minutes trying hard to convince a charming fellow-student, bless her heart, that my antecedents and background really were as I claimed them to be. She persisted in thinking my parents remarkably enlightened in having sent me to what was then called an elementary school.

No, it wasn't snobbery. It was just that I found it all so damned dull.

A working-class adolescent in London grew up quickly in those days. Quickly by the middle-class standards of the day, that is; at tortoise-rate by anyone's standards today, of course. But I had known freedom and independence; had gone out when I liked, with whom I liked; had listened to the speakers at Hyde Park Corner; was a frequent visitor to the Old Vic gallery (ninepence a time); had been taken by my school to lectures, museums, picture galleries.

School itself had been full of interest. A London secondary school had a cross-section of society; the pupils ranged from solicitors' and doctors' daughters down through clerks and petty tradesmen to my father, who was a jobbing gardener and anything else that turned up until his early death. I'd known the seamy side of life too: real poverty, and heartbreak. So Newnhamites never seemed quite real to me. They all seemed to come from the professional classes and from quiet homes in the country. They didn't seem to know what life was all about. I joined the Labour Party, or Club, or whatever it was called. *They* didn't know either, though they tried terribly hard. I remember once listening to an impassioned talk by some good soul, who was horrified because there were households in Britain where the only hot water was obtained by boiling kettles. I'd been filling my weekly bath that way all my life.

But of course if there were things they didn't know about, and that I did, the reverse was also true. I didn't know you had to be introduced to a man before you could get to know him; at home we picked up our boy-friends on the street corner, just outside the Public Library. It was all perfectly innocent, and an established social custom. We all met there every evening. It was like an open-air coffee bar without the coffee. I didn't know, either, that whereas it was all right to have a lot of men friends, in those days it was very questionable to see a lot of just one, unless he had 'intentions'. In my circles it was just the reverse – as with the young today: as long as you stuck to one young man, even with no intentions at all, you were respectable. The Newnhamites shocked me a good deal. As for me, I made a fool of myself in my first term and never got over it.

Another thing was that I didn't know how to eat asparagus. Asparagus wasn't a thing one encountered much in the Newnham of that day, but somehow, somewhere, I contrived to get myself involved with the stuff, and tried to eat it with a knife and fork. And I didn't know about things like Ascot and Henley, and rowing Blues, and bumping races. I wore *terrible* clothes, and too much lipstick.

Work might have made it all worth while but, alas, there too I'd seen it all before. I was reading English, and I'd already at school achieved London University Intermediate B.A. standard. Now I was back to an elementary course in English Literature, designed for the products of the public schools who, as far as I could see, had read absolutely nothing. In any case, I have asked myself ever since if one can really read English for a degree. When you've read all the first-rate people, what do you do? Read the second-rate? And then the third? And of course I knew there was going to be no job at the end of it all. There weren't in those days, the early thirties. And I desperately needed a job. In the event, I became a shop-girl – a graduate trainee, it was called. It was the last straw for my long-suffering family.

Well, that was my Newnham. I was lonely, bored, frustrated, humiliated, insecure, frightened, resentful. And I didn't stage a sit-in, nor a demo; never so much as threw a tomato; just sulked my way through three long years.

Of course if one could have one's time over again now... University is really too good to be wasted on the young.

I'm sorry I didn't like you, Newnham. I feel a little better now I've explained.

And the remarkable thing is, of course, that I'm no longer explaining a minority of one. I'm explaining now, today, the majority to the bewildered few. Today there are thousands of me: not so much in Newnham, I daresay (I'd be interested to know), but in the new universities.

Maybe, then, for that small service, Newnham, you'll forgive me that I didn't like you better.

K. A. Rees (Reed, 1929)

*

A ROLL OF HONOUR

I treasure the vivid recollection, while at work at my bench in the Biochemical Labs. in 1930, of receiving the roll of my long-coveted Ph.D. (Titular) Certificate from the hands of the Vice-Chancellor's proxy – in this case Mrs Onslow's red-headed fifteen-year-old lab. boy, in stained overalls, on his round of errands. It had the flavour of being knighted on the field.

R. Meares (Scott-Moncrieff, 1926)

MRS PALMER AND PEILE

When I was up (1930 to 1933) it was still possible not to be aiming at a career, although most of us rather looked down on the idea of 'staying at home to do the flowers'. I was in Peile, and every evening Mrs Palmer, our Tutor, would put up a notice saying 'I should like to see the following at the High Table tonight', and five or six names were listed. It meant putting on a slightly better bib and tucker, though we always changed for Hall. Miss Elles, the Vice-Principal, was usually in Peile, and being deaf she talked in a very quiet voice, but it was well worth the effort to hear her stories of the supernatural.

At the beginning of each term a meeting was held, presided over by the Senior Student. At this we voted for representatives to deal with newspapers, the fire service, etc. There was usually a lot of humming and ha-ing before anyone was proposed, so before one such meeting my friends, Eleanor Dobson and Kathleen Potts, and I decided whom we thought 'suited' to each job. We then proposed and seconded them before anyone else could think, and the meeting was over in record time. The next term, however, we got what we deserved. Someone proposed Eleanor and me for the least coveted of all the jobs, Maids' Dancing.

There were in those days about a dozen maids in each Hall, and every Monday evening a sort of social was arranged for them, when they all gathered in Clough Hall, and were entertained (we hoped) by conversation and ballroom dancing to the gramophone. The students acted as the men. The Maids' Dancing reps had to press-gang other students to go along, and somehow they always seemed to have prior engagements for 8.30 to 9.30 on a Monday evening. So to liven up the Peile interest in our allotted ploy, we copied Mrs Palmer's High Table summons, and wrote, I regret to say in an imitation of her handwriting: 'We should like to see the following at Maids' Dancing tonight'; we listed some of our more lively friends, and pinned it at Mrs Palmer's end of the notice-board. It worked surprisingly well, and I think they enjoyed the evening more than they expected.

Mrs Palmer used to give us kindly pep talks from time to time, in the course of which she mentioned how putting off it was to find people's laundry left in the bathrooms long after it was dry. (We were delighted that she pronounced laundry 'larndry'.) So, being able to copy her handwriting, I wrote a note to Peggy Hansford: 'Kindly remove your laundry from the bathroom. It is so putting off. H.E.P.' Peggy luckily came at once to my room to complain of the note, satisfactorily outraged at its 'unfairness'. Peggy was very pretty, with lots of glamorous undies, and had bought a wildly expensive pair of crêpe de chine frilly pants from Debenhams because of the iron staircase outside the Geography School. She was often in difficulties because there was only one waiting room in which to see male visitors before lunch, as she did not want her various beaux to meet each other. We could only have men friends in our rooms between 2 p.m. and 6.45, and then only if we had written a note to Mrs Palmer explaining that 'Miss So-and-So would also be there'. We did not actually need chaperons, but Miss Anna Paues was still in Cambridge, who 'in the old days' had often chaperoned students to tea-parties and dances.

Our first February we began to ask in Heffers and elsewhere if they sold Valentines. Nobody did. So we bought small paper doyleys, cut flowers from bulb catalogues, and made up verses to each of our male acquaintances, some forty in number. Best of all was a copy of the *Matrimonial Times* which a Caius man had had sent to Eleanor. Extracts from it were pasted to strips of card and slipped among the flowers with a string to which a heart was attached, saying 'Pull'. The forty Valentines were only just finished in time, and I can remember how my feet left the pedals in a frenzied ride to the G.P.O. to catch the last post on February 13th and get back by 11 p.m. T. R. Glover acknowledged his neatly at our next lecture on Vergil. He referred to his book *Greek Byways* as just the thing to send as a Valentine next year.

While I was up traffic lights were installed at the bottom of Sidgwick Avenue, and I remember how interested we were that they cost £80 per annum, which was cheaper than employing a policeman. My brother-in-law, P. H. L. Ling, a member of Queens' College and a native of Cambridge, remembers the old crossing-sweeper, lame and infirm, who used to operate there well into the twenties. He used to hang his coat on a nail driven into a large tree at the corner.

M. Ingledew (Mathieson, 1930)

*

FLYING...

After some discussion, (the Tutors) decided that leave should not be given to learn to fly except for a serious purpose and that therefore Miss Barnard's application must be refused.

Extract from the minutes of the Tutors' Committee, 15 October 1931

*

...AND RIDING

Leave was granted to R. Kitching (2nd year O.H.) to ride in the Ladies Point-to-Point Race at Cottenham on March 10th, her father being in favour of her doing so.

Extract from the minutes of the Tutors' Committee, 9 February 1932

*

1932

TALKING

My mother never went to university, and as a result she felt, all her life, that she'd missed something. Her father, her sister and both her brothers were at Cambridge, and she would have gone if she hadn't had an untimely illness at the age of eighteen, which made her doctor advise – wrongly, I think – against her attempting any further education. When I was eighteen, and her only daughter, she was determined that I shouldn't suffer, as she had, the deprivation of going through life without a degree, and she bribed me with a fur coat to take the Newnham entrance examination. The absurd thing is that I didn't want to go to Cambridge and I also didn't much want a fur coat. But I did want my mother's approval, and as, according to my school, I hadn't a chance of getting a place, I rather defiantly took the exam. No one was as much surprised as I was when I got in. I was convinced that it must be entirely because a friend had lent me a volume of Edward Thomas's poetry that autumn, and this was the volume put into my hand by Miss Welsford in the interview, so that instead of staring at it blankly, which was what might well have happened, I was able to say that, yes, I knew it, and that, yes, this was the poem I liked best and I'd read it to her.

This is to explain why, when I arrived, the following October, in the cool dark corridors of learning, I was more than usually equipped with a sense of inadequacy which I now realise was universal. Just as my mother, who was an extremely intelligent woman, had an idea that anyone who hadn't been to university was somehow lacking in some unspecific but obvious way, so I now, too late, realise that most of us freshers who arrived that autumn – and every other autumn – in Cambridge, came with the idea that we ourselves were the only ones who were somehow there by mistake. Everyone else we saw prowling along the passages or collecting their breakfasts in Hall – even the other obvious new girls collected in our Tutor's room for the preliminary briefing – was either beautiful or clever, or both. I, horribly conscious of that grey squirrel coat which had proved so much more desirable than I'd anticipated, was certain that all these other women were potential academics. I knew they had sweated blood to get here. I knew they would, at the drop of a hat, break out into original poetry, or theses on someone they knew all about but whom I'd barely heard of, like T. S. Eliot or D. H. Lawrence. Or they would be Scientists, knowing all about atoms and what made the physiological clock tick. Or Chemists. I knew nothing of

Chemistry. But it was clear to me at once that they were all learned and experienced – I hadn't even been properly kissed, oh God! – and serious. Whereas I knew, though I couldn't admit it, that I was frivolous. No one who was at all serious would read fiction to the extent that I did. And though I enjoyed *Richard II* enormously when I saw it acted, I was bored stiff by the effort of going over it line by line in order to discover just how Shakespeare had attained his dramatic effects. I knew, at that first convocation of us freshers, that I'd never fit in to this eclectic and frighteningly high-powered society.

I suppose what Newnham gave me more than anything else was the realisation that I wasn't for ever beyond the pale. I wrote my first essays trembling, convinced that at any moment Miss Welsford or Miss Hoare would denounce me as the impostor I felt myself to be. When they didn't, when they actually seemed to think that what I wrote made sense, I stepped on to a different level altogether. I actually began to wonder whether perhaps I could begin to compete with the chosen ones of Newnham, at least on the academic plane. I don't think I ever really believed I could; it's a sad indictment of middle-class, intellectual British families that they seem to produce in such great quantities these frightened, gifted – and I now realise that I was gifted, though the idea would have seemed preposterous then – inhibited, children. I looked again at my terrifying, high-powered, staggering contemporaries, and saw, to my astonishment, that they weren't all geniuses, they weren't all femmes fatales (though some of them were, and I know so today), they weren't all quite different from, and immensely superior to, me. I suddenly realised that quite a number of them were approachable and friendly. A good deal later I discovered that some were actually frightened of me. One day one of them, I can't at all now remember who, said to me, 'You have such poise.' I was astonished. I'd thought that I wore my lack of self-confidence on my sleeve for everyone to remark on; but when I considered this comment I realised that the mistake arose because my sense of inferiority had the effect, thank goodness, of making me silent. At that time I hadn't learned, either, that what looks like an air of superiority often covers intense shyness and an inability to join spontaneously in a conversation.

So it took far more than that first term to convince me that I had the right to be in Cambridge at all. In fact I think I left at the end of the three years still believing that any successes I'd had were due to mistakes, and that my failures were a far better criterion of my ability. But in spite of this, that first autumn taught me that, however unfit I was to be there,

I wanted to stay until I was actually kicked out. All sorts of different things made me feel this. My last year at school had been depressing from the work point of view, I'd got bored with English Literature and convinced that I'd never be any good at reading it for a degree; here at Cambridge it suddenly became exciting again, and once I'd faced the fact that I was ignorant of an enormous number of names with which everyone else seemed to be familiar, I enjoyed trying to catch up, and enjoyed reading in quite new fields. I loved Cambridge; I'd never spent the autumn in the country before, and I wanted to see all the changes that take place between the half green, half gold of the opening of the term, and the scene of misty skeleton-branched trees that we left in December. I was intoxicated by the flowers in the market and went there just to look at them often when I'd already bought enough for my room. I enjoyed the sort of pretence of being grown up; the being called Miss X instead of having my first name shouted across the hockey field by a gym mistress maddened by my incompetence, the choice of attending lectures or not, the freedom to arrange my own time as I liked.

But most of all I enjoyed the talking: the talking with a lot of people, mostly of my own age, but all quite different. I enjoyed not having to stop talking because it was late, or because my parents wanted to go to bed, or because they thought I ought to be asleep, or because anyone had a long journey home. It seems now as if I never went to bed before three o'clock in the morning that first term, but I'm sure I sometimes did. And perhaps the thing about the opportunity for these conversations that seemed to me to belong most of all to Cambridge, to Newnham, or to my newly discovered self, was the sense of freedom in being on my own, rather than on someone else's ground. When I'd had friends to visit me at home, I suppose I'd felt slightly constrained by the fact that the house belonged to my parents, and I was somehow responsible to them and for them. Here, in Newnham, I was responsible only to myself, and in a quite irrational way, this liberated my feelings and my views on every subject; I wanted to discuss everything, to find out about everyone, to try out, to explore. Don't let me appear to claim more than I should: at that time it was very much a theoretical exploring, I wasn't at all living dangerously; I have always been more cowardly than I could wish, too anxious to enjoy taking risks. But that first term at Newnham I felt a great liberation in the way I thought and spoke; and for this, which isn't probably what my mother had foreseen as the prime advantage of a university education, I'm grateful, and remember that and the following terms with affection; though I'm also thankful that I need never live through that time again.

C. Storr (Balogh; Cole, 1932)

*

SERIOUS TRAINING

I was up from 1934 to 1937, and it was a period of interesting event. There was the Silver Jubilee of King George V's reign, and his death; the accession and abdication of King Edward VIII; the accession and coronation of King George VI; war between Italy and Abyssinia; the Civil War in Spain. Less dramatic, but clearly remembered, was the opening of the new University Library by George V and Queen Mary; the building and occupation of Queens' new building in a surprisingly short time; and new rooms added on the top of Peile.* These memories will be shared by many people, but one group of my recollections will only be shared by a limited group, and these are of the Boat Club.

I think I am right in saying that none of us had rowed before coming up. Perhaps that is what attracted us to it. We used Banham's boathouse, near Victoria Bridge. I pass it almost daily now, and its out-dated and decrepit appearance makes me wonder if I am the same. We had a coach from Jesus College each year, and started our tuition in tubs to Jesus Lock. When we could handle an oar with a little dexterity, we graduated to the clinker eight. Down to the Pike and Eel each afternoon, and sometimes a little farther, and on very memorable occasions we even got as far as Baitsbite. There was no question of our entering the Lent or May Races, as women were not yet recognised by the University. Girton did not row so we were never more than a College boat, but we did challenge Oxford each year. We rowed against them on the Tideway one year and at Oxford the next year.

We went into serious training in the Lent Term, and had our meals together in Clough, with a special diet laid on. Each morning we had cold baths, weighed ourselves – and kept a record of it – and walked an appreciable distance before breakfast. If we smoked, we were expected not to exceed four cigarettes a day and we were supposed to retire at about 10 p.m. At the end of term, we went to the White Hart at Barnes for a week on the Tideway, to row against crews of women from the

* The Flat (see p. 204) was not designed to be self-contained. It probably acquired the name from its particular atmosphere: a cosy, faintly privileged separateness from 'ordinary Peile' a short staircase away.

London colleges. We used Quintin boathouse near Chiswick Bridge, and rowed above and below there, but mostly between Chiswick and Barnes Bridge. It was there that I first learned the difference between what was said to a newspaper reporter and what appeared in print. We even appeared on a newsreel at the cinema, and it was shown in Cambridge in term-time. We did not know it was to be shown, but we heard that it had been greeted in a typical undergraduate fashion.

The Boat Club seemed to attract a normal cross-section of students, and the records show that we followed a wide range of activities in later life. One of the members married one of the coaches, and another is now the College Vice-Principal.

W. Blayney (Shaw, 1934)

*

A GOOD DAY'S WORK

The maids called us around 7 a.m. which gave one enough time to be ready for the morning prayers, led by Mrs Palmer, which preceded breakfast at eight – if one wished to join in. For the domestic staff it was compulsory – they all lined up from the senior maid down the scale, and then stayed on to help with breakfast. Five of us became great friends – known in Peile as 'The Family'. One of our members did attend daily prayers; we other four waited until we knew the latest riser would appear and then breakfasted together. The newspapers had been delivered, and the College porter had brought our mail round to Peile so that it was waiting in our pigeon-holes for collection.

I was a Geographer, which often meant 'Niners', so the mad rush on one's bicycle followed the breakfast chatter – up to the splendid new Department of Geography, of which we were the first 'full generation'. Once there, there was no need to dash to other centres as we had everything under the one roof: lectures, library and labs. Miss Mitchell had primed us: 'If you work a full morning, nine to one o'clock, and follow that with three more hours – say between tea and Hall – you will have done a good day's work, and enough, if it *is* work.' We very frequently did just this. So one o'clock would mostly see us in the bicycle jams dashing back to Peile for lunch. After lunch we usually gathered in one of our rooms for coffee and the *Times* crossword. I was hopeless at this, apart from a claim to everlasting fame when I supplied 'The Abominable Snowman' for my duly impressed friends!

How would the afternoon pass? A multitude of occupations: as freshers we played hockey vigorously, but eventually gave that up in favour of squash. In summer we had tennis parties to which we invited our men friends and, of course, to the inevitable tea-party afterwards. Sometimes we shopped or, in the fresh spring days, walked and chatted, or just lazed and chatted. And of course there was the river. We were not allowed to go either punting or canoeing until we had satisfied our seniors that we could handle the craft safely! This meant early morning (pre-breakfast) sessions on the Mill Pond 'learning how' – a chilly but hilarious pastime, under the watchful eye of a second-yearer. I don't recall any of us volunteering to teach our successors!

If you were not caught up in the daily tea-parties, tea and buns was provided in Hall at 3.45 p.m. in order that you could get that three hours clear before dinner. There was never a very full house for this – but it was useful. So maybe one did work between tea and dinner, or perhaps one had a supervision then – in the old Lecture Room Passage, between Old Hall and Sidgwick. Or one might be throwing a tea-party oneself, in which case one's men friends had to leave at 6.30 p.m. – after which we stacked our cups and saucers and dishes ready for the maids to wash up for us – the exception to this being on Sundays when we washed up ourselves to give them a holiday. One was expected to appear for dinner in Hall neat and tidy: and, if one found one's name up on the daily list of those six or so chosen to dine on the High Table, one was definitely expected to change into an 'afternoon frock', and converse intelligently with the dons.

After Hall coffee again – if one was not rushing out. I think I was the only member of The Family who did not play (the new craze) a recorder. Mercifully for me the noise of all musical instruments had to stop at 8 p.m.! Only a very few had their own wireless set – and if you did you had to listen to it through headphones only, so as not to disturb others who might be working. After eight more work, if Tripos loomed; if it didn't – well – conversation (the burning subject of our day was the Spanish Civil War) or society meetings – or perhaps one was going out. Fred Astaire in *Top Hat* – or, in my last term, the new Arts Theatre, where Margot Fonteyn danced at the beginning of her career. It was possible to get back from the cinema before 11 p.m., after which one needed special permission up to 11.30 p.m. or midnight or, for balls, into the small hours. So we would bike madly back to the then main gates at Old, and leave our bicycles in their bicycle sheds overnight. Newnham Walk presented a nightly show of couples' tender farewells till the next day's dawn brought it all around again. We from Peile had the good tramp round the entire College before we got to our beds, and we were not renowned for our lightness of foot!

We were gay, we were happy, we were carefree. Munich came after we were down – the war after that. We married our Cambridge boy-friends, and thirty years later have enjoyed it all over again, in the company of our daughters and sons who sensed there was something in this Cambridge business and happily followed us there.

B. D. Chapman (Rennell, 1935)

*

AN OUTSIDER

I was an outsider for several reasons, some of which will appear below, but one is that until a day in May 1935 I had not even heard of Newnham. That day, not long after hearing I had been awarded a travelling scholarship, I went into the library of the University College and studied a fat book called *The Students' Handbook to Cambridge*. It named Girton, which I had once before heard mentioned, and Newnham, whose fees were £1 a term less than Girton's. Though the £240 a year I was to receive sounded like incredible wealth to a young woman whose friends were teachers at £60 a year, I had been told that living in Cambridge was expensive, and so I applied for Newnham, never, in my ignorance, doubting that I would be accepted. However, I was accepted, left New Zealand in August and arrived in Sidgwick Hall early in October.

Between May and October various people told me, or warned me, a little about Cambridge or similar institutions. A Rhodes Scholar told me that the English reserve was such that I must expect to be friendless for at least the first year. He advised me to change my plans and go to London, where for some reason he thought it might not be so bad. A Professor of Education warned me that the standard was so high that I must not expect to excel any more. Having heard the same sort of thing before, when I went to secondary school, and again when I went to our university, I listened politely but did not believe it. This time, though, it was devastatingly true. Worst of all was what I read in a series of articles in our students' paper, written by a young lecturer who had recently been a student in Cambridge. He described, among other things, the festivities of May Week, and the presence of debutantes from outside the University. My father being an Anglican clergyman, we were poor, and my social life sketchy. How would I know how to behave in such surroundings? I began to think I should not go, though this scholarship had been my dream for three years. My mother tried to reassure me by telling me that I would probably be the only girl there who knew how to make jam and bottle fruit. I couldn't quite see the relevance, and never enquired about its truth, but I went all the same, as the alternative was unemployment. My culinary abilities did me no good. One day at Hall the girls were criticising the food. My contribution to the discussion showed clearly that I knew what was wrong and how to fix it. So I was snubbed, and ignored for the rest of the meal, and I thus learnt to hold my tongue. I wonder if things are quite as bad as that now, in these days of lack of servants? Are there still any girls like R, who invited some undergraduates to tea and then didn't know how to make tea?

The last major piece of advice that I remember came from a compatriot who had lived for some years in a Sussex village. She told me that I must never let anyone know that my father had not had to pay for my education. I remonstrated. In our town the state schools were then far better than the private schools, and I knew how little my father was paid. I made no contribution to my keep, and would not have dreamed of asking for school or university fees as well. I was proud of the fact that I had won my way on scholarships. 'Yes,' said my informant, 'I can see your point, but *English people wouldn't understand.*' With all this sapping my small confidence, and with the person who was going to meet me not arriving (held up by a traffic jam), when I finally reached the reception room of New Zealand House in London, I tripped over the mat and fell sprawling. No, those May Week debutantes wouldn't have done that.

At tea on the first afternoon in Sidgwick Hall, I met a group of North Country girls whose various accents surprised me. I had met the Oxford accent before, as my father had had a supercilious curate who had read Metaphysics at Oxford and referred to one of my hardest-won scholarships as 'Your – ah – little distinction'. And I did know there was such a thing as Cockney. But this – Durham, Newcastle, Yorkshire, and a girl from Derbyshire whom I could hardly understand at all! She, incidentally, could not understand why it had taken me six weeks by ship to get to England, as she thought New Zealand was somewhere off the coast of Denmark. They were most friendly, and three of them later invited me to visit them during the first vacation. So much for the Rhodes Scholar's gloom. Later I found that all of them, and a number of others too, were like myself on scholarships and ex-pupils of state schools. I was fortunate indeed to meet such a group. With one of them I still exchange yearly letters.

I took delight in writing to the Sussex lady, whom I disliked, and telling her that she was wrong. And for two years I had most enjoyable friendships with people whose backgrounds were somewhat similar to my own. But before the two years were over, something began to dawn on me which becomes much clearer when I look back. That is the deferment to people of wealth or position. Some examples. A, who read the *Daily Worker* at breakfast but did not associate with the state-school girls. B, who led a breakaway musical group when the Musical Society, the Raleigh, elected as its conductor one of the state-school girls. Perhaps the conductor was not the only reason, but there it was. C was interested in University societies, not Newnham ones, but when it came to the election of a students' representative for the Hall, the girls elected C, whose father was a national figure, and not D, who was far more active in Newnham affairs, but whose father was not heard of. Both were capable young women.

I heard of an undergraduate at one of the men's colleges who said that, if he befriended a certain student of his college whose background was state school and scholarship, he would be dropped by his own associates. I doubt if anything so bad would have happened at Newnham, but, as I have pointed out, there were elements of that attitude. Also, it was not only the grouping of like people, but that one group expected to lead, and the others appeared to accept this. However, the College was big enough to allow for class or interest groupings. All the same, I never felt at ease with those whom I mentally referred to as the 'public-school type'. I always had the uneasy feeling that underneath their beautiful manners they were laughing at me. Perhaps this is the sort of thing the Rhodes Scholar was talking about. Perhaps it was worse at Oxford. I know that my successor in my scholarship went to Oxford and rather disliked the people she met, but then she boarded with Lady Something, and may have met that sort of person and not my friendly North Country girls.

The Halls had their characteristics.* It was said that Mrs Palmer of Peile Hall looked over the new applicants and selected the best-looking for Peile. Clough girls were said to be more wealthy and, on the whole, to come from more influential positions than the others. In Sidgwick we used to wait in the passage before the lunch gong, thus gaining the criticism that we were the Sidgwick Lions, lining up to be fed. I remember no special characteristic of the girls of Old Hall.

* See p. 53.

Some of the rooms in Sidgwick were small and cold, and were called 'the Sidgwick slums'. I am told that they afterwards became bathrooms. Mine, though not so small, was called one of the slums because the roof leaked. Coming as I did from a country of small houses with bathrooms, I was surprised to find that every room had a small wash-stand complete with basin and jug, and that a maid would bring a jug of hot water each morning if one wanted it. This took me back to my childhood visits to a farmhouse too remote to have modern plumbing. I, like many of the girls, banished the jug and basin, and used the pedestal cupboard as a store for books. We then indulged in the pastime of 'chase the bathroom', and soon grew to know which ones were occupied for long periods and which were readily available.

At the beginning of the year, elections were held for the various committees and jobs. There seemed to be many of them, but I can only remember one, Maids' Dancing. There was a custom that when a girl was proposed she at once replied 'Beg to withdraw', and if she did not do this quickly enough she was considered to be elected. I thought this custom rather silly and unreal. Perhaps a girl who wanted to be elected would be slow to withdraw, pretend not to have heard her name, or use some other device. However, a friend assured me that it was real enough. Many of the girls, she told me, had been Head Girl at school, and were thoroughly tired of doing all kinds of jobs.

A compatriot whom I met in London suggested sending my name to her uncle, who was a professor in Cambridge and had afternoons for students from time to time. Knowing that she, too, was vicarage-bred, I presumed that her uncle was some theological professor and his afternoons would be dull, but I agreed, politely I hope. As an afterthought I asked what her uncle was professor of. When she replied that he was Professor of Physics at the Cavendish, I was overcome with awe. But it appears that I conquered the awe, for a diary entry after the first meeting reads 'Lord Rutherford talks loudly all the time, but he seems a nice old thing.' Coming from a country with a small, scattered university, I found it a great pleasure to be in a place where one could from time to time go to public lectures by world-famous figures, or even, on occasion, to meet them.

Another pleasure was meeting students from other countries. There was my Chinese friend, graceful in her tight, straight dress which looked so bumpy if one of us tried it on. Another Chinese, a Greek, two Indian sisters who were so vivacious as to be thoroughly exhausting, undergraduates from India, Africa, Canada, Wales, all are ones I readily remember.

For a practical person like myself, the then emphasis on Mathematical Analysis, though this was the University, not Newnham, was a tedious grind, the price I had to pay for being there. I had always liked Mechanics, and took happily to Hydrodynamics, in spite of the first chapter of the book making assumptions that I had found to be untrue when, as a three-year-old, I had sat my doll on the water-race. This book explained why it made the assumptions. Mathematical Analysis did not explain what it was driving at. However, my difficulty of those years has been useful in teaching. It made me careful to explain the aim of any topic, particularly if the pupils found it hard or irrelevant. It led me to the abandonment of formal geometrical proofs of obvious properties long before the New Math made such abandonment respectable. Above all, it meant that I knew from the inside the feeling of utter confusion, being expected to make intelligent replies, but instead guessing hopefully because I did not know what my supervisor was talking about. Being now in the main a teacher of average and below-average pupils, I cannot overrate the importance of this insight.

When I asked my Director of Studies whether a certain arrangement in Electricity could actually be performed, she replied that we left such considerations to the Physicist, and added that I had too literal a mind. Yes, the Hunger Marchers, the Basque children, and what was happening in Germany were much more real to me than proving that a continuous function of a continuous function is continuous. But even the continuous function was worth it. It was the price I had to pay for being at Newnham. Nowhere else have I been in surroundings where the main emphasis was on learning, where one's mind was stretched to the utmost in the attempt to keep up. This applied not only in study but in leisure pursuits: going to meetings and public lectures, discussions with friends – in short, the life of a residential university, by contrast with my previous four years of study interspersed with parish work and with friendships with factory girls who had left school at fourteen. There was an obverse side of course, the worst instance being one day in the boathouse when we were waiting for some reason, and accidentally it became known that I had an M.A. degree from the University of New Zealand. The derision and comments ring in my ears still. It is true that these English girls, brought up on a highly competitive system, were more used to concentrated study than I was. I had had to work hard at times, but not all the time. Even the solving of Applied Maths problems, for instance, was often done in the intervals of baking a cake, or doing the ironing or washing-up. I was accustomed to using the holidays as holidays, and, with the invitations received from Newnham girls, did not realise that Cambridge students were expected to do a good deal of study in the vacations.

We were not members of the University. This did not worry us, as we felt more free under the regulations of our own dons than were our counterparts at Oxford. But our dons were keenly aware of the anomaly. Perhaps it is poetic justice that I now find it hard to interest young women in equal pay and opportunity for women generally.

What else do I remember? Miss Milner-Barry's kindness and sense of humour. The beautiful Newnham garden – but when I climbed a tree I had to go in and change my dress – soot, I suppose. The claustrophobic feeling induced by the constant mists of East Anglia – how I longed for the clear air of our mountains, the only time I felt homesick. The Advent procession with carols at King's College Chapel – had my great-grandmother, who lived in King's Parade, heard just such music, or was it a recent development? The Lent and May Races where, if there were debutantes, I did not recognise them as such. The narrow, crowded streets and the bookshops and the market. The Backs, of course. The University Library where one soared up in an automatic lift. The undergraduates with their varied gowns which they had to wear after dark. The Proctor and his Bulldogs. Plays at the Arts Theatre, and foreign films at one of the cinemas. The crowds of bicycles, so like my home-town except for the bicycle baskets. Going hatless, even to church, except for Holy Trinity. Sunlight and shade patterns in Sidgwick Avenue. The girl who came home from a matinée of *Night Must Fall* and insisted that I precede her into her room, for fear there might be a man hiding behind her balcony curtains. The girl who went to the first meeting for the term of the Socialist and Labour Club because she thought it arranged socials and working bees, presumably for some charity. Missing the evening meal to march in a demonstration where 'someone gave us a torch, which dripped wax on B's coat and nearly set my hair alight'. A League of Nations Union meeting in the Guildhall, where some students threw tear-gas down from the gallery. One of my friends, M, had weak eyes which took some time to recover. The girl who had not finished her essay but went on 'reading' until her supervisor, who probably knew what was going on, asked her to repeat something a page or two back.

Trip lunches, earlier than the normal time, where the second-year girls were waitresses. Punting up the river in the evening light to a fen (I forget the name, we skated there in the winter) after exams were over. And finally, hearing the Mathematical Tripos lists read in the Senate House. One undergraduate, who did well both then and later, was there in evening dress after a May Ball. Was his partner a debutante? I do not know. I had never failed an exam before, but as Mr Cunningham read 'Page, Newnham, Pearson, Newnham' I grew fearful. Would 'Powell, Newnham' follow? It did. What relief. And so to breakfast with a friend, and back to complete my packing.

F. U. M. Dromgoole (Powell, 1935)

*

INVASION, 1938

In 1938, when there was the scare that war would come, Newnham had agreed with the authorities in London that we would take in nursery-school children. I think it was to be five children to one member of staff, or maybe ten children to one staff – I can't really remember. Sidgwick had just been redecorated, so Margaret McFie arranged to have palliasse mattresses – four in all the ground-floor rooms in Sidgwick – to accommodate these children. The day came when evacuation was to take place, before Munich, and nothing happened. We were just about to go over for dinner when Margaret McFie rang from the Porters' Lodge to Kennedy Building, and said, 'Anybody who is there – maids, Fellows, anybody – come over at once to the Porters' Lodge, babies have arrived!' So we all rushed over. There were relatively few of us there (we were most of us away), but those of us that were there were all marshalled.

And here were two busloads of babies with mothers, and it never dawned on us that the mothers weren't going to stay – but oh no, they just handed out these infants. Each infant had a bundle of clothes and a large label which said JOHN, WILLIAM, HENRY or what have you, but no indication of its age or whether it had bottles or ate rusks or anything. We took them all over to Sidgwick Hall, which was empty, and we laid these babies all in rows on the floor in the Hall. Gwen Woodward, who was the Librarian, established a little table with a card-index at the door to record the names and ages of these babies.

The first thing we had to do was bath and wash them, because they had been travelling for I don't know how long. So we each took a baby and gave its name and all its particulars to Gwen Woodward, who wrote them down in the card-index, and off we went to the nearest bathroom or washing cubicle, bathed and washed the baby and put on clean clothes if it had any. Somebody rang all the Newnham mothers in the district and said 'Do come', and we also rang the Mill Road Hospital and, when they asked what did we most need, we asked for something to make napkins and something to make feeding bottles – which they sent.

After bathing the baby you put it on one of the palliasses. I did know one end of a baby from the other because I have got lots of nephews and nieces, but lots of people didn't. I can see Betty Behrens with an absolutely filthy little chap clinging round her neck, saying 'Oh no! I'd do anything that I needn't have this baby'; and Mary Beare holding up an infant with a napkin nicely tied round its middle but just hanging loose, saying 'I don't think this is very effective!' Eventually we got them all bathed and popped into the rooms on the ground floor of Sidgwick; and it was all right for the tinies, because they couldn't move, but anything that could crawl wouldn't stay in the rooms – they came crawling along the passages, and you couldn't shut the doors: so you pushed the babies in, and then kept on fielding them in again.

There was one little boy, I don't quite remember how old, a tiny little thing, who kept on coming out of his pigeon-hole in Sidgwick, saying 'Baby, baby' and weeping. I happened to notice that his surname was the same as the surname on a tiny infant, and I took him in there and popped him down and he crawled over to her, said 'Baby, baby, baby', put his hands round her and fell asleep. He found his little sister.

At last we got them bedded down somehow or other and came and had an exhausted meal. Mill Road spared us a nurse for the night, and we were to go back at five o'clock the next morning and feed them. Then again it was pandemonium. Those that were fed with bottles (some of them were only about eight weeks old, or even smaller) were well and good; but the kind that could eat! There weren't enough of us and we had about four babies per grown-up. While you spooned porridge into one, another took its fist and threw porridge at someone else. We did get them all porridged and pottied, and (fortunately it was a gorgeous morning) we brought them all out on to the Clough lawn. We put any crawling ones on that lawn and we stood round on the paths, and if any baby came off the grass you just pushed it back on again. It was priceless. And it was then that we heard that Munich had been arranged, war wasn't going to come, and they had (fortunately!) all to go back that night.

The buses arrived; and, would you believe it, they had sent buses for these infants, of which there were something like eighty, with only one grown-up per bus. We had to marshal everybody, we had to pop them into the buses and to hold on to them; and those of us who had cars drove up to London in the wake of the buses to bring back the various members of the Newnham staff. I arrived with my little car at Westminster almost simultaneously with the buses. Mothers and whatnot were boarding the buses to carry off the babies, and I went into County Hall with the card catalogue and said, 'These are the babies from Newnham College: here they are; what shall we do with them?' 'Oh,' they said, 'that's all right, the mothers will take them.' They didn't even count them.

London was pandemonium because Neville Chamberlain had come back, or was coming back; everybody was out in the street, and special constables on duty at Hyde Park Corner. The traffic was an absolute tangle. I didn't tell anyone that I had never driven in London before.

The reason we had the babies was that the London clinic had thought that the baby clinic in Cambridge was a resident clinic, and it wasn't. When they arrived all unannounced at the baby clinic in Cambridge they couldn't cope with these infants to sleep, and the clinic knew that Newnham had arranged to take nursery children. Margaret McFie, having survived the First World War in Serbia with refugees, was ready for anything.

It was then that we did the hasty A.R.P. blackouts. Miss Strachey and I sat for two or three days on that lawn outside Old Hall (it was wonderful weather), and kept on stitching curtain rings on to these acres and acres of black sateen to hang up. Miss Strachey kept on saying, 'Oh dear, you're much better than me at this – I'm not very good at it!' We did curtains for all the students' rooms – every room in College. I don't think they were all finished in time for the first scare, but they were later on, for the real thing. The corridors were all painted in blue paint, and if you look very carefully there is some blue paint (there was until recently, at any rate) in the cracks of the Kennedy Passage windows.

When the real thing came in 1939 they collected up into Cambridge a whole lot of women in their last month of pregnancy, and Newnham was more or less full of these women who lived here until the baby was about to be born, when they were transferred to Mill Road, or Chesterton, or wherever was coping. We never had any baby in the College; our nurse was very skilled, she could see them off at the right moment. On one occasion I was over sleeping in Old Hall and my doctor arrived at Kennedy to see me, and one of the little maids at Kennedy was sent with him across to Old Hall to show the way. He looked at the women who were sitting about on garden seats and said, 'Dear me, who are these women?' And the little girl said, 'Oh, they are the unexpected mothers, sir.'

Then we had women nurses who were going to be drafted to various parts of East Anglia, as the blitz demanded their services (because we expected the blitz at any moment). After them we had evacuees from London. Quite late at the end of the first day of the evacuation, Newnham was rung up and asked to cope. The last lot of evacuees had come in rather too late to be dealt with, and we had them for the night. They were from Soho, largely Greeks, some Turks, mothers and their children. Very many of the women were not able to speak English, so that they were turning to little tots for interpretation. We summoned Professor Ellis Minns, who lived just down in Millington Road, because his Modern Greek was marvellous, and he came trundling up: I can see him now coming up Newnham Walk wheeling a perambulator that had belonged to his grand-children, full of loaves of bread – I think we were so short he had brought them to help us out. He took on as interpreter for all these women.

War broke out on the Sunday, and during the night of Sunday there was the first air-raid warning. I was sleeping in Old Hall, and the hooter went; and then there was a knock on the door and in came the Old Hall man, wearing a gas-mask, with a hatchet in his hand – he had been drafted to evacuate me. This was all part of the drill, but it was very terrifying.

J. B. Mitchell (1923). Extracts from a tape recording

3 SEPTEMBER 1939

Memories of 1939 are often connected for me with the garden at Newnham. It was difficult to dig the air-raid shelters because of the wetness of the ground, and they could not be sunk deeper than three feet. There was also another hazard: during the digging of those outside Peile Hall, some ancient burials were found. Moved by a rather recent interest in archaeology, I went along to help, and spent most of Whitsunday removing the earth from the bones with a tablespoon. There were a number of burials; I particularly remember a grave where two adult skeletons lay inextricably mingled, and one where three – apparently man, woman and child – lay side by side. They were not straight, but lightly flexed; their bones had acquired a beautiful red-brown patina, and they looked wonderfully comfortable. White cherry-blossom petals from the tree outside Kennedy Building drifted down on to them, and inevitably recalled A. E. Housman:

> I hear my bones within me say
> Another night, another day.

I remember thinking how far they were from any suggestion of sadness. We were the people under stress, held in a horrible suspense, and they were reassuring in their quiet sleep.

A few months later, on September 3rd, I stood in the garden early in the morning. It was a lovely autumn day, and I was more or less on duty, as the College had accepted a number of evacuees from London, mothers and children from Soho. Although we were not officially at war, a mistaken air-raid warning had sent them all into the shelters for the first time, and the garden which appeared empty was full of people. It was odd to stand there and hear the whisper of talk rising from the ground, as one might expect to hear leprechauns talking in an Irish hillside.

Later in the morning, also in the garden, I met Nan Robertson (Tutor of Old Hall) leading an unusual-looking group of people towards the hockey field. 'We're going to St Mark's Church,' she told me, so I joined them. On the way she told me what had happened. The Rabbi had come to speak to the Jewish element among the evacuees, offering them the friendship of the community in Cambridge and saying prayers with them. The others sensed a lack. 'Where's our church?' they demanded. 'Who's looking after us?' So we all went to St Mark's, arriving I think during the sermon, and the congregation, astonished but respectful, moved up the pews to make room, and when we came out we heard that Britain was at war.

M. Mann Phillips (Somerville, 1924)

*

ONE SHORT WAR YEAR

I have very vivid memories of my one short 'war year' at Newnham – from September 1939 to May 1940: the cold of the winter and the warmth of so many new friends; helping arrange blackout curtains and strips of black paper around the windows of a big dining-hall – Clough? – because there was I, all alone in England and a month to go till term started. When it did I was very happy in a little room at the top of Old Hall, looking south over the grassy playing fields – I think I have a picture somewhere – I know I have a picture taken on the roof one sunny Sunday in spring, while the church-bells were pealing and answering, a new experience for one from the wide open spaces of Canada.

There were so many new experiences, such as discovering the way to warm up in winter was to go out for a walk! From a country where central heating was taken for granted, and winter could bring frozen noses and toes, it was quite a change. Wartime rations meant trying to light a fire with six little sticks – I never forgot that – and you left off lighting it until as late as possible because you had only a half scuttle of coal for the day. Of course it had to be one of the coldest winters in many years. The snow lay on the fields for weeks – even the Brussels sprouts froze – and I was obliged to eat parsnips, which I hated and have never eaten again to this day. I became most adept at rolling newspaper into curls to get and keep a fire going, and my next-door neighbour, Helen Epps, introduced me to the delightful custom of hot chocolate made over the fire in one of our rooms at the end of an evening of studying. Another custom we developed that year was saving up our daily butter rations until we had enough for a 'crumpet party' at tea-time. There was Margaret Moxon, Margaret Myddleton, May Haddock, Daphne Sisson, Phyllis Tettenborn, Gladys Bartell, and another dear Margaret (Canney) who became a librarian in London. The latter was among those who helped me with my washing and packing, for I had to leave for home within three hours of finishing the last of my Tripos exams – what a heartbreak. I didn't get back until 1962 when I passed through Cambridge with my three children, and had a wonderful visit with Miss Chrystal. I missed connecting with Miss Grimshaw, who was such a patient supervisor, or with Miss Robertson. The latter was in charge of Old Hall when I was a student there, affectionately called 'The Rabbit' behind her back – she was so kind to me when I broke up over one of my exams right in the middle of the session, and undoubtedly saved me from failure.

I almost forgot the terrible time that I banked my fire with ashes, hoping to be able to revive it in the morning and save a little wood for next time. I awoke in the middle of the night to find it blazing up merrily – and my curtains had been thrown wide to the night air! Did I close my curtains? Did I douse the fire? I don't remember, but I didn't waste any time, I can tell you! Sure enough my brilliant display was spotted and reported by the Fire Warden and I didn't try that again!

Spring came early (I thought) that year – it was only February when we rode 'miles' into the country (by bicycle of course) to a little wood where the aconites were blooming. I had never seen bare ground at that time of year before, just snow, snow, snow. Oh! the coldness of some of those colleges, such as the oldest part of John's, downstairs, walking and slipping on ancient cobblestones and under low arches – riding by bicycle, with a dim blue light that showed you next to nothing, to the opposite side of town to sit in the top balcony for *Macbeth* – or lining up

Monday morning for sixpenny standing-room places at the Arts Theatre. We saw a lot of good things there that were trying to avoid or spend less time in London.

D. F. Johnson (Burt, 1939)

*

THE UNDERGRADUATE COUNCIL

The French family with whom I had intended to spend the summer holidays could not believe that we were on the brink of war. 'Come early and bring your tennis racquet,' they had written. Had I taken their advice I might have been trapped on the Continent as some of my friends were. Instead I stayed at home in Cambridge, and was working with a sandbagging party at what was then the Central School when the fateful broadcast came over the air. For a time it seemed as if the world had come to an end, and I could hardly believe that I should be allowed to take up my place at Newnham and continue my education. It was a constant source of amazement to me to find how many things seemed to go on almost exactly as before.

In my second year I was made Secretary of the University Undergraduate Council, the only attempt at undergraduate representation in those days. Because women were not members of the University there had to be a male co-Secretary as well. Conditions were not favourable to the formation of a coherent representative body, and I doubt if the Council achieved much, but I found the organisational experience useful in later life. At times I became over-engrossed in extra-mural activities. On one occasion, I was at a meeting when I realised that Commemoration was due to commence in less than half an hour. I pedalled furiously back to College, only to discover that, as was usual on such occasions, all but the main gate had been locked. I flung discretion to the winds, flew up to the door of the Fellows' building and rang the bell. Presently the little maid opened the door. 'Thank you so much,' I cried to the astonished girl as I rushed past her and disappeared in the direction of Peile. I don't think my heart stopped thumping till halfway through the speeches.

Imperturbable, or so it seemed, amid the vicissitudes of wartime and the erratic behaviour of women students, was Mrs Palmer. She was a Christian and also a Socialist, but of a moderate school and she disapproved of extremists. Some people may have thought her hard, but she was invariably kind to me. Each year she gave a short series of lectures on architecture for first-year students, and I attended these, though I have to confess the only one I recall even slightly was about the Roman basilica. As Registrar of the Roll Mrs Palmer took a great interest in her past students, and I corresponded with her until shortly before her death.

There were times at Cambridge when you could quite forget there was a war on: like punting up the river to Grantchester on long June afternoons. At other times you would be assailed by pangs of conscience and feel you must do something for somebody: like going up to blitzed London in the vacation to relieve the helpers in the rest-centres. The night I arrived there, a bomb damaged the students' sleeping quarters while we were out distributing hot cocoa to the people in the shelters; and the day I returned home, incendiary bombs were starting to fall on Liverpool Street station as my train pulled out. Such narrow escapes happened all the time, and engendered a rather fatalistic outlook.

I feel that most of my contemporaries shared my belief in a better world after the war. Poland, France, India, even Scotland would be free and England would be one big beautiful community experiment. There would be opposition of course, but it would be overcome: that would be part of the fun. I did meet one or two students who did not believe in anything, but their attitude seemed unimportant at the time. Education, we thought, should be reorientated so as to serve the community better, but we were thinking as much of moral concepts as of technical progress. The triumph of technocracy was alien to our thoughts, and the words 'scientific breakthrough' did not even feature in our vocabulary.

C. M. Leach (Blackman, 1939)

WARWORK

I was in Clough Hall from 1939 to 1943: Part I, Part II, Part III Maths Tripos. During the war years I had a buttercup yellow blanket made into a stylish siren suit with many zip pockets for identity card, torch, etc. If not on duty, we slept during an air-raid warning on the passage floor of Fawcett. We were crowded together, and I recall awakening at 6 a.m. utterly alone! The warning had soon been followed by the All Clear, but even jostling and the hard floor did not wake me from sound sleep. Thus that day began, and after breakfast I had lectures alternately in the Arts School and in Trinity College; the hectic bicycling was refreshing and aided concentration, and I heard of no one killed in the mad dash – I think the residents kept off the roads for ten minutes of every hour.

After lunch we did some warwork. I discovered one could think about

Uniform Convergence while washing 400 spoons, or while fixing coloured rags on to camouflage netting. But as we raced while pulling up onions, concentration on simple properties of Quadrics was all that would fit well! When we did roof drill to be ready for incendiary bombs, I did no Maths *at all* in case I got involved in experimental projectiles. Lunch had been inadequate – I discovered the exact time-interval between a better-than-average meal and the consequent brain surge was fourteen hours, and I used this discovery to eat the 'food on points' this exact time before any particularly challenging work – but lunch in Hall in the war was always inadequate, and as the afternoon continued I was always hungry and so would stop studying in my room, and go down to study in the Library or the University Library where the books were very engrossing.

Supper was always very enjoyable – groups of friends would include people from many faculties and conversation was lively. One day at supper we had rolls and anyone who got a large red bean inside could claim an orange! This was a very good way to distribute the twelve oranges received for sharing between all the College.

After supper we usually went to a society meeting such as the delightful 'Informal Club' inspired by Miss Welsford (for which club we wrote poetry), or perhaps we'd go to the Trinity debating society, 'The Magpie and Stump', or we might study in College in the semi-gloom of a 40-watt bulb. (This caused me such eyestrain that the oculist *prescribed* a 60-watt bulb – like a prescription for medicine!) While we studied we assembled transmitters for paratroopers, or fixed rubber sleeves over the turned-back outer covers of wires, keeping to a colour code. We used as a tool little pieces of glass tubing drawn to a point (in place of expensive three-pointed scissors), and this brilliant idea of Miss Chrystal's set people at Pye's factory wondering how it could happen that a specialist in Hebrew and Theology could have such *practical* brilliance.

I recall one evening when I did a daring thing. To be out late we had to sign the Late Book at breakfast to have permission. At lunch-time on this occasion the eminent G. T. Bennett, Senior Fellow of Emmanuel, invited me to dinner and discussion the same evening. I believe it was June 30th – his birthday – and he would be seventy-four that day. could not miss this opportunity. He had a delightful personality, and his remarks on Mathematics and on life in general were able to cast special light. In the evening as he politely escorted me back to Newnham, I stopped near the bicycle shed outside the main gate and told him I would have to climb in, as I had no late permission. I vividly recall his expression as he said, 'I have felt for fifty years that I have known appropriate behaviour and etiquette, but now I am stumped. Do I say "Goodnight, and it was very nice to see you", and go – or do I help you to climb?'

A. C. Dillon (Falconer, 1939)

*

A SIREN AT THE FEAST

20 October 1940

The most wonderful thing has happened this week – we have had 3 whole nights without a single air raid siren! It was decided on Monday that we could not go on spending half our nights in the shelters, so we now only have to go down to the ground floor until there is 'urgent danger'. On Tuesday we were all in our rooms just after dinner, at about 7.30, when suddenly we heard a plane and then two terrific cracks. Of course we all rushed downstairs at top speed, and then the sirens went. We were down for about three hours before the all clear, and had just gone off to bed and sleep when the siren went again at 11.30. This time the all clear did not go until 4.30, so we had a pretty good night of it. Next day we heard that the two loud bombs we first heard had fallen on a bank manager's house about half a mile away. He was sitting in his study and was killed outright, but his wife was in the kitchen and just escaped.

Another evening the siren went in the middle of the College Feast, just as we were beginning on our plates of roast chicken. Miss Strachey got up and requested us all to leave for the shelters, but everybody just laughed, so she had to repeat the request, very much more firmly this time, and we all trooped off, some of us carrying plates of chicken down to the depths!

26 January 1941

I have been kept pretty busy by practices for A.R.P. The stretcher-bearing is uproariously funny, and most of the time we can hardly lift the people for laughing. Practising bringing unconscious people down-stairs, and squirting stirrup pumps on the roof, also causes great merriment. We had a very interesting lecture on incendiary bombs, given by one of the Physics dons. We had four sirens in one day this week, but nobody now takes any notice of them. All the lecture rooms are fitted with a 'buzzer' system, which is a signal given by the Observer Corps and is supposed to signify urgent danger. Unless the buzzer goes, the lectures go on as usual.

C. M. Davies (Hollingworth, 1940). Extracts from letters home

*

1941

FIRE PRACTICE

Mrs Palmer was Tutor of Peile Hall, and a governor of my old school as well as an occasional visitor at my home. Much loved, she was nevertheless a formidable character; when she pronounced that, as Miss Brooke had been at Bedales, she would already be trained and a suitable person to captain the Peile fire brigade, I did not like to confess that I had never even been a novice in the Bedales brigade. Greatly doubting my ability, and rather fearful of the more senior third-year members, I felt it would be easier to shoulder the greatness after all.

At school, there had been plenty of canvas hoses and brass couplings, and the great treat was the annual testing of the Davis escape harness. At Newnham, the accent was rather more on stirrup-pumps and buckets of sand. It was suggested to me, by the Fellow with responsibility as Fire Officer for the College, that we should test the equipment. I remembered about the great treat; it did seem rather tame to test a stirrup-pump by transferring two gallons of water from one bucket to another, and anyway in the preceding Long Vacation Term we had had a real air-raid and we might have another at any time. A little exercise was prepared and duly carried out.

At that time, only Clough dining-hall was in use and rather a squash it was, for Old and Sidgwick dined together, as did Clough and Peile, alternating for early and late meals. As I came into Hall that evening, the Fire Officer Fellow was alone at the High Table. She rose from her chair, and came down a step. 'Did you have a successful time?' she asked. 'Oh yes,' replied I, 'we had a marvellous time; we imagined that an incendiary bomb had landed on the roof of the Flat,* and obviously the best way up was through the skylight in Miss Pilsudska's room. We passed lots of buckets up, and tested all the stirrup-pumps. It all went very well.'

So green and so inexperienced, I was quite unprepared for the effect my words would have. Her hand really did fly to her mouth. 'You *didn't*!' she gasped, her voice a mixture of horror, amazement, and I think just a little envy. I realised that I must play it down a little, and did my best to reassure her about the perfect safety of the whole operation. Another member of the fire brigade was with me, and an excellent story we made of it to everyone at our table. We sat so that we could see the

* See note, p. 185.

High Table, and each Fellow who appeared heard the saga with varying reactions, from disapproval at the risk to amusement at the enterprise. We watched with apprehension as Mrs Palmer came in; I am glad to say that she seemed disposed to break into her famous chuckle.

E. Hollingsworth (Brooke, 1941)

A TIDE IN THE AFFAIRS OF THE BOAT CLUB

Most college clubs suffer fluctuations in their fortunes, from flourishing like a green bay tree to struggling for existence. Changing fashions in student life affect the membership and this in turn affects the income. Few clubs can count on stability in popularity or finances, and for those whose activities require considerable expenditure on equipment the problem can at times be acute.

To such ups and downs Newnham College Boat Club is no stranger. It was founded in the Easter Term of 1893 with thirty-three members, originally as the Rowing Society though the name was later changed. At some periods it controlled all activities of College members on the Cam, and at others only rowing and sailing on the lower river. In its prime it was very well supported, with enough members to form three divisions, several grades of proficiency, and an uncommonly large number of regulations.

There are early references to competitions, mainly with Girton College, and in 1918 a crew was described as the first Cambridge University Women's Eight. Yet not long after that there is an ominous reference in the Club's records to a 'fresh start'. The early twenties were a period of controversy, over shorts versus tunics, sliding versus fixed seats, and Fairbairn versus orthodox style. The Club reached a peak in the late twenties and early thirties, when frequent outings as far as Clayhithe, a coaching by Steve Fairbairn himself, weeks on the Tideway and Upper Thames, and numerous races and cups, feature in the minutes. This high tide in N.C.B.C.'s affairs was followed by an ebb in the late thirties, and when I went up in 1939 there was no rowing by Girton College, and in Newnham the Club had only nine members. We got quite used to going out with only seven or even six oars in the boat. We actually rowed a race with a crew one short, which of course means that the cox has to use the rudder against the stronger side, but only lost by half a length. I recall one outing in which a member who had been having flu thought she was sufficiently recovered to row again, but rapidly found she was mistaken. We off-loaded her to walk back to the boathouse and continued the outing without her. A small boy who was fishing on the bank and had seen us go out nine and return eight shouted excitedly to a friend, 'Coo, they've draowned one!'

He was not the only one to comment on the Newnham Eight. There were always a few superior persons who thought the sight of girls rowing was unattractive, and therefore could not imagine why we should do it; they were apparently unable to grasp the idea that we rowed for our pleasure, not theirs. We went out at lunch-time, because several of our members were Scientists and had to be in laboratories in the afternoons, but even so there were usually a few bystanders, wolf-whistlers and chiikers on the towpath, to say nothing of the soldiery practising on an assault course near Ditton. We grew so accustomed to this barrage that when I was coaching two freshers and one said, 'There's a man on the towpath shouting at us', I replied without looking, 'There often is; pay no attention.' In that instance it turned out to be our coach, who wanted a lift across the river and was somewhat hurt at not getting it.

The war presented a few unusual hazards to rowing, in addition to some prior claims on our time. Aircraft-spotting is a laudable activity, but awkward in a cox. It is exciting to be in an eight which is rounding a bend at a spanking pace with its cox gazing heavenwards and exclaiming, 'Oh look, Wellingtons!' The fields by the river were used extensively for Army training and on one occasion we encountered a pontoon bridge built nearly across the Cam, the negotiation of which was an interesting exercise.

Because of examinations, we did not row in the Easter Term but had all our races late in Lent. This meant that much of our training had to be done in January and February, when the weather was often unfavourable. On such an occasion in 1941 the Club suffered the loss of its shell eight, which was sucked through the flood sluice at Baitsbite Lock with all but one of its crew. The accident resulted from the coincidence of some half-dozen adverse circumstances, which separately would have been trivial but in combination overwhelmed us. No one was injured but the financial loss was severe. We managed to buy a second-hand boat from one of the men's college boat clubs, but my particular recollection of that period concerns a boat which we did *not* buy. It was offered to us by another club and we went to try it. It had been out of the water for four years, and its would-be vendors did not have the forethought to soak it before our trial. We returned it to its owners within a quarter of an hour, with a tart enquiry as to whether they thought we wanted to row in a boat on the Cam or in the Cam on a boat.

At that time we rowed as the Newnham, not the Cambridge Women's, Eight and were not awarded Blues. Thus, when in the first year of the war the Oxford University Women's Boat Club declined to row us, it was a disappointment, but did not disqualify us for the College award of oars to those who had been in the Newnham First Eight for three years. In 1941 the Club's committee decided to see what could be done towards establishing Blues for rowing for women. Approaches were made to the College authorities, to Girton College and to the Amalgamated Games Club (then the authority on sport for the women's colleges, which were not at that time part of the University). Girton students were invited to join N.C.B.C., as a temporary measure until they had enough experience and backing to re-form their own club. A race was rowed against Oxford, and in due course the negotiations were successful and Blues were awarded to this crew.

That was an exciting race. We found at breakfast-time that a sudden thaw had caused the Cam to flood overnight. It reached such heights that the arch of the old Silver Street bridge was covered, Grassy Corner disappeared, and the University Boat Club forbade the men's clubs to go out even in clinkers. We were too late to stop the Oxford crew coming, so when it arrived we decided after discussion to hold the race despite the submersion of some of the landmarks of the course. The only misfortunes were that our coach rode his bicycle off the towpath into the river at a point where the boundary between them was hidden under several inches of water, and that Oxford beat us by three-quarters of a length.

Nevertheless, for the Boat Club's affairs the tide had turned, and it continued to flow in the 1941–2 season. Once again Clayhithe was reached. Once again we discovered the pleasures of single scullers and light pairs. We did not manage to revive the races for these classes which had been a feature of the Club in its early days, but I recall a challenge, successfully met, to change over sculls in midstream in a 'funny'. With more Girton students rowing with us we even had two eights, an achievement which in 1939 seemed wildly improbable. It meant unfortunately that, in order to leave the clinker for the Second Eight, the First Eight had to take out the shell whatever the weather. However, an obliging friend who was reading Engineering made us an ice-shield for the bows and they never suffered any damage.

Both Eights had races and won them all. We could not challenge some of our old adversaries such as London University Women, but did row its Bedford College which had been evacuated to Cambridge. We had two away races, for which we borrowed boats from the host club but took our own oars. I had to cross London with them on one such occasion, and remember selecting an old-style taxi with a rail round its roof and sitting inside for some entertaining minutes while every other driver and porter at King's Cross advised, encouraged and occasionally even assisted my cabby to lash them over my head. We went to Oxford where we tried out a new racing start designed in Jesus College Boat Club and taught to us by our coach, and won by three lengths. Lastly, we had the hardest and most enjoyable race of the year against Reading University Women, and beat them by a canvas.

Thus in the short space of three years Newnham College Boat Club passed through minimal membership, no major fixtures and considerable money trouble to two victorious crews, a reduced debt, the promise of a rival club at Girton, Blues, and a First Eight which according to veteran boatmen was one of the best women's crews ever seen. And we had enormous fun with it. Despondent officials of any college club should cheer themselves with the reflection that truly there is a tide in the affairs of clubs, as of men. I wonder how it is flowing for N.C.B.C. now.

I. W. Preston (1939)

MOCK BLITZ

17 October 1942

On Thursday we had stirring times! Cambridge had a mock blitz, and ten people from each hall had to volunteer to act as casualties. Helen and I went, and really! talk about inefficiency; if Cambridge had a real raid I tremble to think what would happen. We were told that we should be collected in ambulances from Newnham at 7.30, so prompt on the dot we paraded, all in piles of clothes and looking like round balls. At 8.20, one ambulance turned up and took seven people to the H.Q. and then returned for the rest of us, and so on until we all landed at the Post Office. There we were very soon split up into groups, and five of us went off with an umpire and a large sack of straw which was labelled 'corpse'. The wretched man strode off at a terrific lick with his hands in his pockets, while we trundled along behind, Helen lugging the corpse! Eventually he stopped on a street corner, took the corpse and two 'casualties', and went off to stage an incident near Queens', promising to come back for us later. The incident came off at 9.0 p.m. and at about 9.25 he came back, when we were afraid he'd forgotten all about us, and said we weren't needed for his next incident (timed for 9.45) but he'd use us at 10.30! So we stood and watched while he arranged for a bomb to explode on the Pitt Press, and then while he interviewed wardens, fire-watchers, etc. who told him what they'd do about it, we stood and shivered and talked to some Cat's people. At about 10.15 he marched us off again, this time to the Low Temperature station, which is behind Downing. By the time we finished finding it the time was getting on, and when the bomb went off I think people were getting a bit bored, for we lay and yelled for help for nearly five minutes before some wardens trotted up and sent for an ambulance, which never arrived. Finally we walked home, where we landed just on 11.30, very cold and bored! Still, it was fun, and I got to know two new people, so it wasn't entirely a wasted evening. Even if I'd been in I couldn't have worked, as all the fire parties were out doing things; Joyce had to patrol the roof of Old most of the time.

What do we do with our rooms? Well, once in a blue moon, certainly never more than three times a term, a maid comes round with a carpet sweeper and ministers to us. I believe on that occasion she also dusts. Apart from that we do ourselves, with a brush and shovel out of common stock. Vacuum cleaners have never been heard of in Sidgwick!

I've also been busy getting in Fire Guard practices; we have to do eight per term and we're trying to get them in early so as to leave the end of term freer. I went to two this week and am doing three next so that I'll soon have finished. We sleep in the fire-post one night in eight, more or less clothed, and on the floor, and of course we have to get to know the building and do our hour's training per week, so it all takes time. On Thursday evening we climbed all over Sidgwick roof, learning where bombs might stick among all the Victorian stone work, and how they could be dealt with. One morning I went out at 7 a.m. for a stirrup pump practice, and for my other hour I went to a lecture by Dr Harding (one of the dons) on types of incendiaries and how to deal with them.

20 October 1942

You ask about supervisions. We have two a week, of an hour each, up in Miss Edmonds' room. She has a very squashy sofa, and she sits in the middle, with one of us on each side, and writes on an upturned tray! It's all very comfortable, sometimes rather too much so, as it almost lulls me to sleep. She is very particular about our work, everything has to be frightfully accurate in wording, of course the first thing I did was to write $4a = 8$, $a = \frac{1}{2}$. Just to give her a good opinion of me!

E. M. Hartley (1942). Extracts from letters home

1945

RESOLUTION ABOUT THE CALL-UP

Resolution about the Call-up A resolution had been passed at the Sidgwick Hall Meeting urging (1) That the limitation of the numbers of women students should be relaxed so that those going down under the call-up regulations would have an opportunity of finishing their courses after the war, and (2) That since women were now serving on equal terms with men, they should be recognised as members of the University. It was decided to consult Miss Curtis on the matter, and in particular to emphasize the strong feeling of the College on the first point.

Extract from the minutes of the Students' Representative Council, 24 April 1942

*

VE AND VJ

How, I wonder, have the rules in College changed in a quarter of a century? When we went up in 1943 the Tutor of Peile, Miss Ines Macdonald, soon called a meeting of freshers and told us about silence hours and music hours, and male visitors – none were allowed during the morning, and in the evening they were allowed in College only if their names were submitted beforehand. Gentlemen had to leave the College through the old Porters' Lodge in Pfeiffer Building on Newnham Walk by 10 p.m., which was the time by which someone who had not 'signed out' had to be back in College, for the gates were then locked. Gate fines were threepence for someone returning between 11 p.m. and 11.30, and sixpence between 11.30 p.m. and midnight. To most of us – still very unsophisticated schoolgirls – these regulations were very reasonable.

The supply of fuel to the College was, of course, rationed, and rooms in Peile were heated by either coal or gas, both of which were restricted. Owners of coal fires were allowed a ration of coal – two scuttles a week, I think, in the Michaelmas Term, while gas-fire-owners were allowed to use only a certain number of shillings each week in their slot meter. Even with the aid of patent fire-lighters bought in town (cardboard contraptions stapled together and soaked in paraffin), we found it difficult to start a coal fire. After the long walk from dinner in Clough Hall through very draughty and dimly-lit corridors, some of them with props of reinforcing scaffolding, we would group together to offer advice on lighting and 'drawing' the fire in the room of whoever was to be host.

We envied those whose gas-fires gave them instant heat. Without some form of sharing fires we would certainly have been cold. The common room must have been heated, but did not seem to be used to any great extent, except that people went there to read the newspaper.

After dinner we usually made coffee, which was not rationed, though sometimes a drink from our ration of 'Namco' (National Milk Cocoa). This was a powder issued to young people – I suppose under twenty-one – and was considered very nourishing, presumably because of the milk protein it contained. Some of us thought it more palatable taken cold and very strong. In our first term there were some students still under eighteen, and they were issued with a ration of bananas and were the envy of the rest of us. Occasionally we all had a ration of oranges issued to us.

All our meals were in Clough Hall, with two sittings of lunch and dinner (6.30 p.m. and 7.15 p.m.) and we had half the term at early and half at late Hall, although exchanges could be arranged. The housekeepers of all the Halls did duty in Clough at meal-times, and one clear recollection is of the housekeeper of Peile (Mrs Morrison was, I think, her name) pouring gravy from a gravy-coloured kettle as we queued up to help ourselves to our meal served from long tables at the side. To help in the domestic running of the College, we were all expected to help once a week with the washing-up after dinner in Clough or with dusting the Library before breakfast. After dusting chairs and tables, we followed on from our predecessors with the dusting of books, by consulting a plan on which we marked what we had done in our allotted time. I suppose it was an efficient system; at least the dust on the books never seemed to be very thick.

The war did not affect us directly in Cambridge; we heard that a bomb had fallen in Portugal Place before we went up, but we experienced no air-raid warnings after 1943. Of course we had to observe the blackout, and one's Tutor was liable to call if any chink of light was visible from the garden, but we wondered if perhaps sometimes this was a device to inspect one's gentlemen visitors! Then we were aware of bombers – Halifaxes, Lancasters and Liberators – passing over Cambridge; one vivid memory is of walking late at night from the Porters' Lodge to Peile across grass which crunched with frost, and looking up to see a hard, bright moon with an enormous halo round, and a large aircraft droning across it. Firemen, several of whom had been present in the blitzes on London or the North West, instructed us in the running of the trailer pump and the handling of hoses, as well as taking us on inspection tours of Newnham's roofs. At the end of the instruction course, we disregarded the usual rules, and finished up very wet, by turning the hoses on each other and on our instructors. Tempers, however, remained sweet, and we adjourned with the firemen to dry out and have hot drinks in Carroll Hele's (now Holland's) room in Sidgwick.

In spite of rationing, we were well fed, and presumably the vegetable garden was put to good use. On one occasion we were given a boiled green vegetable which did not seem to be one of the known varieties, and we decided that it must have been boiled lettuce, but whether this was so or not we never found out. One memorable meal was served on the day that Paris fell to the Allies in 1944; one of the dons (probably Miss Robertson) announced that to celebrate we were having ice-cream. It had pineapple pieces in it, and this was at a time when ice-cream of any sort was a very rare occurrence, and was never sold in shops.

As the Boat Race was not rowed during the war years, there was an unofficial Boat Race which took place on the Ouse at Ely. Ely was within cycling distance, and the road was filled with young people in college scarves cycling there and back. How Oxford got her supporters there I do not know, but they cannot have been so pleasurably exhausted at the end of the day as those who went from Cambridge by bicycle. Another consequence of the war was the evacuation of some London colleges to Cambridge for a year or two. In Science lectures we had students from Queen Mary College, and Professor Robinson of that college gave the series of Physics lectures on Electricity. Women students of the London School of Economics, with their black, purple and yellow scarves, were to be seen going into Fawcett Building from the Sidgwick Avenue boiler-room entrance to supervisions held in Fawcett lecture rooms. St Bartholomew's and Bedford College students were also to be seen in Cambridge.

VE Day and VJ Day (which was during the Long Vacation Term) were memorable days in Cambridge. On each occasion most of the junior members of the University, it seemed, flocked to Market Hill – a meeting place used on similar occasions through the centuries – and there danced in large concentric circles amid an immense throng, to music amplified from some unknown source. A huge bonfire was later lit there. There was on VJ Day the horror of the responsibility of the A-bomb to think about, but the sense of relief at the end of war lifted everyone's spirits. By the next term, it was obvious that many students were coming up after war service, and there was a noticeable rise in average age of first-year students. Celebrations on November 5th became more boisterous, no doubt because of the familiarity of these young men with gunpowder and similar things. After the war, too, we became aware of 'D. P. Camps' round Cambridge, where displaced persons with no homes were housed. Members of the University Strathspey and Reel Club made several visits to these camps to entertain the inmates by dancing to the music of bagpipes; although this must have seemed very strange and noisy, it must nevertheless have been appreciated, for the Club was invited back more than once.

The system of numbering students' bicycles in each College extended to Newnham in about 1944; it was rumoured that this was because so many unidentified bicycles were 'borrowed' by Air Force personnel returning to base and then abandoned. In Peile Hall the numbers began with N 300.

In the lecture room, one impressive lecturer was Dr Alex Wood, whose course was on his own subject of Acoustics. He also gave lectures on gyroscopic motion, and one demonstration in this subject was particularly popular. By sitting on a swivel-top stool while holding a spinning bicycle wheel, he showed us the phenomenon of precession, which caused him to rotate on the stool at considerable angular velocity, to everyone's amusement. Students who had seen this in previous years had probably come to see it again, for the lecture theatre seemed more than usually full. Dr Wood was a very approachable person who obviously enjoyed the company of students, and in more serious vein he gave an S.C.M. sermon. In Optics practical classes we were often able to talk to Dr G. F. C. Searle, who was then a very old man, but still very sprightly, and keen to help line up optical benches. His skill at producing interference patterns, where students would have no success, was legendary. He was always very friendly, with bright eyes behind small metal-rimmed spectacles, and a pink face with a slight stubbly white beard. He was recognisable in the distance by the haversack which he carried over his shoulder.

As the lecturer to introduce the subject of Biochemistry to new students, Dr Ernest Baldwin was a suitably dashing figure. He was very tall with a slight stoop, and had a dark beard – less common then than now. He wore a navy blue siren suit of the sort made popular by Winston Churchill, but still rather novel. The following lectures were given by Dr David Bell, who also sported a navy siren suit but was shorter than Dr Baldwin, though equally dapper. They were good friends and had research labs next to each other. Sir Frederick Gowland Hopkins, the 'Father of Biochemistry', was very old, but came to the lunch for those in the middle of their all-day practical examination for Part II in 1946. There he told us that we could not all expect to get Firsts, but that we should do our best and that a Second is a very worthwhile degree. During the Part II Biochemistry course, while doing practical Microbiology, students made the acquaintance of Dr Marjory Stephenson, a Fellow of Newnham, who in 1945 (with Dr Kathleen Lonsdale) was the first woman to be elected to the Royal Society.

G. B. Treacy (Mills, 1943)

*

DOMESTIC WORK

When we arrived it was to find that the lower corridors of Newnham, particularly by the Library, were sandbagged against damage by blast. Because of the shortage of domestic staff all had to do some domestic jobs. These were allocated to third-year students first, so the first-years were left with the 'worst' jobs. The ones that stick in the mind are sweeping and dusting the corridors *before* breakfast! If one was crafty this was done in slacks and sweater over one's pyjamas, so that one could return to bed for the extra ten minutes. However, one was likely to be disturbed by the housekeeper enquiring if one had in fact been up at all!

Since fuel was scarce there was a bath rota giving everyone three baths a week: Monday, Wednesday and Friday for surnames in the first half of the alphabet, Tuesday, Thursday and Saturday for the second half. I cannot remember whether anyone bathed on Sundays. There was a five-inch depth mark on the bath which was the maximum suggested by His Majesty's Government. There were still the Flying Bombs (the V1s) around, and we were informed by one of the male lecturers that should the occasion arise when we had to depart to the air-raid shelters, 'Let there be no nonsense of this "women and children first"!'

Considering the food situation existing then, the meals were very good. It helped to come from a home where it was understood that one ate everything one was given. We always had sausages for Sunday breakfast, although I must confess that I was willing to sacrifice this for extra time in bed. In case I give the impression of sloth, let me hasten to add that this love of lying in bed was due to the fact that one lived a very full life, and there was really not enough time to get even a good seven hours' sleep. This was, in part, because we would spend hours of the night in discussing and generally putting the world to rights. It all seemed so easy then.

We all had our rations of sugar, butter, Namco and jam. This was collected on Saturdays after lunch, and a very pitiful amount it looked. Cakes were virtually unobtainable, unless one was lucky enough to have a paper bag from Fitzbillies which entitled the owner to one cake a week, and that at the expense of a nine o'clock lecture. Namco turned up in every conceivable way: ice-cream, chocolate sauce, puddings and so on, and we also had some of the raw product each. This was sometimes eaten neat with a tea-spoon and, unless one has actually experienced the complete dehydration of the mouth due to a spoonful of Namco, it is impossible to appreciate it.

Turning to more sporting topics, I remember afternoons or evenings punting, but not before one had passed a 'punting test' conducted by a senior member who had passed the test herself. As I remember, it consisted of going a certain distance in a straight line punting on left and right, turning in a reasonable distance, and bringing the punt in tidily to a mooring.

The main event of 1945, of course, was VE Day on May 8th. This caused the usual collection in the market square, for which the police were unprepared as it was announced, I think, during the day. The Proctors and Bulldogs were magnificent, even to calmly treading on a thunderflash which landed at their feet. The American forces seemed completely astonished by the behaviour of the cold-blooded Englishmen really enjoying themselves. It is odd to remember that the new part of St Catharine's was then the Bull Hotel, later the self-styled 'Bull College', and was full of American forces. Lectures were suspended for three days, which must be a fairly rare occurrence. Whether this was because the lecturers wanted to celebrate, or whether they assumed no one would turn up to lectures, I am not quite sure. There was a great celebration on Parker's Piece, and the search-lights were put on and crazily swept the skies. There were no fines for being in late that night, and I think very little sleep. By contrast VJ night was very quiet. This was due partly to the fact that it was in the Long Vac Term, but mainly because the local regiment was the Cambridgeshire, which was largely lost out in Malaya I think. There was a certain macabre interest as the initial work on the A-bomb which had just been dropped in Japan had been done in the Cavendish, and everyone concerned who was still in England was very interested to see that it 'worked'.

The next special memory is of the very cold winter of 1946–7. There was frost for months and it looked superb. The trees were outlined in ice and Sidgwick Avenue was just like an illustration from a fairy-tale book. Every tree and branch sparkled in the sun and there was skating for weeks. It was very cold, and as we had only utility shoes we envied the returning R.A.F. men in their flying boots. There were no 'kinky' boots for us in those days. When the snow finally thawed it was right at the end of the Lent Term, in fact the night of the Newnham Ball, the first I think held in the College since before the war. The river rose rapidly and the partners could not get over the Silver Street bridge, but had to go round by Magdalene Bridge. There was the fascinating possibility that they would not be able to get back at all, giving rise to all sorts of speculation. However, the river had by then fallen, because it had in fact burst its banks at Ely and flooded that. Going home some days later, the train ride to Ely was on lines lapped with water, with water as far as one could see on either side. This is when food and fuel were at their lowest level. Even bread was rationed, and we got two buckets of coal a week each. Sometimes odd pieces were saved and stored in a cardboard box in the wardrobe. The Library was always reasonably warm and so quite a lot of work was done in there.

This was followed by a marvellous summer. We were swimming in the river long before the end of term which must have been in early or mid June. We were now eating in separate Halls, and exams were now in the various parts of Cambridge and not in Sidgwick Hall as in previous years. It was so hot that we took to sleeping out on the hockey field, much to the astonishment of the gardener's boy, a gentle youth who was not quite up to military service.

The arguments pro and anti allowing women full membership of the University were going on at this time. It all seemed rather a foregone conclusion to us, but it probably had its objectors at the time. It is interesting to record that I and many of my contemporaries took a B.A. 'through the post' with 'The Title of the Degree of Bachelor of Arts', but an M.A. from the hands of the Vice-Chancellor. Incidentally I took it under a different name too.

The year, and my time at College, finished with one of the May Balls almost back to pre-war glory, or so it seemed to us at the time. Eating roast swan by candlelight under a perfect carved ceiling and drifting down the river as dawn was breaking, but the fairy lights still burning in the trees, was a suitable romantic ending. The other lasting memory on a more serious note was the performance of the Bach B Minor Mass in King's Chapel. This was on a perfect summer's evening with the big west doors wide open and the swallows flying in, and the sacred grass outside with people sitting on it listening to the glorious music. We were not to appreciate the glorious glass of King's, however, until some years later when it was replaced.

M. Wood (Richardson, 1944)

AN EXCESS OF GOWNS

When I went up to Cambridge in 1945 at the supposedly mature age of twenty, I was an eager and ambitious student, like many others I imagine, and an earnest admirer of Dame Myra Curtis. It was my susceptibility to gowns (women didn't wear gowns in those days) which proved to be my weakness!

Newnham had been my Mecca for a number of war years when I slaved in a gas plant factory. Newnham! Peace! They were synonymous in my mind with freedom from England's unpleasant war demands. 1945 came at last and soon I was walking with wonder round the most beautiful buildings – St Catharine's, King's and King's College Chapel, Clare, Trinity, John's, Magdalene, and the term had begun. I had lovely lists of books and an exciting selection of lectures: Mr Rylands, Mr Rossiter (alas, now departed), Brigadier Henn, Professor Willey, Mr Tillyard with his bright blue eyes and rising nose, Dr Leavis, F. L. Lucas... Miss Welsford warned us with her diminutive finger not to go to them all – there *must* be time for reading.

And then John, a family friend also 'older' at twenty, asked me to pop round to Clare new buildings to cook breakfast on Sunday morning. Oh, the sheer massive majesty of that pale courtyard with the imposing Library background. Before I had time to settle to a work routine life was crowded with entertainment. Next Sunday, frying eggs for colourful pyjamaed figures lasted till elevenses. Elevenses turned into a party with 'Ed', an American at another college; lunch materialised at the Blue Boar. The term continued with parties on punts; dancing at the Dot; rehearsing with the Mummers – when was I to work? We had to give in our written work to Miss Welsford on Wednesdays, so often I found myself writing Monday, Monday night and Tuesday without sleep, but it was worth it. One term I went out separately with twenty-five different young men. I made a colossal mistake when I asked a select twelve of them to the Newnham dance – that night when the Backs were flooded – to meet eleven girls who had no 'contacts', for my efforts were a failure, and I felt the author of *Emma* watched me with contempt from her honoured position on the wall. But life went on at a hurtling pace. In the spring of my third year, I was baffled one week when three men separately suggested marriage. I accepted one, now an M.P., but fortunately a month later he withdrew. Only two years after leaving Cambridge did I feel ready to 'settle', and I did marry a friend from Trinity!

Many memories of Cambridge have a magical quality, perhaps the most perfect being that of standing on King's Bridge with the madrigal singers below on punts, voicing their exquisite harmonies. I also remember in 1948 standing with pride in the Senate House square while Sir Winston Churchill and General Smuts paraded round in scarlet gowns on their way to receive Honorary Degrees. Those three years are ones I will never forget: certain embarrassments still make me laugh; some triumphs still make me glow. Although I only achieved a II.2, for obvious reasons, I would like to take this opportunity of expressing my immense gratitude to Miss Curtis who allowed me in, and to Miss Welsford and Miss Burton who tutored me.

A. M. McEwen (Sackville Hamilton, 1945)

WAR AND WEATHER

The words that are in my mind, as I remember Newnham from 1945 to 1947, are War and Weather. They should, of course, be War and Peace, for ninety per cent of the undergraduates at the University were ex-servicemen and women recently demobilised, come to make peace with the world and with themselves. Newnham, although it had its share of ex Wrens, Ats, Waafs and Land Girls, had far less than this ninety per cent of older students. I was one of them and, as it took me the best part of my time to find that peace hadn't come with the ending of the war, it is 1947 that I remember most clearly.

Everywhere (along K.P., the Backs, in town and colleges, in the Whim, the Copper Kettle, the Red Lion, the British Restaurant) there were signs of the remnants of war. Men in flying jackets, seamen's boots, military top-coats, some with Merchant Navy beards, others with Army and Air Force moustaches, escorted us in our coupon-rationed garments. 'I used to work up at Newnham when I was a girl,' I heard a middle-aged woman say. 'The young ladies then had more style somehow. You could always pick them out from the town girls. Of course with coupons they can't do much in the way of dress.'

Yet I remember going to a May Ball in an evening dress made from my aunt's silk bedspread, and I wasn't dismayed at the thought. Around me were others resplendent in gowns made from old blackout material cunningly devised. In our everyday life we were short on stockings; slacks were the best investment, and because of the cold that winter, some wore bedroom slippers at breakfast; one or two had fur-lined boots they had bought in Canada when they had been evacuated there; others wore jackets of Army or Air Force battledress. For most, the tweed skirt, the twin-set and the pearls, now so despised, were the stylish standby.

The weather that year was dastardly. The wind blew across the Fens like a scythe; six-foot snowdrifts were on the outskirts of town. There were few gossiping groups of undergraduates in the streets. Some of the colleges were forced to ration coal, only allowing students to use it at night. Lecture rooms at the Arts Faculty were deserted. In Newnham, there was a small room in Fawcett where we were asked to sit together during the day, so using one gas-fire instead of several. For weeks the snow hung like crêpe mourning on the trees. Every day light powdered snowflakes covered the footfalls of the day before.

What was the earth like beneath our feet that winter? I used to ask myself that question. A student of twenty-eight, at university for the first time, separated from the age of the essay and the examination by an eight-year gap, I felt I had forgotten. For me, as for most of that ninety per cent of 'older students', there had been no path with sure-footed steps to lead us here. We had come with our own knowledge of Hiroshima and Belsen and our own individual experiences the world over, to what seemed the isolated isle of Cambridge, where we could not feel the challenge which somehow we felt it should proclaim. We had come here, battles over, voyages completed, many of us on a two-year course which gave us little time for 'being' and placed too much insistence on 'becoming'. The snow, which brought uniformity of landscape, seemed to reflect the editorial comment that 'now after a year the undergraduates have settled down into some kind of external conformity'. Indeed with sharp individuality, yet not exhibitionism, most of us were trying to discover this 'external conformity'. You might even say that many were seeking it now that uniforms no longer gave true identity.

I lived in The Pightle, a grey stone house in Newnham Walk, that looked across the Principal's garden to what was then the red-bricked front of Newnham, with its wrought-iron gate. The Pightle, like other houses in the neighbourhood, had been taken over to accommodate the overflow of students, for the town was still settled by civil servants. Cambridge was now overflowing with demobilised students, the men doubling up in rooms; some of those who had married during the war were living in villages outside, and others in what I heard described as 'tumble-down places, roofs leaking, have their babies there too. Why, in the old days, the students kept their horses in stables better than that!'

At breakfast that winter, in our different Halls at Newnham, with the windows still rigid with improvised blackout devices, as I've said, the subject was the Weather. It filled every newspaper, and those wireless programmes which had not been cut by electricity shortage. 'Worse than in our unit in North Italy,' someone would say as we queued for porridge or bacon, and coffee made with powdered milk; then we would make our way to a trolley to collect the jar of marmalade and the pot of butter ration, each with our own name on it. Because of an acute domestic shortage, recognised then with some surprise, we made our own beds and 'did' our own rooms, and other chores such as dusting the Library. Most of us took all this for granted, and it was left to an elderly domestic to comment on the 'change both in quality and mode' of Newnham living. Meals were in relays. 'More stodge' we said so often, as we examined our main meals; meat was still rationed.

As a matter of fact, the Weather was a heaven-sent standby for conversation that winter. The rigours of specialisation were building up, and the general cultural life was not yet so very rich after the years of war when the colleges had been sparse of students, and those very young indeed. The Arts Theatre and various revues had, at times, items of excellence, but the town itself was not yet back to any social shape. We even resorted to discussing the Weather at our once-a-term invitation to dine at High Table. I can also remember dons and students alike discussing clothes, with minor patronage, that were in Marks and Spencers. And, oh how dreary it sounds now, but how important then, the question of Government grants. And (can it be possible?) some of the elderly women dons telling us how different things were from their day, when they were chaperoned! 'Of course we found ways of meeting the men students. I often wonder if we didn't get more fun out of it than you all do today when it's so easy.' It was easy, I suppose, but it seemed foolish too that, after visiting an undergraduate at Christ's (who might have been a thirty-year-old ex-colonel), we had to slip out after eleven at night through a chapel door, like a member of an underground movement; write our name in a book in the Porters' Lodge at Newnham if we returned after 10.30 p.m. for a fine to be imposed; and climb over the walls of Fawcett if it was after twelve; especially since some of us had known bomb attacks from midnight until dawn.

If we were late back at The Pightle we always found a welcome awaiting us from Professor E. M. Butler, then Schröder Professor of German. She would be sitting up in bed, wearing the most feminine of bed-jackets, smoking a cigarette through a long black holder, in a room so exquisitely feminine I always thought of it as that of a movie star. And she would discuss her research into Ritual Magic. Whether in bed or riding her bicycle in town, she presented a most elegant figure, with her white hair banded with a thin black ribbon which stretched across her forehead, like a Red Indian Twiggy. It was said that the first thing she did in the morning was to scan the personal column of *The Times* for second-hand clothes, so building up an extensive wardrobe without the need for coupons.

But, at last, the unnaturally prolonged abundant snow cleared, and there came the great floods. Brown river water rushed over the fens; the meadows on the walk to Grantchester had meaning only in the sight of the roof of a cottage just above the water, crosses of telegraph poles, stumped trees that we knew were tall willows or old oaks; a swan swimming where the summer picnic had been held. The way to the lecture rooms in Silver Street was now along the Backs, for the old Silver Street bridge was under water.

Spring was more than a little late that year, and with it came Tripos. The newspapers had noted:

> It is encouraging that the ex-service students who form a high proportion of the present university population can be rightly described in the Universities Review as 'serious minded and hard working'. This opinion of them is general, and it is a happy contrast with 1919 when, although brilliant students were not few, the majority tended rather too much to live like roaring boys in the Elizabethan tradition.
>
> If anything the present students take their studies and examinations too seriously, and so subject themselves to harmful strain.

Yet we realised how much time we had spent trying to look as attractive as possible in order to get married; how much time we had spent talking about men friends. There was a strong emphasis on the importance of human relationships and making a home. Only a few Newnham girls seemed to possess an isolated intensity of application.

The week before Tripos there was a quietness over the town while lilac bowed over old walls; wallflowers like brown velvet edged the peacock-green grass; grey stone opened its crevices to the sun and revealed moss and lichen. Heavy chestnut blossoms around the Senate House; needles of grass straying across paths while ink spilled on paper in the examination rooms.

'Well, it wasn't too bad.'

'Too bad! I thought it was worse than bloody.'

Then the May Balls, dawn, tight ashcan faces, going for breakfast by punt to Grantchester or to someone's rooms.

'We must meet tomorrow otherwise we won't see each other for some time.'

Never? Going down, 1947. Some of us, most of us older students ('you have got so much more out of it than the younger ones'), feeling intruders, isolates, bound by war and not by University. The farewell cocktail parties; the eager, anxious to impress, talking as if even their voices were on a tight-rope of aphorisms which no one dare pursue, the very obscurity a mask of shyness. And the plodders who would leave and have, perhaps, their flare of brilliance, and those who even now had matured to their fullest capacity. And those who never spoke at all, and who would be remembered as part of the oak panelling of some undergraduate's rooms, or as quiet part-time gardeners amid the sunken rose-beds of Newnham. Like ourselves, the University had roused itself, stretched itself, examined itself.

We had a lot of private fun, but as graduates, especially those in the Arts, we wondered which part of the strange, odd pieces of treasure we had gathered, we could offer to a competitive, unacademic world. 'Unless you teach,' we were told, 'an Arts degree isn't very useful. You need secretarial training. Or training for industry.'

Perhaps the Newnham of 1947, as part of the University, was experiencing early a malaise which is now chronic, and which again is recognised by a leader-writer of that time:

> This queue for learning, and the recent increase in State grants and scholarships, has prompted a natural discussion whether, in any case, the universities do not need rapid expansion. That we need more universities and that certain university colleges might well take a new and extended status is indisputable. It is not simply a question of residential buildings, of libraries and lecture rooms or of staff – though all these offer practical difficulties. It is rather that our universities set out to be something more than teaching institutes. They are, above all, social entities. The present undergraduates may indeed find themselves already deprived, by force of present circumstances, of some of the most valuable factors in a corporate life.

Some of us may have agreed with this last sentiment, or explained our feeling of not having come to grips with a 'spirit of Newnham' in terms of War and Weather. We didn't, however, require newspaper editorials to tell us that 'undergraduates, male or female, who somehow find their way to the books of an overcrowded university, may rightly count themselves fortunate, remembering the disappointed thousands outside who must postpone their entrance or forgo it altogether'. In most of us, I suspect, there was somewhere an inner sense of privilege.

E. G. Capel (Hots, 1945)

*

MISS CHRYSTAL'S BLESSING

Former inhabitants of Clough Hall who knew Miss Chrystal will, without doubt, have each her own special memory of a woman who inspired in her students about equal quantities of holy terror, admiration and – on further acquaintance – affection. She regarded me with a severe eye when at the end of my first term I went to pay about eleven shillings in gate-fines, all incurred, though the 'signing-out' book discreetly concealed the fact, as a result of evening excursions with a certain young man who was, as the 'signing-in' book triumphantly pointed out, my constant and apparently my only visitor. Miss Chrystal disingenuously expressed the hope that I was making the acquaintance of a large circle of interesting people.

During the second term of that first year, I was laid low, one cold, wet afternoon, by fever and a miserable cough. I retired to bed, hoping that the certain young man would assume that my failure to arrive for tea could only be due to an emergency, such as the sky falling on Newnham. At about half past six he arrived in my room, examined me with the eye of an experienced medical student, and pronounced me unfit for Hall; he would return shortly, he said, and make me some supper. He returned in due course with his one egg (they were still rationed in 1947), and proceeded to make up my decidedly ineffective coal fire – the room was big, the grate small, and our coal ration dreadfully inadequate for the damp Cambridge winter. It was at this moment that Miss Chrystal, having learned from one of my friends that I did not seem well at lunch-time, came up to see how I was. Her appearance was awe-inspiring. Visitors were not allowed in College from tea-time until eight o'clock, when they were admitted only if their names had been signed in the book. My visitor was out of hours, unrecorded and male; I was tucked up in bed. Miss Chrystal's intelligent eye surveyed the cosy domestic scene, and she invited my nurse to step downstairs to her room.

My mind, admittedly feverish, ranged wildly among visions of expulsion, public disgrace, and official letters to the young man's Tutor, while my imagination conceived only too easily what Miss Chrystal might be saying downstairs. In ten minutes the young man returned. 'She's wonderful,' he told me. 'She gave me another egg so that we could both have one, and she lent me her egg-poacher; and she says I'm to put these logs on the fire because the room isn't nearly warm enough for an invalid. Oh yes, and she signed me in the book.' Humanity most skilfully combined with discipline – that was exactly Miss Chrystal. My nurse returned the poacher on his way out that evening. When I next saw Miss Chrystal, some two days later, she merely remarked in answer to my thanks: 'The poacher was washed up very well. I should marry that one if I were you, he's been brought up properly.' As a matter of fact, I had already decided to do so; but I was oddly glad of Miss Chrystal's approval; and we are both still grateful for her kindness.

N. S. Rinsler (Lee, 1946)

EDITH AND ENID

Miss Edith Chrystal, Tutor of Clough Hall and Vice-Principal of the College, was the first person I encountered when I came to Newnham in the spring of 1946 as a research student to read for a Ph.D. degree in English. I had taken my first degrees at the University of Cape Town, I had been a junior lecturer there for some two years before I came away, I was married, and in the easy colonial air of South Africa I had never since I left school known any constraints on my personal freedom. My astonishment and dismay may therefore be imagined when, at my first interview with this formidable-looking lady, who bore a striking resemblance to a well-known portrait of George Washington and spoke English with a strange, distinguished accent which I barely recognised as Scots, I was told that until my twenty-seventh birthday I would have something called 'B.A. status', which entailed being under 'Tutorial jurisdiction', which in turn entailed keeping, with the utmost punctiliousness, an object called a 'Nights Book'. This, it transpired, was a small ruled notebook, in which I was to enter, in straight columns, the date of each and every one of the fifty-six nights of Full Term, request my approved landlady's signature against each date as proof of my having spent the night under her roof (I was to live, I understood, in 'approved' lodgings, and cleverly inferred that the landlady must therefore also be approved), and at the end of each term I was to bring the little book, complete with all the dates and signatures, to Miss Chrystal for inspection and counter-signature. Miss Chrystal was kind, and even a little apologetic, but quite firm about the business. She understood perfectly that it might be rather a 'nuisance' to me (pronouncing the word 'nuisance' with a short, sharp snap of the diphthong which I found very fetching); but Cambridge rules were Cambridge rules, and she hoped I would get used to them before long and would mind them less as time went on.

I bore the daily signature sessions with my landlady for one week, and then rebelled. I marched with my little book to Miss Chrystal, and said: 'Miss Chrystal, I'm very sorry, but I can't, I just *can't*, do it. I can't do it *every day*. I've been having nightmares about forgetting, and I'm sure I *will* forget, and – well, it's all just too much. Wouldn't it be enough if the landlady signed just once a term – for the whole term, you know?' I saw the expression on Miss Chrystal's face, and added quickly: 'Or perhaps just once a month? Or even – 'I ended desperately, 'even just once a week?' The look I received was grim and bleak, and I was sure I would be asked to leave Cambridge the next day, thus bringing to an early end my dreams of a scholar's career. But I had underrated Miss Chrystal's flexibility, humanity, and plain common sense. In a moment her expression relaxed, she laughed in a kindly way, sighed out something about 'you research students', intimating that we were an irregular class of being – neither fish nor fowl, neither undergraduates nor dons – and that one didn't quite know what to do about us, but there it was; and as to the Nights Book, once a month would not be enough, and once a term certainly would not do, but, yes, perhaps, in the circumstances, one signature for each week of Full Term would serve. I went away pleased and relieved, and much impressed by this first proof of the British genius for compromise about which I had heard and read so much.

This, however, was not the end of our troubles with the Nights Book, or of the proofs of Miss Chrystal's resourcefulness. Some six months later my husband joined me in England, and found himself obliged to accept a research fellowship at another university. Knowing that I had to 'keep my nights', he planned to come to Cambridge most week-ends during term, and as there was no provision for a husband in my approved lodgings, we decided to spend those week-ends with various friends of his in Cambridge: he had been at Cambridge before the war, and had lots of nice friends who had repeatedly asked us to stay. But: what in that case was to be done about my Nights Book? My landlady could not conscientiously sign for nights I had not spent under her roof; and if she didn't, who would?

Again, nervously clasping my little book in my coat pocket, I confronted Miss Chrystal. She heard me out, and this time looked at me not grimly but only sadly and thoughtfully. She said: 'You know, you research students *are* rather a nuisance' (again, with the short, sharp diphthong); 'and when you're married, you're *worse*, you know.' But after a moment's thought, she had found the solution. 'I think,' she said, quietly, triumphantly, 'I think *your husband* had better sign the book for the nights you stay with your friends. Yes, your husband,' she repeated with satisfaction. 'It's never been done before so far as I know; but I suppose' – sighingly – 'if one has research students, and they're married, there's no other solution, is there?' My husband crowed with joy over the solution, signing merrily for his nights and begging me to let him sign for all the other nights as well. His friends all begged to be allowed to sign too, and I had great difficulty in saving my little book from desecration at their impious hands.

A Commonwealth research student's life in the bitter winter of 1946–7 was not an easy one. There was quite a group of South African research students at Cambridge at the time, who like myself had been waiting for the war to end to come away; and having known no serious hardships during the war years, we were unprepared for the grim discomforts of post-war England: the food rations, the fuel cuts, the cold, tomb-like bedrooms, the cold, grumpy landladies serving awful unappetising meals at long shabby tables in dreary kitchens. I learnt that winter to dress and undress in bed, to wash like a schoolboy (face and hands only, nothing else), and to scrape to the last drop my precious one-pound jar of marmalade – a habit I have compulsively retained to the present day. I think what we missed most of all was hot water; and twice a week, or only once if it was snowing hard, after lunch, I used to walk the length of the Backs from my lodgings in the Chesterton Road area to Newnham, trotting quickly against the cold (I had not yet learnt to ride a bicycle), clutching my sponge-bag and towel in a rather tatty shopping-bag, to have a marvellous boiling-hot bath in the Newnham Out-students' Cloakroom. The O.S.C., as we came to call it lovingly, became a great meeting-place for frozen female research students waiting their turn to enjoy the supreme physical luxury of the week. We were sure it was the only place in Cambridge where there was *any* hot water, and we vowed to leave huge bequests for more and more out-students' cloakrooms if we should ever become famous and rich.

In spite of the cold and the discomforts, we adored Cambridge. We loved the beauty of the snow-bound Backs, the University Library, where we spent most of our working day, the intellectual excitement of the lectures we went to (with no examinations at the end to spoil the pleasure); and, most of all perhaps, we enjoyed our own interesting, stimulating company, over long coffee breaks in the Library and at our lunch meetings at the Women Graduates' Club in Mill Lane, where at least once a week, along with husbands and male colleagues, we gathered to compare notes about our researches, our supervisors, our Tutors, our new English friends (some of whom presently became honorary members of our circle), and English life and institutions in general, which we analysed, dissected and speculated about with never-diminishing zest. We thought ourselves a rather superior group. We looked down a little on the undergraduates, who seemed to us callow and immature, and boringly anxious about their Triposes; and we were rather sorry for the younger dons we knew because they were always complaining about 'having no time for research', and indeed were seen only at sherry parties and hardly ever in the University Library, where we sat reading our heads off, growing cleverer every day.

Accordingly, the hint of reservation in the attitude of Miss Chrystal and the other Tutors to 'the research students' seemed to us misconceived, injurious to our dignity and value, and even a little tasteless; and one day, at my weekly meal in College, sitting next to Miss Chrystal at High Table and hearing her hold forth again in her teasing, provocative way about that troublesome body, the research students, who (she said) were never satisfied with their lodgings, their landladies, their supervisors, their Tutors, and so on – I decided that, now or never, she must know the truth. Putting down my knife and fork, agitated but resolute, I addressed myself to her, telling her that she was *quite wrong* about the research students. They were the flower of the student body, the cream of its intellectual life, and (running out of dead metaphors) the best thing, the very best people, in the College. Because (I went on, determined to prove my point, something I knew she hated, especially at High Table) we were obviously better than either the undergraduates or the dons. The undergraduates were silly, immature creatures compared with us; and the dons, poor things, were so taken up with teaching and College administration that they had no time for *research*, and never, never read in the University Library, not even in the Long Vacation.

(This was, of course, a polemical exaggeration, but I was in no mood to be accurate or fair.) I must have said other things as well, more confused and incoherent, but this is what I mainly remember; and this (alas) is what Miss Chrystal, too, remembered.

At the time, she only smiled faintly, murmuring something non-committal. But afterwards, for many months, she punished me over and over again, by introducing me to College guests and senior members of the University with the words: 'This is Mrs Krook, one of our research students. She is reading for a Ph.D., and' – with a smile and laugh full of kindly malice – 'she thinks research students are *the only good thing* at Cambridge. She thinks undergraduates are foolish, ignorant young things, and dons are foolish, ignorant old things, and only research students are any good at all: they're the *cream* and the *flower* of the intellectual life of the University – *isn't* that what you said, my dear?' I tried to take it with nonchalance, but never succeeded; and though I was not sorry I had said what I said because, of course, it was nothing but the truth, I did wish Miss Chrystal would more easily forget it since it had obviously done her no good whatever to know it.

The great day came, in 1948, when women were at last admitted to full membership of the University, and those wonderful, anomalous old proctorial notices, beginning 'To all Members of the University *in statu pupillari* and to Members of Girton and Newnham Colleges', disappeared for ever. Miss Chrystal was charged with the onerous task of devising a suitable costume for women graduands, who were now, for the first time, to receive their degrees in the Senate House. I remember clearly the instructions that went up on all the Newnham notice-boards before the first Degree Day, signed by Miss Chrystal, the College's first Praelector. Women graduands were to wear 'a plain, dark coat-and-skirt' (we shrieked with mirth over the 'coat-and-skirt', which we had never seen used except in pre-1914 novels), 'a plain white blouse, plain dark low-heeled shoes, dark stockings, no jewellery, and no varnish on the finger-nails'. At our first briefing, Miss Chrystal carefully explained that the 'dark' colour of the coat-and-skirt might be black, brown or grey, but ought if possible to be black; that the shoes were to be low-heeled because high heels might catch in the hem of the gown when the graduand knelt before the Vice-Chancellor, causing her to fall – forward into the Vice-Chancellor's arms or backwards into Miss Chrystal's – when she rose to her feet; and that the prohibition about varnished nails was designed to protect the Vice-Chancellor, who if he should suddenly find himself gazing down at ten bright red talons clasped between his hands, might from nervous shock forget his Latin words.

When, four years later, I was to receive my Ph.D. degree, I remembered this impressive rationale and appeared in the prescribed costume, looking impeccably plain, sober, and dowdy. But did Miss Chrystal herself? Not she. *She* under her gown was wearing an elegant black suit indeed; but, with it, a dazzling white blouse richly, elaborately frilled, ruched and ruffled, the frills and ruffles foaming daintily over the black silk ribbons of her gown; and at her throat a huge diamond brooch – round or square, I forget which, but very large and conspicuous – shooting out fires enough (I thought bitterly) to blind the Vice-Chancellor for life. I gasped at her dreadful duplicity as she beamingly led us forward to receive our degrees; and I only forgave her because she really did look so handsome in her ruffles and her diamond, and her white George Washington coiffure showing to splendid advantage against the formal black. I hadn't that year actually seen the notice about the plain dark coat-and-skirt, plain blouse etc.; but I remembered it distinctly, and when I taxed Miss Chrystal with her breach of her own sacred rules, I gasped again to hear her shruggingly disclaim all knowledge of any such 'rules' or of her alleged authorship of them. 'You must have imagined it, girl,' she said; adding that she saw no reason why *she* should look a frump on Degree Days merely because '*you girls* care nothing about your appearance'. I resolved to expose her by producing the documentary evidence whose existence she had denied. But I never succeeded in tracking down any of those first notices, and Miss Chrystal as usual had the last word.

In due course I ceased to be a research student and became a Research Fellow and a University lecturer, and Miss Chrystal became 'Edith', and a very good, devoted friend. But she never quite lost her sense of me as a researchy sort of *Luftmensch*, who had my head in the clouds, knew little of what was going on in the world about me – and nothing at all about University rules and regulations, of which she herself had an expert knowledge, and loved dearly, almost with passion.

Edith Chrystal's expert knowledge, however, was not confined to University regulations, but extended also to life. I had been asked to a small dinner party of three, on purpose to meet a distinguished old man of letters living in Cambridge. The party had been a distinct failure. The D.M.L. had made observations and expressed opinions about Henry James (who had just then entered my life) which had seemed to me foolish and perverse, and though I had said little, he must have felt what I thought, and no doubt thought me stupid and unresponsive. We had no better luck with St Paul – another of my passions at the time: he disliked St Paul and thought him a disaster for Western civilisation. I thought, and this time said, that we would all at this moment have been howling barbarians but for St Paul; and the party ended early, in an atmosphere of polite chill and disenchantment. Edith, knowing the D.M.L. and about the dinner party, asked me the next day how I had got on. I told her about Henry James and St Paul, and how bored and cross we had both been, and how our poor host (whom she also knew) had struggled to save the evening, but without success. I also mentioned that I had worn a high-collared, long-sleeved velvet dress, which I knew Edith disliked, and had felt suffocated in it, so that I had been uncomfortable as well as unhappy. Edith's expression at the end of my report was wonderful to see. 'You stupid girl!' she said, her voice full of honest revulsion. 'You *stupid* girl!' – pronouncing 'stupid' like 'nuisance', with the short, sharp diphthong, which made it sound ever so much more cutting. 'Henry James and St Paul! At a *dinner party*! Whoever *talks* about such things at a dinner party! What you should have done, you stupid girl, was to *vamp* him. You should have worn your prettiest dress, not that ugly velvet thing, and vamped him. Yes, vamped him – *vamped* him!' she repeated, her voice rising with her disgust at my stupidity.

I was too taken aback to laugh. I had never before in my life heard anyone *use* the word 'vamp'; I had only seen it in print, in the film magazines I used to pore over at the age of eleven or twelve. And who would have thought that Edith Chrystal had such *ideas*? And what an awful depraved old woman (I thought) to suppose that 'vamping' an old codger was better than talking to him about Henry James and St Paul. But I have since learnt that she was right, and have got on much better at dinner parties as a consequence; and I have rejoiced to think that, just once in my life, I actually heard someone use that funny, forgotten word. I cherish in this episode, one of several of its kind, the memory of her uninhibited common sense, her forthrightness, and her wicked, teasing Scots humour. Once one had learnt not to be afraid of them, they were among her most delightful traits.

My friendship with Enid Welsford began soon after I came to Newnham, where she was then Director of Studies in English. It started from my hearing her on Hooker, in an informal College lecture which on the spot converted me to a love of the English Moralists, and grew and flourished during a term's work with her on Plato in that same dreadful first winter of 1946–7. I remember long so-called supervisions, lasting two to three hours, in which we hammered out differences about points I can no longer exactly recall; what I do see before my mind's eye is the picture of Enid *kneeling* on the floor, with her *Republic* or whatever in her hand, staring fixedly at me and saying, 'No, Doris, I don't think you quite understand it. If you don't mind my saying so, I don't feel you *do* quite, you know.' I am sure I didn't, whatever 'it' may have been, and the mystery is only how she came to be kneeling on the floor.

If Edith Chrystal treated me as a *Luftmensch* with no sense of time and no care for the normal responsibilities of life, she took almost exactly the same view of her friend and colleague Enid Welsford, who was nearly thirty years my senior. As my friendship with Enid grew and we fell into the habit of continuing our discussions after Hall until well after midnight, it became our chief anxiety not to be 'caught' by Miss Chrystal, as we crept past her rooms on the ground floor of Clough on our way to the Kennedy outer door, through which I was to be silently precipitated into the black wintry street to hare back to my lodgings. She had caught us once: I can see her now, emerging from her bedroom just as we were passing it, an unforgettable, almost unrecognisable apparition in dressing-gown and with long white tresses hanging down to her shoulders (so *that's* what the George Washington hair-do looks like at night, I had said to myself, and told everyone about it afterwards), stopping to gaze at us, silently, accusingly, like the female ghost in *The Turn of the Screw*. We had giggled helplessly like two schoolgirls; and the next day Enid had got a tremendous dressing-down, as if she really were a schoolgirl. The life of the spirit was all very well (Edith had said to her), and she had nothing whatever against the pursuit of truth. But there was such a thing as *sleep*, and (cruelly) Enid was to remember she was no longer as young as she used to be and *needed* sleep. If we went on like that she (Enid) would ruin her health, become a nervous wreck, incapable of any useful activity – and so on, rubbing it in hard.

Enid, unrepentant, with lovely splutters of laughter, had reported it all to me, and I had taken care to keep out of Edith's way for a while – even though she had disdained so much as to mention me, evidently holding Enid (as the elder) responsible for everything, treating me as a delinquent minor who could not be held fully accountable for her actions. We were never actually caught again; but Edith somehow always knew when we had been 'at it', no doubt from the bleary, weary face Enid presented at breakfast the next morning; and (according to the reports of eyewitnesses) she used to look at her sardonically and say, 'Ah ha, Enid Welsford, I can see that your friend Doris Krook spent the evening with you again. I don't suppose it's any good asking when you went to bed.' Then with a sort of fierce Scots moan: 'You look dreadful, Enid, *dreadful.* I don't know what will come of it all.' For me, certainly, nothing but good came of it. Most of my first book came out of these intense, protracted, disapproved midnight sessions with Enid Welsford; and when I dedicated the book to her, I mentally added a sub-dedication to Edith Chrystal, whose disapproval (I fancied) perversely increased our enjoyment of our intellectual communications, making us the more determined not to stop until we had got to the end.

How right Edith Chrystal was about our having no sense of time or place once we were 'at it' was proved by an amusing episode which, luckily, she did not witness. I was by this time a Research Fellow, living in Kennedy; Henry James had replaced Plato as the man of the moment; and my talks with Enid now turned on such things as the ambiguity of *The Golden Bowl*, the absence of low life and nature (which Enid deplored) in James's world, or the refinements of the late style – which Enid thought were perhaps sometimes a shade over-refined and I thought were always just right. We had been drawn into talk over coffee in the Combination Room – I believe it was about something arising out of *The Princess Casamassima*, though I cannot remember what – and we were walking towards our respective rooms, determined to settle our differences another time as we both had pressing things to do that evening. We stopped at the foot of the small wooden staircase in Clough – not the main staircase, but the side one next to the gyp-rooms, which led directly up to Enid's rooms – just to say one last thing each and then goodnight. The time must have been about half past eight, and I noticed as we stood there groups of students passing by us, evidently on their way to the Porters' Lodge to go to their meetings, theatres, or whatever, looking at us curiously as they passed.

We each said our last thing; but, somehow, it led to another last thing, each of us feeling, as usual, that just one more sentence, one more quick, oh ever so quick, explanation of a point obviously missed by the other would really, finally, settle the matter. 'Yes, Doris, I do see your point. But, you know – I feel I haven't perhaps made *my* point quite clear. What I mean is... For instance, now... Think of what you yourself said...' I listened, feeling I understood *her* point to the last nuance, but had she quite – completely, perfectly – grasped what *I* was getting at? So we went on, standing there at the foot of the side staircase, with our faces half turned in the direction of our rooms, on the point of going, going, going, with always only that one last, conclusive, decisive thing to say. Suddenly, I sensed rather than saw, through the pores of my skin, as it were, the resumption of human movement in our immediate vicinity. I looked up from or out of the world of Henry James, and saw groups of students passing us again, from the direction of the Porters' Lodge, this time looking at us not just curiously but with distinct, definite grins on their faces. I glanced at my watch, and then said in a low, hissy voice: 'Enid, do you know what the *time* is? It's nearly a quarter to eleven – and the students are coming *back*. They *know* we've been standing here all the time – since after Hall – more than two hours – and they're grinning like horrible little hyenas.' At that moment three of the grinning hyenas passed right by us into the gyp-room, and I whispered, 'I think we'd better stop now, don't you?' Enid whispered back in stricken tones: 'A quarter to eleven! Is it *really*? Isn't it *awful*? Aren't *we* awful? Yes, do let's *go*.' And without pausing to say goodnight, we fled in the directions we had been facing for more than two hours.

I draw out of my store just one last little episode which remains in my memory as a typical expression of Enid's humour and spirit, and indeed of the whole rare, beautiful blend of energy with amity and civility in her intellectual personality. The subject this time was theological, as it almost always was in those years, and we had been at it over an extended lunch at the Women Graduates' Club in Mill Lane. It was my 'religious humanism' against her 'historic Christianity': where they overlapped and where they diverged, and how radical the divergences were, and how, being as radical as they were, they could probably never be reconciled; yet (as I seem to see it now) how the yearning for reconciliation persisted, on both sides, and how it pressed and goaded us on – to go over the ground again and still again, in case we had missed something last time, all the previous times, which we might, suddenly, miraculously, come upon this time. We had finished our lunch (as usual, in an empty dining-room), and were winding up, and had somehow come back to one of the radical divergences, which turned upon our respective attitudes to the Created Universe.

Enid was definitely not happy about my religious humanism's view of the created universe. She felt it didn't satisfactorily account for it; it didn't give it the place it ought to have in any proper scheme of things; and she suspected – she voiced her suspicion with delicacy, but she voiced it – it was because I, the author of the religious humanism, didn't perhaps take the created universe as seriously as I might and ought. She was right; and perhaps from weariness, or perhaps because I was a little nettled at being thought a philistine about the created universe even if it was true, I said, incautiously, complacently, even a trifle flippantly: 'Yes, dear Enid, I don't suppose I do take the created universe very seriously. I don't, I think, find it really interesting. It doesn't somehow kindle my imagination. I find that I'm not really concerned about it – don't, really, *care* very much about it.' At this, Enid, already standing up, seemed suddenly to square herself, becoming very stiff and erect; she thrust one foot slightly forward as if in a fencing posture (I remembered she had once been an enthusiastic fencer), and with eyes sparkling humorously and fiercely, she flashed back: 'Ah, *yes*, my dear Doris, that *is* the difference between us. *That's* it. You don't care and you're not concerned; but I must tell you that I, for my part – I – I am a *passionate partisan* of the created universe!' The picture of Enid, small and fiery, in her fighting posture, as if ready on the spot to take on single-handed the defence of the created universe, was too much for me. I laughed until the tears came, thought how wonderful she was, and could only say feebly, 'Dear darling Enid, I think the created universe ought to be very pleased and grateful.' But I meant it with all my heart, knowing the value of her passionate partisanship to those, like myself, who have had the blessed privilege of enjoying it.

D. Krook (1946)

A SEQUEL

Sequels are rarely successful. After a St Andrews B.Sc. degree, a two-year Part II course came as a shock that was both academic and social. Academic, because the 'experimental' Zoology of Cambridge started where the Victorian Natural History of St Andrews left off, and social, because hot dog and coffee 'sophistication' was suddenly – and disloyally – compared to sherry parties. Edith Chrystal, Tutor of Clough, was my godmother; all around were dons who had known me from infancy, so, more in defence of anonymity than in deference to my late mother's* fellowship of the College, I was given a brand-new room on the second, Sidgwick, floor of Fawcett. The gas-fire, divan bed, and built-in cupboards were luxury after my old room at St Andrews, but

* M. D. Haviland, Research Fellow 1919–22.

there I had the Northern Lights, and a distant view of the surf pounding the West Sands, and here there were only plane leaves and mist, and, worst of all, no friends. For there is no more hollow a fall than that between the stools of the academic years: I was too old – and too toffee-nosed – for the freshers, and my own academic year had long since made its cliques. The blandishment of societies, pinned on notice-boards, left me cold: I had tried them all, elsewhere, and made my juvenile mistakes.

I sat lonely and rather aloof (looking back on it, I might have tried harder) for three whole days, not sure where to go in the dining-room, and probably giving an impression of superiority that was rapidly and deservedly becoming undermined. The first person to speak to me was an Indian girl, a senior student whose kindness was as striking as her beauty. She knocked on my door one evening, and, immaculate in sari, drank cocoa made with the dried milk left over from my St Andrews ration, for during post-war austerity students were issued with extra cocoa, milk and sugar. There's a lesson here somewhere: she's the only 'coloured' student I remember.

From then on personalities emerge: Alicia,* the eccentric of the year, with a hair-style for each day, and mostly piled high, titupping incongruously through modern corridors in a purple, velvet-bowed bustle on the night of the Newnham Ball. She adopted me voraciously, outlining my future with pouted lips and an Edith Evans voice. She swore she would get me into the Marlowe Society, and engineered an introduction to a terribly tired young man with a gold cigarette-holder and apparently half my age, whom I met in the Whim and who eyed me scathingly before pronouncing that 'if I was lucky I might be taken on as a scene-shifter in three weeks' time'. As I was hot from being Secretary of the St Andrews Mermaid Dramatic Society, I was hardly gratified, and told Alicia so. That evening, a girl I didn't know told me bluntly and kindly that Alicia would forsake me – 'she adopts freshers and then drops them' – so I was forewarned when Alicia cut me dead, but not before her omnipresence had passed the word to the newly re-formed Queens' College Bats Society that here was a not-so-green fresher who wanted to act. Alicia may have been fickle, but she was kind-hearted.

I applied for one of the two female roles in J. B. Priestley's *I Have Been Here Before*. Two other girls were auditioned at the same time, Pauline, now a well-known journalist, and April, who wore fewer

* Author's note: all students' names are fictitious.

clothes in a Cambridge fog than one would have dreamed possible. April was defeated, and drifted, smiling vaguely, out of my life for ever, but not before she had earned with her pink cotton shifts and strapless sandals the nickname of 'Droopy Lil'. Poor dear, she was up against a gang of hard-bitten 'de-mob' Law students to whom art, nouveau or otherwise, meant nothing, and who probably dismissed her less because of acting inability than because her Veronica Lake flop of hair obscured her face. Pauline got the female lead, and I found myself a Neurotic Character with a Yorkshire accent. John, now a leading barrister, played opposite Pauline, and fell briefly and violently in love with her, so that the production was fraught with tension, especially when Pauline's verbal frankness (later to make her famous) threatened to arouse John's friends loyally on his behalf. Invariably, as the only other woman, I was called upon to mediate; the worst occasion was when an engagement ring, borrowed as a 'prop', was mislaid, and Pauline, surely for the first and last time in her admirably professional career, had histrionics behind closed curtains in our dressing-room. It consoled me slightly for the time when I went to Pauline's room to see her about a rehearsal: perched on the window-sill and surrounded by sophisticates, she managed by a look to make me feel not only a virgin but a foolish one.

Wartime St Andrews was no training ground for world-weary post-war Newnham, but I soon learned to giggle at the 'scholarship' freshers who appeared at meals with PREFECT on their blazer pockets. Newnham society in the late forties consisted of definite strata comprising Social Butterflies, Eager Beavers, Social Beyond-The-Pales, and Do-Gooders, and a sort of floating mass that tried individually to emulate the first or second, according to whether an off-the-coupon dress-length or approaching exams was uppermost in the mind.

Gradually, I found my own level, with the third-years. Who of course went down, and I had to start all over again. I couldn't – and now I believe wouldn't – keep up with the work, and was disapproved of in the Zoology Department because I appeared wearing an engagement ring: marriage was a frivolity not compatible with limited places for women. I'm afraid that that Part II class trailed me – they approved my flippancy to the extent of electing me to the Tea Club, which met for lectures by its members on the lighter side of science, but disapproved my addition of a *Punch* cartoon to the end of one of Dr Parrington's Palaeontology demonstrations. The only socially acceptable light relief from dedication to the Zoology syllabus was the Bird Club; and, possibly, music. Small wonder that my addiction to acting was frowned upon, and when I asked for leave to go sailing for a week in the Long Vac Term (an invention of the Devil that permitted Arts undergraduates to laze about in punts, while we dissected 'high' fish in a heatwave and studied every insect known to man because there wasn't time during the rest of the year) the ceiling nearly dropped out of the lab. Coming from a family, and a university, where narrowness was a sin, I came to hate my subject a year before I took my degree.

However, there were compensations in Newnham, so that twenty years on this Cambridge child is hard put to it to differentiate between the time when she watched a frog croak in the Newnham lily-pond as a small girl, and the other time when she spread wet handkerchiefs on the tiles in Fawcett to save ironing. Friends emerge. Carol, bursting into tears at breakfast: 'It's all right, dear, it's just that I was writing an essay on Strindberg until three o'clock this morning!' and the same Carol, glorious in pink gingham: 'Ducky, if Alan calls, say I'm lying down with a headache, only really I'm out with Stephen, so head him off from my room, because I won't be there...' And horrors, when the dreadful Australian Don Juan, whom I thought I'd ditched successfully in St Andrews, walked unannounced into my room long after hours, to be escorted back past the grinning Porters' Lodge, where afterwards, upon apologising, I was told: 'That's all right, we asked Miss Pybus, and she said you'd have him straight out again!' And anger, too, when I fought the editor of *Varsity* single-handed (yes, really) in my room because he had refused to alter his distorted version of my article on St Andrews. Loyalties lie deep for our first love.

Personalities emerge. Miss Pybus, Tutor of Sidgwick, was always attainable, comfortable, and, above all, down-to-earth, while managing at the same time to appear totally dissociated. When the Senior Student informed her agitatedly that a Parsee and a Hindu had been listed to share a washing cubicle, she replied briskly: 'Nonsense, dear, we can't have any of that colour-bar stupidity in Sidgwick!' (The two students were instant and firm friends.) No sartorial genius herself, her dictum on the wearing of slacks holds good today: 'Perhaps, dears, you would just look at your back views in the mirror, and then possibly put on a little jacket or something.' It was the Pye, escorted at night along the road to the main gate by a highly embarrassed student, who remarked: 'Dear me, what a lot of little birds there are in the bushes tonight...'

Fawcett is sufficiently far from the rest of the College for me to think of it as Newnham. During my two years at Cambridge my room, if never becoming as loved as the one I had had at St Andrews, at least became a valued friend. I sneaked into it briefly last year to see how the view from the window had changed with the erection of the new buildings. It was still aloof, and a bit unlived-in, a hotel room with memories the only permancence between what went before and what has happened since.

I suppose I never, quite, belonged.

Audrey Hulme [A. H. Ackroyd (Brindley, 1947)]

*

ACADEMIC DRESS

The Principal outlined proposals for academic dress which were then discussed by the meeting.

1 It was decided that the gowns should be made in the same style as those worn by the men.

2 The question of the length was discussed. It was pointed out that while the robemakers had stated that gowns should reach to two inches above the knee, the Ordinances laid down that gowns should reach to the knee. The general feeling of the meeting inclined towards the former length; the Principal said that the Ordinances would have to be followed.

3 For the sake of appearances it was thought advisable that the sleeve of the gown should be sewn up the entire length, as it would then not matter what length of sleeve was worn underneath.

4 Headgear. The official headgear would be the standard 'squares' as worn by the men, but the Principal thought that individuals could decide whether they would prefer the actual fitted cap to be hard or soft. The soft topped caps as worn in Oxford were definitely rejected. It was requested by the students that women should be allowed to wear some headgear other than squares, when wearing gowns after dark in inclement weather.

It was pointed out that 'squares' would be worn by women on the same occasions as the men, and that they would not be worn in College Chapels or at the University Sermon.

Extract from the minutes of the Joint Committee of Fellows and Students, 20 January 1948

*

THIRTEEN AND FOUR TO PAY

After the *Messiah* rehearsal, he accompanied me to where our ways parted. I did not want to say goodbye. It had been a long rehearsal, with the contraltos placed well away from the tenors; and there had been time for only a few minutes' conversation before we reached the place where I must turn right, and he must turn left. I fiddled with my bicycle while we talked. It was a busy T-junction with a high wall on one side. There was so much to discover – 'What subjects did you take?', 'Did you enjoy the rehearsal?', 'Are you going to the next one?' People and buses and bicycles passed by, ignoring us, as we ignored them. Then suddenly it was dark, and out of the greyness a voice boomed:

'Are you a member of this University?' (Oh golly, the Bulldogs!)

'Yes, I am.'

'The Proctor would like to speak to you.' (Heavens, what have I done?)

'What college?'

'Newnham.'

'And where is your gown?'

'Well, er...'

I reported, when summoned, to the Lodge at Corpus Christi, wondering if the Porter would guess that I was not a genuine 'visitor'. I was led up a wide staircase past a room from which came the sound of someone playing Chopin. It was so elegant, and here was I, gowned this time of course, furtively slinking past to the study. (What would happen? A severe reprimand? I should like to peep into the room with the piano. Well, it wasn't anything serious, was it? Anyway, it was afternoon when I set off to the rehearsal. I didn't know I should be talking until nightfall, did I? Oh, he's coming.)

'Would you like some sherry?'

'No thank you, I don't drink.'

'There is thirteen and four to pay.' And that was that. I scuttled down the stairs.

I married the tenor, and he has been well worth the 13s 4d, but I do wish I had been able to accept the sherry. I might have been invited into the room with the piano, though I am afraid the gauche undergraduate would have been very much out of place in the Proctor's drawing-room.

J. K. Bowker (Boardman, 1948)

*

'HOW DIFFICULT EDUCATION IS'

25 October 1949

I am sorry you are both so shocked by my denunciations of the history lectures. There are the good ones like Butterfield and Knowles who have something creative to say, but they are not the prescribed people for my courses. The economic historians like Habakkuk and Postan are doing active work but for the rest, modern history is pretty dead, apart from the junior lecturers such as Hinsley and Miss Behrens... This year's work needs an entirely different technique as I have found to my cost with this week's essay. Far more concentration, far less sheer absorption of books is the new demand, with the correspondingly different or more intense approach to essays. Any writing has to be taut, logical, and undecorated. I can't get away with my usual 'flow' which unfortunately *Varsity* has fully encouraged. The habit of writing to an ordered length, however little the subject matter, has become a habit which needs alertness to break. How difficult education is! As soon as I begin to learn how to write, I find that one advance is an obstacle in itself to further progress.

I had to write: 'Can you justify the assertion that all men have rights to life, liberty and the pursuit of happiness?' What I should call plunging right into the subject of The Theory of the Modern State without any mercy at all...

I have been fairly quiet and stay-at-home this past week, mainly on account of my tiresome cold, which I've been nursing beside big fires. The trouble is that staying in Newnham is hardly the same thing as constant study. By the third year we all live far more in each other's rooms. Coal difficulties and the temptations of everyone else's wirelesses make it even harder to get down to things. I have evolved such a comfortable pattern of living with unlimited books, music and conversation that time goes past far too quickly.

On Saturday and Sunday for instance I went out very little. The weather was appalling. Odd jobs, washing, seeing people on petty details, filled most of the morning. In the afternoon I prepared tea for Trev and Ris who were supposed to be coming after a rugger match but they never turned up. I have since had elaborate explanations and apologies but at the time it wasn't worth doing any work so I filled up the application for the Civil Service and read *Sons and Lovers*. I am trying to keep up a policy of detached reading. I begin this every term and collapse in the middle.

After Hall I had one hour's reading and then went to Morwenna's room to listen with Ellen to a quartet recital. We chose Morwenna's room because she had both a fire and a wireless. She, poor darling, with very different listening tastes, had to sit in silence and do her mending.

On Monday night Jean and I listened to Attlee. It's extraordinary how moral the current style of political speaking is becoming – back to the days of Gladstone almost. Also it's depressing how more and more Conservative the papers are going – *The Times*, *The Economist*, and *The Observer* as well as those which lay no claim to be impartial. Cambridge economists are all as gloomy as usual.

Looking back now it's easy to see what a change Cambridge has made in all of us. We argue and try to understand the economic measures which in our first years we would have ignored as being beyond us. Politics, too, come into conversation far more as is likely in an election year. I have had useful peeps into both camps through Elizabeth Ewins who is Secretary of the Labour Club, and Jean, College Rep. for the Conservatives. She lives in terror of the party discipline which demands of her an hour's personal canvassing round the college *every* week. She has to go to all the big meetings in order to collect her posters at the end.

31 October 1949

I am sending you a copy of this term's first *Varsity Supplement* and also my first appearance in print in the newspaper itself for this term. You can judge from all this that it has been a *Varsity* week more than anything else.

I vaguely remember telling you in my last letter about the Profile of Hugh Sykes Davies which was impending. In spite of my nervous forebodings about the interview it went off very well. En route to Sykes Davies' room I collected my photographer, hitherto quite unknown to me, from his haunt in Trinity. I should think you'll agree that his photograph is a jolly good piece of work and I was grateful to him for more than that. Sykes Davies was still taking the line of trying to escape, but became so engrossed in watching the camera gadgets that he almost forgot about being interviewed. Then, too, Geoff Marshall, the photographer, joined in the conversation, fired bright questions at Davies, and found they'd spent part of the war in the same part of Wales. All this made my job far easier. Davies got thoroughly warmed up, kept us from 6 to 7.30, drinking sherry and arguing about lectures and the university. He's a most stimulating and unorthodox person. Before we left he took us into the bathroom to see his fish swimming around in the bath. He is an ardent angler.

I have just been for a brutally frank interview with Miss Behrens. You can never hoodwink her. What can you do when somebody says 'Why don't you work, Faith?' All I can manage is to grin and say 'Because I'm lazy'. She says all the usual stuff that you have always told me, that it's the only chance, and really does affect what you do afterwards etc. She says she wouldn't know what chance I have of either getting a First or into the Civil Service because I have never done for her the kind of work which would show those higher qualities in either their presence or absence. It's quite true, for so far her subjects have always been those I've been grounded on at school and have just scamped through. At any rate her advice is, try a little more work to see what happens. I am starting to act on it this week. How long the campaign will last I don't know.

22 November 1949

Last Monday was an exhausting day for I had two supervisions with Miss Behrens, one at 12 on Peter the Great and one at 5 on Liberty. The best she could find to say for me on each occasion was that I had tackled a very difficult question. At least she was kind in a slightly pitying way and obviously thought I had tried for a change but by the end of the day I was feeling fit for a mental institution instead of a college for higher learning. This third-year work has much the stiffest beginning I can remember. Of course, that is largely my fault in choosing some of the most demanding subjects but I don't regret it. Things should get easier after the first plunge.

I visit the University Library as we are allowed to get books out in our third year. I have established good relations with a kindly man at the reception desk who is most useful in tracing the whereabouts of books I want which are missing from the shelves...

Saturday was another busy day. Jean and I spent most of the morning shopping and getting my room ready for our Pooh Party in the evening for the King's group. It was intended as a counter-blast to Brenda and Hazel's party and because we had never entertained the whole crowd of them...We divided the labour of organising, Jean arranging the readings and me the coffee. The room looked very nice with flowers, extra cushions, and a collection of everyone else's chairs. We sacrificed some of our sweet ration, bought cigarettes, had stuffed dates and preserved ginger, as well as honey, an essential at any good Pooh Party. We had an interval for coffee, sponge cake and biscuits which cost all our end-of-term points. It was great fun collecting all these special foods and arranging them. I love being extravagant on occasion. The only drawback to the evening was turning them all out at 10. As the party only began at 8.15 it meant a very short evening. The readings went very well and Michael and Ted who had never been to Pooh readings before, enjoyed them more than anyone. When our guests had gone we called in Ellen, Carol and Morwenna to eat the remains and go on reading Pooh. I went to bed in the middle of the debris.

F. M. Aitken (Morton, 1947). Extracts from letters home

MORNING

Morning on Cambridge lies like an unworn dress
Dropped on the bed by a girl who couldn't care less
Waiting for use but waiting without any hope
While she in the bathroom fumbles and swears at the soap
Later of course the girl will look charming and gay
Later of course we shall do such a lot with the day
But now she has lost the soap and her face is a mess
And morning on Cambridge lies like an unworn dress

A. L. Laski (Harris, 1949)

SIDNEYS

Yesterday evening a television programme featured songs that we sang along the corridors during my first year at Newnham, 1952, and today came an impassioned plea for a description of what it was like to be a student twenty years ago. The coincidence has made me write this.

Although it seems only a short time ago there have been changes. At my first J.C.R. meeting we decided to eat margarine at breakfast, butter at tea, and be issued with half our week's butter ration after lunch every Saturday.

Our rooms were heated with coal fires. To help them to burn the College provided what in Peile we called 'Sidneys', one to each floor. These were square pieces of metal with a handle on one side which were put in front of the fire to improve the draught. When the fire was burning well the Sidney was put outside the door for the next user. In other ways we had too many draughts and used our gowns to stop those coming under the door. In April, when we were carefree and gadabout, the weather was always warm and we saved our ration of coal in cardboard boxes hidden under piles of oddments locked in the cupboard. Every year on May 1st the housekeeper found every last lump and took it away until October, so that when the weather turned cold as exams drew near we shivered as we sat revising. Nothing ever happened about our illegal bottles of sherry that were very carelessly concealed.

We could only cook on the two communal gas-rings in each common stock. Although meat could only be bought by presenting a ration book we still managed to give dinner parties. As these always needed more than two gas-rings the preparations involved a great deal of running up and down stairs.

In 1954 we moved into the post-war era by buying a wringer for the drying-room, paid for by a subscription of threepence per term for three years from each student in Peile. Washing was a problem as we wore calf-length full skirts over the same length full petticoats, which became very muddy. The first A-line dress caused a stir, especially as it was worn by a girl with pink hair. There were three irons in the drying-room for all these skirts; one old penny gave twenty minutes' ironing time. It was not surprising that there was an unofficial uniform of black trousers and white polo-necked sweater covered by a duffle coat.

I hope that someone else will write a description of our intellectual pursuits. During my student days the Raleigh Society flourished although the Chess Club foundered. Most of the time, however, we were a frivolous set of students, even the one who found a block of ice in her pigeon-hole on St Valentine's morning, and so I have only written of the trivial side of life in Newnham while I was a student.

V. M. Middleton (Palmer, 1952)

HIGH MORAL TONE

At the university, my mother said, you will meet really intelligent people. This apocalyptic was supposed to palliate my irritations with playmates, classmates, school examiners and school-teachers, none of whom gave any evidence of being Homo Sapiens. I suppose it was not very sapient of me to look for anything better in a nice, expensive and very religious girls' boarding-school where happily for my sanity I didn't board, but the day started with the imposition of silence at 8.50 and ended, still in silence, at four. Stimulating conversation and the intelligent exchange of thought were not likely to arise under these circumstances. The regime made extroverts become giggling silly, and introverts sullen – that was worse, they would rather you were naughty than sullen. 'Joan,' one perturbed teacher rebuked me, 'I never know what you are thinking.'

I continued not to tell them what I was thinking, survived (some didn't and had breakdowns, then, or later, at college) and passed the necessary exams to secure my release to a Better Place: at college, my mother kept assuring me, it would be quite different. So I stuck at it: I never saw the roses in June, I was always cross-eyed trying to remember irregular verbs. It *was* quite different at Newnham. There, with exams in May, you went up straight after Easter before the cuckoo, and missed the cowslips.

No one at Cambridge seemed to mind about cowslips. The countryside wasn't fashionable. Since people, even at home, did not at that time have two cars in the garage as a matter of course, they were not in the habit of going out, and of course no one would have dreamt of walking. It didn't occur to them to cycle out either, though we were all most proficient on the machine – had to be, as lectures were all over the place and the only way to get from one to the other in time was on wheels. We prided ourselves on being able to put up a skilled performance in all weathers – snow was most exciting, it blinded you, and strong winds came a good second. There is a stretch of the main road west of Newnham, perfectly flat, where I reckoned, if the wind lay in the right direction, I could travel a quarter of a mile without pedalling. I used to try it on Sunday mornings. In the exam term I walked to Grantchester Meadows every evening; the ducks came to expect me (biscuits). The man working in the allotment gardens beside the path, who watered his produce every night with two buckets from the river, after about three weeks actually nodded to me. His was the only acquaintance I made in Cambridge, and we never spoke.

I had chosen Cambridge in preference to Oxford because the stonework was less heavy and more golden, and the willows quite ancient and miraculous – budding in spring and shimmering in the breeze in summer, and a bit Chinese when bare in winter. At the corner where the river turns sharply into the meadow you can see the Burning Bush, around sunset when the fiery colours in the sky get reflected by the water up on to the grey trunks of the willows that bend over the water there. When the wind ripples the water the red reflections ripple over the smoky grey bark, and the tree burns but is not consumed. It is unpaintable: I know, I tried. But I could find no one to walk there and look with me then. Walking wasn't fashionable. A young dog-collar sympathetically stopped his car in a downpour once to offer me a lift back: I explained I was walking and he looked as if someone had just demonstrated that Exodus was a nineteenth-century forgery, and drove off.

It was in respect of dog-collars that I made my first howler. All clergymen who appeared at school were either governors or much-approved-of parents come to preach at Sunday service. One was expected upon meeting them to give them a nice smile, on behalf of the school. The first innocent Cambridge Divinity student to encounter my now automatic nice smile for dog-collars reeled and fled, as if he were certain I was after his virtue. Should they have built Ridley next Newnham?

But it wasn't only in this matter that I had been misled about university. It wasn't Paradise, as advertised – though it took some time before this sad conclusion began to take hold of me; about forty-eight hours, actually. My mother escaped from a Victorian upbringing where you went to church in white kid gloves on Sundays and daughters stayed home till marriage, to a redbrick where she was to read Horticulture – a 'nice' subject for girls. On arrival, the feast of reason – and the intellectual excitement of the early thirties – went to her head. She changed to Geology, and married her free-thinking lecturer from Ulster. She was far gone with me when the Vice-Chancellor gave her her M.A. Her friends said that the degree was consequently conferred upon me also and that I was born academic. I never had a chance to be anything else. Naturally, my mother held up college to me as a kind of promised land where one entered into enlightenment, and one's life up till that point – school etc. – was just a kind of embryonic darkness. So the first night in Peile I felt as doubtless the Blessed feel having at last got in through the pearly gates, suffused with a warm glow of righteousness, all things being made perfect and all weariness dropping from them, and starting to pluck harp-strings frenetically while waiting for the milk and honey to flow. Harps twanged in me all night, I couldn't lie still for them, I was warm from top to toe with an actual physical excitement: I'd got there. I never slept that night.

Forty-eight hours, and the *next* night, now *very* tired, I found the imperfections. First, the fanlight above the door that permitted the corridor bulb to beam right in my face (shades of Soviet brainwashing of which we heard rather far too much those days, shuddering; not a comfortable thought to go to sleep with). I hung a towel over it; later, I substituted a coloured map of the Highlands (more decorative, lots of nice browns).

Add the cold. Autumn 1954 started with a cold snap. To wit, the water in the cup on my window-sill froze. It was weeks before I learned to operate my gas-fire sufficiently well to produce a flame more than half an inch high. Sitting on the hearth-rug I could see the steam of my own breath. I went to bed in flannelette pyjamas, a jersey, bedsocks and a dressing-gown, with two hot water bottles, six blankets and two eider-downs. I was still cold. Probably the weight of bedding impeded my circulation, but reason omitted to suggest this at the time.

Finally, the noises off. Even when summer – in time – arrived, I had to sleep with all my windows stuffily closed to keep out the awful din of all the college clocks, which otherwise numbered out my sleepless hours all night. At certain times there were other noises. More regular even than the clocks, at 9.58 p.m. precisely the door next mine opened, there were tender whispers and then the headlong clatter of heavy male shoes on the wooden stairs as the fiancé made it to the Porters' Lodge by ten o'clock – else had they both been ruined. He always did make it, everyone did, so high was our moral tone those days. Nobody offended – nobody got sent down except once (I don't know who she was, her name was only mentioned in whispers and soon forgotten). There was one more unbearable noise and that was the pianist downstairs. I admire anyone with the patience to practise the same passage in the same part of the same piece by Beethoven day after day after day, all day – but not when I'm trying to revise. When maddened thumps on the floor failed to affect her, I retaliated by taking out my very decrepit, cheap and second-hand fiddle, and drowning her with Bach, out of tune, for hours.

I was always out of tune, partly through a happy inexactitude which is natural to me, but mostly because the peg of my bottom string, being defective, always slipped and came to rest flat, whilst the adjustment of my top string was jammed altogether. Eventually someone heard me practising and amiably told me to come along to the Raleigh Society, where I sat it out at the back of the seconds, still out of tune but less happy about it. However, I can boast that I never spoiled an actual performance because on these full-dress occasions I was always so nervous that my bow missed the string altogether – or once, in the Brandenburgs for which the orchestra had rehearsed the accompaniments only and not run through it all with the soloists before the performance, the sound of a solo trumpet coming in suddenly and gloriously right behind me so took me by surprise I stopped to listen, lost my place in the score and never found it again.

I don't know his name who played it: I never knew any of their names;

that was the trouble with Cambridge – you found yourself under the same roof with lots of people, but you never got to know any of them – not unless you had the nerve to push in, and I hadn't. One didn't. The snobbery was absolute – as if they felt now was the last chance to re-establish things as things ought to be and as life had been before the war – now, or bust. Like all last-ditch movements it was narrow – strict and clannish, and demanded an abolute conformity if you wanted to join it at all. We sat that first evening lined up along the pale polished wooden table – eating cold meat, tired lettuce and beetroot served with sliced raw onions and too much vinegar, a recurrent depressing meal I grew to hate, but it was so soon after the war (ten years!) that we didn't look for better or think ourselves underprivileged when it left us still hungry. Nobody ate their soup the wrong way. Nobody helped themselves to the cruet: it was passed you or you went without. We inquired of each other, in quiet drawing-room tones and with no great interest, where we came from. The question was superfluous because the answer was always either Cheltenham or you would have been forgiven if you thought it must be. 'My referee,' said one young lady, discussing entrance requirements, 'was the Archbishop of Canterbury. The form said,' she explained in just the right off-hand tone, 'a doctor or a clergyman, so I just popped along and asked him.' She was immediately made student rep. for our year.

They all spoke the same B.B.C. Oxford. They all dressed the same – tweed skirts in quiet colours, four inches below the knee and full; in summer, cotton, cut circular and worn over several petticoats – the aim apparently being a complete concealment of the female contour below the waist. No trousers, ever, though they did creep in later on. Plastic covers over the back wheel of the bike prevented the skirts becoming entangled. It was also necessary to be careful of one's precious, expensive and fairly recently introduced nylons. One girl, knocked off her bike outside – of all humiliations – Woolworths (a shop for the lower orders), told the policeman who bent anxiously over her that she was unhurt but her nylons were damaged. He wrote this down in his notebook as if it entitled her to claim compensation against the motorist. Above the waist, bosoms were as large as you could make them and covered in cashmere twin-sets. You wore lipstick – bright red – and pearls. And your hair – mousy, because tinting had not come in (except for one ash-blonde who coloured hers pink, laboriously in the common room every other week or so, with a toothbrush) – was worn just above shoulder-length and frizzled round the bottom with a perm like the Queen had.

I wouldn't have been seen dead looking like her, so I wore mine straight and greasy, with two hair-clips at the sides – and, in the day-time I wore ankle-socks. No one else did except an American on a visiting studentship, and she dropped it after her first year. I don't know what she felt about the Queen, but to everyone else the throne was something like the true name of Jehovah that couldn't be mentioned because of the overwhelming reverence it aroused in one's breast. The Coronation was only just past and the glory hadn't faded from the earth. Everyone had answered questions in their A levels on the place of the monarchy in British life. I thought the sooner it didn't have a place any more the better because it was being so overworked and overdone, and the kindest thing to do with modern royalty was to shoot the lot and put them out of their misery. But I'd have been keel-hauled if I'd said so.

For evening occasions, you even dressed like her: it had to be long, full, heavy, and silk, and must come from London. A slight problem was posed, if you were the social type, by the rule that you could not go out with the same boy-friend twice in the same dress. You got round this by adapting the dress. Magic could be worked with separates, or with net overskirts adding yet a further layer upon the piled petticoats beneath. But the problem was not a common one, because we didn't go out with the young gentlemen very much. One of the things my mother had impressed upon me was the importance of selecting, as a marriage partner, a person of similar I.Q. and academic attainment to oneself. Such, she said, one found at college. But college was now no longer a marriage bureau and romances were rare. The engaged third-year next door to me was an exception. Only two of my year, to my knowledge, got fixed up. One was an actress (which explained all) and the other was marrying a top-line editor, which was so obviously a good match that it just *had* to go through.

I did get taken to the A.D.C., and to eat beforehand and take coffee after in the places one was supposed to get taken to; but the boys who took me were the sons of friends of the family that I knew already. We made tediously polite conversation and rarely felt that we needed to repeat the invitation. Girls, if they felt it incumbent on them, repaid dinner and theatre with tea in Newnham gardens – or crumpets by the fire in winter – this was even more tedious because there wasn't anything to watch.

All casual acquaintance was out. There was one Newnham student who came from parts of London we didn't know and had a face that would be glorious to paint – or for the stage (every feature twice as large as life and vulgarly flamboyant – or flamboyantly vulgar) – chain-smoked in the common room, combed her waist-long hair like the gypsy in the song and lived on buns and instant coffee. She was wonderful. I longed to draw her but didn't dare ask – she came in one lunch-time in our first week having been accosted by a young gentleman in a college blazer who took her off to eat tea-cakes. 'It's all right, isn't it,' she said, 'if they're undergraduates.' We thought not; an introduction was essential. (Yet this was 1954. I told you our moral tone was very high!) Actually we appeared, under our nice cashmeres, to be quite passionless. Boy-friends didn't feature in our conversation. (The only one that ever knocked at my door unasked I sent packing because he looked like my uncle. Not that I have anything particular against uncles, but one doesn't marry them, does one?)

In fact our conversation featured very little of anything. The feast of reason of which my mother had spoken was gone. Politics, for a start, were out. There was one general election whilst we were up; we might as well have been in our cradles for all the notice we took. Those old enough voted Tory without a second thought, with occasional Liberals. You were, of course, canvassed by the parties on coming up, but only to buck up their subscriptions so that they might hold even grander annual dinners, which was all they existed for; there was no campaigning. Even the Labour Party had forgotten its crusade. There weren't any starry-eyed socialists still around to preach the cause of the invisible masses. I went to one meeting only, it was dry as dust and the members quite unashamedly curled up in armchairs and went to sleep. The Labour membership was minute, and very apologetic. When they came canvassing to my door they entered droopily dispirited saying they begged my pardon for disturbing me etc., etc., but they didn't suppose I wanted to join...; and fell on my neck in astonishment when I said yes I did.

There were, of course, Communists about – somewhere. One was warned against them by a Labour Party circular. They were infiltrators, all very underground at that time. One girl said she was a Communist, but we didn't believe her, she just couldn't be. We even felt a frisson of treason while we watched the Bolshoi ballet on television. And that was before Hungary. Hungary was awful. For once, we found ourselves bothering to read the newspapers attentively (instead of merely queueing up for the gossip column in the *Express* to see the latest French gossip re the royal family). And as we read, appalled, the Government took the opportunity, whilst everyone was looking the other way, to walk into Egypt.

We were taken completely by surprise. I went up to the common room one morning (yes, to read about royalty in the *Express* – republicans need to know the facts, don't they?) and found the radio on and a ring of solemn faces. The British troops, it was telling us, had landed in Suez. We were shattered. We had been taught, since our infancy in air-raid shelters, that the objective of British foreign policy was peace, that aggression was the iniquitous prerogative of the Soviets, and up till that minute we had believed it. (How awfully good we were at believing in things.)

There were no demonstrations, no incidents, nobody got arrested or even sat down. We assembled in perfect order and with great dignity, on Parker's Piece, where we stood in awful silence whilst somebody on a soapbox in level tones spelled out to us the iniquity of the Government. There were hundreds and hundreds of us – I don't know how we got there, how we knew where to go or when. It was a little foggy which gave an eeriness to the scene, a coming and going look, now here now not, like an old grey film that animates history for a moment but you know will disappear in a moment again. In this scene in my memory I see no policemen. Nor television cameras, nor press. Afterwards, we all signed petitions which were later with no publicity at all presented to Downing Street. The Government pulled out of Suez. If we had been less green in politics we might have realized this was more due to back-room machinations in the House, the drawing-rooms and the embassies; but we believed the battle honours were ours, and turned back to gazing with horror once more upon Hungary.

Young men packed and disappeared to fight for democracy. Their Tutors got terribly worried and telephoned consuls and things. But I wasn't quite happy about what they might turn out to have been fighting for. The choice was a stark one between the Russian tanks and the alternative to Communism, which was a class-structured society. In England class was a harmless if obnoxious survival, but in Eastern Europe it meant almost back to the Tsars. It meant the return of the middle-class families with money, sort of Balkan Forsytes, who would without compunction reassert their old stranglehold upon the economy of the country. My belief survived that socialism in any form, however perverted, was preferable to *that*. And if Aristotle preached otherwise, well, I didn't think him particularly relevant – and did Budapest? Really it seemed wiser to send bandages than soldier-boys, so I gave all the money I could save.

That was the only time anyone came to one's door – if they wanted something. Except for the S.C.M. They determinedly befriended people; especially people outside the fold, which I was in all ways, not only religious. They asked me to tea, two of them, and a jolly good tea it was, and I ignored all the leading remarks in their conversation until I had finished it all up, and then I fielded the next ball, as if it had suddenly dawned on me what it was they wanted to talk about, and played it back to them. I gave them St Augustine hot and strong. Did they not know the number of the elect was very small and predetermined and what made them imagine they were included in it? By what right did they presume to limit God's right to damn as many people as he felt like damning, like for instance me and how about them? They said very nicely that they found that they and I didn't think quite along the same lines and shut the door quick, and I went away and laughed diabolically, full of their chocolate cake and cucumber sandwiches. Cambridge I am afraid is a place that goads one into wanting to take beastly revenges.

Oddly, religion was talked about at table. At Sunday lunch. Everyone, it seemed, bar me, went to church, and over the roast were recounted the sermons that had been preached in the various churches and chapels that morning. Mervyn Stockwood, of course, was the tops. But it would be wrong to say we discussed religion. The content of a sermon was evaluated on its helpfulness, or edifying effect: nobody stopped to ask if its contentions were valid. Such discussion that wasn't discussion was little satisfaction to me, having been brought up an agnostic. I found only one person with whom to discuss more deeply – and that wasn't discussion either because it consisted of me, the flood-gates opened, pouring out my deviationary views on everything (except the royal family) whilst she – bless her, she saved my sanity – listened and neither interrupted nor argued. She was a quiet soul who wrote poems.

Which was brave of her, because one didn't, not then. There was no outlet at Cambridge at all for normal, average creative activities. You weren't *supposed* to play, unless you were a terribly good performer. You shouldn't paint, unless you could rival Stanley Spencer. All poetry must be like T. S. Eliot and novels like E. M. Forster's. If you didn't like Eliot and Forster bored you to tears then you were beyond the pale. I dared not show anyone the poems I wrote and very fortunately I have now lost them. I hated nice novels, and only read fairy stories. Tolkien came out when I was up. No one read him. He published two volumes – and then kept me waiting nearly two years for the third, in a great sweat because the end of Volume Two leaves our hero bundled up in a dungeon. But I couldn't have explained *why* I liked Tolkien better than Eliot – but maybe people know why now.

One supervisor asked us once in alarm didn't we even discuss our work? We had to disappoint her. One didn't. Work, like the blitz, was a thing to be endured, with a stiff upper lip and perhaps a joke now and then. Nobody – except perhaps the acolytes of Leavis in the English faculty – appeared to enjoy their studies. Certainly Historians didn't. Lecturers realized this and kept their audiences by the comic style of their delivery, not by the quality of their subject-matter. I went to one who did lecture straight – he drew in an audience averaging about six. He gave his lectures in the old Anatomy theatre, which is like a Greek amphitheatre, the seats rising up from a central well. We all sat, each separately, around the top and the poor lecturer bellowed economic statistics at us from down below. He begged us to come nearer down but we wouldn't. The next term he took a smaller room. I stopped going – somehow the atmosphere was lost. The only other small lecture I went to was an obscure Special Subject which drew about twenty, all male and held in the college of the lecturer who taught it and probably most of them came from there. He looked at me as if I ought not to have been allowed to get in and started every lecture with the word 'Gentlemen', although I always sat in the front row in a bright red coat. I dropped my blotting-paper once – I swear not on purpose. He looked the other way as he picked it up and handed it to me.

Cambridge had still not crawled out of the Middle Ages. You still needed Latin to get in – not that you used it, or Greek either, once you were there. Everything was in translations, and I don't think many people read them either. They bought the texts, thinking they would need them, found the lecturers who knew we didn't read books and précised everything in the texts for us, to be sure we got it clear in our heads and passed our exams – and so the books were passed on, clean and almost unopened, from Historians, who did Aristotle in year one, to the English faculty, who did him in year two, and to the Scientists who did him in year I'm not sure what (because intercommunion between the Arts and Science faculties did not exist). That any Arts student should want to leap the divide and take an interest in Science was absurd. Which is why, when a comet appeared in the northern sky, the Scientists all got to see it through the telescope, lucky beasts. Whilst I had to crawl about Peile's attic with a torch that kept showing me huge and terrifying spiders, in order to find a skylight high enough to see the horizon over the top of the cherry tree outside. Scientists, on the other hand, were thought culturally deficient, and wooed to come over to our side – with Aristotle!

To study Aristotle is not mediaeval, but to consider him gospel is. Especially as I am convinced he didn't mean it all seriously anyhow. There is too strong a streak of humour showing through. The nearest equivalent today to Aristotle is Parkinson's Law. Aristotle has a very strong and provocative personality, like a good television interviewer you find yourself itching to disagree with from the very first sentence. But at Cambridge the critical faculty was dead. Lecturers told us what Aristotle meant; we wrote it down and learned it. The whole thing resolved itself into no more than a comprehension and précis act, like school.

So much for college consisting of intelligent companions and the stimulating exchange of thought. The silence at Newnham was more dreadful than the silence at school because it was not imposed, it grew out of the conditions. Days often passed when I did not exchange even a good morning with anyone. When you get to this point it is the choice between the gas-fire and burying yourself in an obsession. I chose obsession – after all that is revocable. I decided I was up there to read History and read History I would. Read and read and read. But not to much purpose. The more you read within the syllabus the more you wondered if your lecturers had really got it right – and to sow doubt in the mind of the candidate for a degree is fatal. So I developed obscure interests outside of the syllabus. I did a strong line in the religio-constitutional implications of *Hamlet*. There are obscure German papers written on this subject, and I had many mad ideas of my own. But Cambridge doesn't cater for obscure interests, except the University Library, which can rise to anything – even an earthquake, once. The tremors, two lots, one at night, made the ground shift and slide beneath us as if the foundations were set on the apex of a jelly-mould. The deafening crash of tiling coming off the roof broke in on the utter scholastic hush in the Reading Room. We raised our eyes for a moment upwards, then returned them to our books. Nobody made any comment, we didn't even exchange glances. When I inquired about the possibility of a research grant after my degree, they said yes, but they chose the subject, and it wasn't about people, as I wanted history to be.

Because actually there were a lot of interesting people to be found in history. Some of our Anglo-Saxon forebears gnawing bones in wooden huts had I.Q.s of 140 plus, and it quite stretches the mind to read them. And if they become a bit stodgy and Teutonic from time to time, it is refreshing to have recourse to the chroniclers. Their I.Q. is less but they are more amusing. There is a dear little German bishop called Luitprand who sweetly believed the best way to deal with the immodest conduct of his contemporaries was to record it in detail for the titillation of posterity. I doubt he'll ever go out of print. These intelligent ghosts became so much more interesting than the Cheltenham mouseheads that I soon came to prefer them. And I soon came to be quite unable to write essays any more. The people became too real to me. If you are obsessed with the colour of Napoleon's hair and his gorgeous eyes, how can you detach your mind sufficiently to produce three succinct pages to the effect that the causes of the French Revolution were *a*, *b*, *c* and more especially *d*? There was always so very much more to be said about everything and which I wanted to think about first.

It never seemed to occur to lecturers that one might want to query the interpretations they offered us or debate the conclusions they arrived at. Perhaps they had reason. It would have saved time not to. After much cogitation and exploration of side-alleys I usually came to agree with what they had said, but I did like to arrive at conclusions in my own way and taking my time about it. It usually took me about a week to agree with anybody. By that time they had passed on to something else. Cambridge had no patience for that kind of behaviour.

To give credit where it is due, my supervisor tried very hard with me. 'I am using, you notice,' she announced, 'the Socratic Method. I ask you a series of questions which must inevitably lead you to the conclusion.' Well, a good Q.C. does that – but it doesn't mean that he arrives at the truth by it or even wants to. It is terribly easy to design questions that will lead to a preconceived conclusion. But I didn't take to being programmed like a computer, so I sat staring into the fire and didn't answer those Socratic questions even when I knew she knew I knew what the answer was that she wanted me to give; and she sat the other side of the fire quivering with the repressed desire to clonk me one – I am sure it is chalked up to her quite immortal credit that she never did so.

There was another approach to history current then, which was the Wedgwood school, saying you should describe the feeling in the air at the time rather than the events themselves. My other supervisor pushed that one. But I didn't quite go that either. It seemed to me the poor chap getting guillotined wasn't awfully concerned with the climate of opinion at the time – only with whether it would hurt much. History really for me resolves itself into the human spirit somehow surviving series upon series of awful events. It is essentially heroic. Unhappily for me, this view of history went out with Thucydides. It has no place in the universities today.

So I came to the end of my three years very ready to go down. One term, I forget which, there was a rail strike on. We all usually sent our trunks by rail, not having parental cars to transport them. So it was necessary to go and negotiate with the road carriers this time. I had to cycle across the housing estates to get there. Everywhere I saw men. They stood at garden gates, not doing anything, not talking, not actually looking at you, but the whole air could feel their anger. I flew past in a panic, but when I got back I found the terror had sown respect. I think that was the only one real piece of education I got at Cambridge. They didn't need Aristotle to tell them how the world went. *And* they knew about tanks.

I got a II.2, didn't get a research grant and went off into a job. I think my subconscious had been plotting that all along, otherwise why should my conscious mind have gone suddenly and completely blank at paragraph two of the all-important essay paper and not recovered until too late? I now wash endless nappies and eat chips in a council house, and I don't want it any different. I keep very quiet about that B.A. and those few friends that do know of it are kind enough to overlook it. I hope my children will not want to follow in academic footsteps. I want them to enjoy the world – Cambridge is only for people who want to make it to somewhere, fast, and haven't time to stop and look at things on the way.

I am sure now there were others at Newnham as miserable as me. Now and again people were found with their heads by the gas-fire. Mystified Tutors would say, 'She never gave any indication that anything was worrying her.' Well she wouldn't, would she? Like surgical operations, miseries are fun to relate in all their detail afterwards, but you don't expect a running commentary at the time. Just be thankful today's generation of students didn't have to do Latin, were never taught that a Stoic is superior to an Epicurean, and let you know, very articulately, what is biting *them.*

J. MacNaughton (Ingold, 1954)

*

MEN IN HALL

Nowadays male visitors in Hall must be a commonplace sight, but in 1956 trousers were never seen there in the evening, except possibly on High Table, where the occurrence was rare enough to provoke a self-conscious blush from the wearer and speculative grins from the 'hai pollai' in the body of the Hall. One day, however, some years before it reached the continent of Africa, the wind of change blew through Clough Hall.

It happened that the Senior Student of Clough and her fiancé were invited to lunch by our Tutor, Miss Morris. The conversation touched on the subject of guests, and Miss Morris remarked casually, 'You know you can invite men into Hall, if you want to?' Stunned silence. Men? In Hall?? Certainly they didn't know; nor did any of us. It is doubtful whether we would have thought of testing a beautiful friendship with Brown Windsor soup, even if we had found any takers. A plot was hatched, however, into which Miss Morris entered gleefully. Four of us were to invite male guests in to dinner one night, guarding the secret carefully.

All went smoothly. Each of us produced a young man carefully selected for his *sang froid* and resilience. As the echoes of the gong died away and we walked into the dining-hall there was an audible gasp, necks craned, eyes bulged. There was no unisex in those days; these interlopers were unmistakably *men*, and some sort of retribution was plainly expected. None came, of course. We sat down and ate soup, then fish, with studied nonchalance. The men played their parts beautifully. 'Why didn't you bring Keith?' 'Oh, I'd never have got him sobered up in time!' Not a word was lost on the rather pi element up the other end of the table.

I don't remember the incident being repeated that year, but it may possibly have set the ball rolling...

S. R. I. Babbage (Gaselee, 1953)

*

AN AMBIANCE OF PEACE

There must be many a man like me, working the world, who remembers Newnham with nostalgia. Whether he fetched his wife from there, like me; or sat an afternoon or two at an upper window savouring the chink of china, the shadows of trees on summer grass, and the blend of polish, powder, books and butter that infuses the Halls.

Every time the heavy door swung to behind me and I put my hand to the broad, smooth banister I felt that I was breathing in an atmosphere of gentle sense and providence, of practicality and charm. Acute intelligence and femininity combined, I felt, as I had always hoped they did, and made an ambiance of peace. The strength and wisdom of those pioneers of women's education who made them seemed caught in the solid walls, from which emanated, also, the humanity and earthy goodness that must be needed to create a hive and haven.

And the faces of the girls I passed as I creaked up the stairs or echoed down the corridors looked upon me with the same admixture of good humour, intellect and health. This particular expression or deportment lasts through life, I think, for I have rightly guessed that many women whom I have met since then were Newnhamites. They seem so calm and yet alive, at ease and still alert.

But it was at tea, in one of those high-ceilinged, simple rooms that I felt most strongly the most haunting mixture of the relaxation and the enlivening. There was scholarly debate which did not exclude the homely things, and kindness which did not indulge. Talk flowed as easily as tea and even had the same flavour as it. Stimulating yet domestic. A poem could be read, a hypothesis propounded, myth retold, or erudition shared without the heat or vanity that men sometimes brew up between them. The chill dark of winter and the yellow dusk of summer welcomed further any visitor.

Always I let go reluctantly that loose brass outside door-knob to go away, because I knew there was nowhere else like this. There seemed a presence dwelling there, created by the living and the dead, the living ever changing yet the presence still the same, informing and being informed by the endless chain of people who reside and then depart. The identity they give and take I always felt among the crumpets and the cups, a subtle distillation of the virtues never to be described and never to be forgotten.

N. J. R. Crompton (St John's, 1958)

FEATURES OF COLLEGE LIFE

When, from as far away as Ceylon, I had to decide between coming up to Newnham to read for the Tripos with, as it then seemed, little or no prospects for research, or working for a post-graduate degree elsewhere,

I decided to come up, on the advice of those who thought that I would benefit from College life.

I did question myself about the wisdom of my choice, when during my first term I had to face the solitude and loneliness of life in digs, in addition to the inhospitable climate and uninteresting food. But soon, through the understanding of my Tutor, I moved into a pleasant room in College. Living in certainly made a great difference. I began to meet more students and became acquainted with those typically Cambridge (so I am told) coffee parties, which went on for hours and hours and at which the subjects of conversation ranged widely – from comments on weather and modes of dress to discussions on art, music, literature and theatre, or arguments on the merits and demerits of nuclear disarmament and the racial policies of different nations. My unacquaintance with the Western arts, as also the obscurity of my subject, often made me only an appreciative listener, but I find that even in such a case the discussions prove greatly beneficial, in that they make one aware of one's lack of knowledge, stimulate interest and prompt further reading.

The individual attention which each student gets at College by being placed under a Tutor who looks after her personal welfare and comfort, and makes persuasive requests to bring up one's problems should any arise, and a Director of Studies who acts as a guardian angel over one's academic interest, recommends and arranges for more supervisions or cancels superfluous ones, who suggests more hours of study or makes encouraging remarks if prospects are good; the opportunity for association, advice and guidance from senior members of the College; the influence of the established traditions of the institution which spur the students to identify themselves with them, the educational atmosphere and all the facilities made available to develop one's talents and interests, are some of the features of College life which impressed me, in addition to its bringing together young people of different ideas and interests.

M. R. M. Handurukande (1957). From the Roll *Letter*, 1960

THE KITCHEN SUGGESTIONS BOOK

The Newnham hockey team was not a serious group of people anxious to play seriously, it was a light-hearted team of unwilling players who liked to spend an afternoon running around a field and enjoy a match tea afterwards. One year Sue was elected captain of the team in her absence. Sue was a vague girl, who stood on the field in a daze generally unaware of what was going on around. When she woke up, a few spurts of effort improved the game for Newnham. If she put her stick out to stop a ball, much to everyone's amazement it stopped.

The games were generally arranged like this: about lunch-time Sue would remember we should be playing at 2.30, so she would find everyone in Old Hall who thought they could play hockey and plead with them to appear on the pitch; some said they would play only if she were desperate; many learnt to avoid Wednesday lunch so that she would not find them. After lunch Sue would hunt out more people in other Halls. At 2.30 she would arrive on the pitch, count the number of players, count the number of sticks (they rarely tallied, and there were rarely eleven of each) and then go inside to find more sticks or players, starting with friends in Old Hall. By 2.40 she would appear from an Old Hall window (she found windows more convenient than doors) with a few more sticks, and the game would start. I cannot remember ever winning a match, though I suppose we must have done so sometimes. That was not important.

After the match we would retire to Clough for tea, and sit under the gallery eating sandwiches for which the bread had been cut, apparently, with a bacon-slicer. We always commented on these very thin sandwiches, and were amused later to find accounts of a visitor to Newnham in 1895 saying 'the bread and butter was so thin you could see through it'. Perhaps the College kept the same bread-slicer for over seventy years!

Collegiate life is a very special experience, and one not fully appreciated by me until I had left Cambridge to spend a year in another university. Although in a 'Hall of Residence', I missed the community atmosphere and the opportunity afforded for intellectual discussion I had enjoyed at Newnham. The formality of Hall and the friendliness of meal-times epitomised what is best and most memorable about a Newnham education. I remember, one Tripos season, a Geologist revising the characteristics of fossils at breakfast. She mentioned ammonites, and a Theologian remarked that to her they were a tribe from over beyond Jordan; the meal ended with a discussion on rams' horns and the connection between the two sorts of ammonites. The Hall–Collegiate system resulted in friendship groups developing across subjects, and meal-times consolidated such friendships.

An interesting record of another aspect of those meal times is found in the 'Kitchen Suggestions Book'. Institutional cooking is notorious, but the quality of Newnham food was generally very good. (I have known none better before or since.) In three years I never mastered the art of eating an orange and cheese with wafers, butter and treacle without getting both hands to the wrists very sticky, but as a dessert the strange combination was much appreciated. An entry in the book read:

I eat my cheese with treacle,
I know it's rash to risk it,
It makes the cheese taste funny,
But it sticks it on the biscuit.

The Kitchen Suggestions Book was read daily by the appropriate authority and all comments were acknowledged, sometimes understood but rarely acted upon, although a plea for milk-jugs with whole, completely glazed and uncracked lips resulted in new jugs appearing overnight. We students used the book to hone our expressive powers to a fine edge. Reading through the comments for one academic year, two particular themes recur: the paucity of food and the state of the College pot-scourers! We frequently felt there was insufficient food; the College authorities nearly as frequently assured us there was plenty. Somehow the difference always seemed to be mislaid in the corridors between the kitchens and Old Hall. Sunday evening frequently presented the problem of how to divide fairly the three lettuce leaves provided for a table of ten. Such an apportionment was recorded on May 22nd. Three weeks earlier the College was more generous: 'One lettuce leaf is not really a salad, and there was no more, except, of course, on High Table!' This comment was annotated by the Tutor: 'A hasty conclusion!'

Perhaps some conflict was caused by inadequate description on the menu. May 5th: 'The presence of 2 bones in the fish-cake I had this morning was all there was to indicate that it was not meant to be a potato cake'; and on May 24th: 'The potato cakes at breakfast had little taste of fish...' To this, the reply from the kitchen was, 'Hard luck I enjoyed mine.' This elicited the following comment from another student, a disillusioned Scientist: 'Surely the distribution of fish in the above dish would conform to the Pois(s)on ratio? It would therefore have a random distribution, a large proportion of helpings having no fish at all. (The Domestic Bursar) was very fortunate to receive a positive sample.'

The Kitchen Suggestions Book for that year ended as it had begun, with comments on cheese. October 7th: 'Not only was my cheese on the point of going mouldy, it had become so greasy that finger and thumb prints were clearly identifiable and embedded on its surface!' June 7th:

'My lunch-time cheese was just like me after rowing – all sweating and grimy.' Despite our efforts the provision of food in Old Hall had neither progressed nor regressed, but we had survived!

R. M. Willatts (1963)

*

RETURN FROM MINNESOTA

In the depth of the Minnesota winter, when the temperature plunges to twenty degrees below zero (fifty-two degrees of frost), and the snow is so dry it creaks, when ice straight from Dante's Hell throttles the land and I realise with a rush of irrational panic that I am 1,500 miles from the sea, then my expatriate soul cries for England as a child away at school cries for home. I want flowers; English gardens pink and blue, sifted with sunshine; tree-dotted fields; hills small enough to be climbed on an afternoon's walk; stone walls and hedges; a landscape scaled down to my size.

So this summer [1965] when I returned to Cambridge, bringing my family, I felt I was giving them Eden. We picked posies of cornflowers, poppies, yarrow, pimpernel and hawkbit. We carried a hedgehog home to live in the garden. (It died.) We acquired a tortoise by the name of Merciful. The children romped in the fields and under the tall elms, and it never grew hot enough to call them indoors.

I discovered, too, another aspect of England whose absence in the American Midwest causes me pain, like the pain, I suppose, one is said to feel in a limb that has been cut off. The physical presence of the past structures one's world, gives the architecture of national life a certain balance, so that it is not easily shaken. The stresses have already been built in. One autumn morning, when the great fingers of the horse chestnuts were turning brown and the roads were littered with their fruit, I cycled to Holy Communion in St Bene't's, one of my favourite Cambridge churches. The tower is Saxon. Brightly painted angels from the ends of hammer-beams smile down benignly on the bowed backs of old ladies (surely the *same* old ladies who have worshipped there these 1,000 years?). We were bidden to pray for peace in Vietnam, and suddenly what had been in the States a matter for writing to one's Senator and the local press, full of the urgency of immediate decision, refocused as just one stretch of the historical process, 'turning and turning in the widening gyre'.

But, as Heraclitus said, you can't step into the same Cam twice. Some time each fall the river along the Backs is drained for cleaning. Unaware of this I was cycling one morning into town over Garret Hostel Bridge. As I topped the rise and glanced towards Clare an astonishing sight met my eyes. The elegant span of Clare Bridge, with its attentive willows, rose not over a placid and well-ordered stream but from a ditch of black primaeval slime that came just far enough up the arch to expose its knees. Tins, bottles and the wheels of old bikes stuck up in surrealistic fashion from the ooze. It was like having one's mother psychoanalysed.

On another occasion I was present at a lecture given by a distinguished American critic. Along the front of the hall a row of black-gowned dons, men who had been bright constellations in the intellectual firmament of my undergraduate days, now so many dishevelled starlings, drooped and dozed unheedful of any crumbs of learning that might be scattered before them, but apparently unable to shake off the habit of coming to be fed.

But Cambridge had a worse shock for me than this. I should have waited to visit my own College until term began and there were people about; instead I went there one afternoon during the Long Vacation when it was empty. The tourists were busy in King's and along Trinity Street, but Sidgwick Avenue was deserted. I turned in at the gate and hitched the front wheel of my bike, with a curiously remembered gesture, into the railings outside the Porters' Lodge. Inside, the smell of the place, a mixture of floor-polish, books and damp walls, rose up at me out of the past. How can a place go on smelling the same for so many years? I found my old room and was surprised to see how shabby and small it was. The gas-ring was a monstrosity. Had I really boiled a kettle on it? I looked through the window. The view into the garden, the graceful white Victorian windows of Clough Hall and the delicate birches, had lain behind so many hours of talking with friends that if I listened, surely I should catch what it was they were saying? Musing rather romantically I walked out into the garden. It was full of ghosts: hockey-playing, bun-eating ghosts, but just as frightening as something in a shroud. One of them was, or had been, me. For a long, horrifying moment I was two people, both child and mother, both a girl trembling anxiously on the brink of the future and a woman returning deliberately to the past. By some quirk of consciousness, the past me and the present were yoked violently together in a monstrous duplicity. The sense of division was distressing and I got out rather quickly. I decided to leave the past alone and went down to the market to ponder over the evening's vegetables.

1966

In a month's time I shall be back in Minnesota. At first I shall be simply glad to be home, reunited with friends, picking up the threads of what is now for me the most familiar way of life. Vietnam and Civil Rights will be my problems again. No doubt I shall be writing to my Senator. But before the ice melts on the lakes I shall be feeling nostalgic again for England. For although I became an American citizen deliberately and willingly, and though I renounced, with all the firmness I could muster, my allegiance to 'foreign potentates and rulers', the flesh is perverse and has its own loyalties.

This pain of wanting to return home, which we call nostalgia, surely depends for its intensity upon isolating certain joyous aspects of the past and suppressing less agreeable ones. We feel we once had something very precious – youth, joy, innocence – which now we have lost and long to taste again. Like Peter Pan we come to the window of the house and find that it is shut, there is no one to let us in. And, like him, we sit on the window-sill and savour our tears. But Peter Pan was the little boy who refused to grow up. Most of us are more like Wendy. She dutifully went about growing up, and married and raised a family this side of the window. But once in a while she returned, if you remember, to Never-never-land, to visit Peter and the little lost boys and darn their socks. I suspect that her own children were the richer for it.

M. Matthews (Howorth, 1946)

*

THE QUALITIES OF PEOPLE

15 March 1966: *Varsity* sherry party...met nobody interesting. Told Suzy (Menkes) that it would do her no harm to mention my name to Caroline Mackinlay, now with *Observer*. Suzy complained the *Observer* paid her nothing (not even expenses) when she organized and appeared in a 'what Oxbridge girls are wearing' feature...

Dress rehearsal of Marlowe *Measure for Measure*. George Rylands (Bloomsbury's 'Dadie'): 'Now just remember this is a melodrama, the juiciest melodrama Shakespeare ever wrote...go on, overact all you like.'

4 April 1966: Still in glow of happy satisfaction about Labour's victory. Saturday night's party for the helpers, with mock-cream cakes and tomato rolls and a bar and dismal speeches everybody talked through. Mrs Kaldor there with daughters. Introduced my husband to Miss Cohen... also X and husband Y. Observed that X's cockney accent, not dented by

Newnham, rapidly disappearing now she lives with Y's received pronunciation. She gets prettier and prettier...was a member of the young socialists, always getting thrown out for being a Trotskyite. We disagreed about immigration and among her points were that colour prejudice not only exists but is rampant, and racial hatred is one of the facts of life in South London among the working class.

23–6 May 1966:...exams, went extremely well...

7 June 1966: Saw Merryn Williams in street outside Bowes and Bowes... about results, I heard somebody appeared with a sword (?!) and read them aloud at nine, and I was able to tell her that Professor Hough had said he didn't think so when I asked him, and she asked what time I was going and I said about 10.15 because I couldn't bear the suspense of watching the notice posted...

On June 1 we gave a sherry party: 50 people came, weather lovely, overflowed into back garden. Heather Ashford, Denise Eveleigh, John and Marjorie Brunner, Ben Akim Oke, Andy Mayer, Richard Harthill, Ken and Yvonne Singer, Dr and Mrs Ron Gray, Nick and Augke Boulter; Virginia Lee, Paul White, Charles Relle, Eleanor Canning, Germaine Greer, Suzy Menkes, Alison Mitchell, John Rowe, Carol and Martin Bailey, Jackie and Chris Sykes, Neil MacInnes who has invited us to sherry in the Trinity scholars' garden for next Sunday, invitation in felt tip on a table-tennis ball, Caroline Lee, Merryn Williams, Lois and Bob Welch, Ald and Mrs Jack Warren, Mrs Councillor Euphemia Davies, Jim Herrick, Liz Evans, Lisa Bronowski.

Nephew Daniel stayed on with us. Took him on river (he paid, I believe); tennis, television, talk. Professor Hough recognized Mike in the street and stopped to chat; Dan was introduced. H said he was busy with marking, I said was waiting for results. Local colour laid on for tourists, as when my American brother-in-law nearly bumped into Lord Butler in full doctoral scarlet in Senate House Passage.

Then to Marlowe *Massacre at Paris*. Super production. Introduced self to producer, Noel Purdon, who lied that he knew my work and introduced me as Valerie Hobson Muggs. Invited to party afterwards to meet cast; night-capped and -shirted professor offered us beer in corridor.

Footlights first night on Monday. Hear on grapevine everybody hates David Frost.

8 June 1966: Am planning to buy Caroline Lee's grey denim suit if it fits for £2 15s. She wants to buy *Piers Plowman* with the money.

15 June 1966: Hot weather holds, but remains muggy. Last night went to wander through the streets and note the qualities of people. May Ball dresses exactly like last year's: the classic dance dress is now high-waisted, slim skirted, Regency line...

When we came up, Miss Everett said we should have to think whether our approach to English studies would be historical or philosophical, and how jolted I was at this...My husband insisted that philosophy was irrelevant to a literary critic. I put this down to eccentricity and showed him recent papers with compulsory questions on 'Art and nature' or 'Aristotelianism in Spenser'. So he fished out some of his old papers and showed me how the special period had changed: in his time, they were asked to discuss major authors, just one book sometimes, not things like 'attitudes to education in the period'. The tragedy paper in his day spent a whole question asking students to evaluate *Lear*. My impression is that evaluative questions have gone out...Gerald Harrison told me that about four years ago there was a 'rubric' on policy change in the English Tripos, saying that people must not repeat Part I answers for special period papers and that 'topics' rather than evaluative judgements must be sought. He says that one paper roused much fury, because it dealt only with minor authors, or at any rate, mainly, so that those who had prepared three or four major authors had to waste a lot. Z. found herself in this hole, because her supervisor told her she must have George Eliot and Dickens at her fingertips...Gerald says the Downing style of supervising, though officially denied, is about evaluating authors.

A week ago I was excited to open an invitation for Michael to dinner at Christ's, talking about being received at sherry with their wives; assumed I was invited to dine...Mike however interpreted invitation correctly. Wives in for sherry only. Furious with rage and disappointment. What are wives supposed to do while hubs guzzle? Wander into street in glad rags, slink away to lonely restaurant meals, return to their hotels unescorted?

21 June 1966: Reading impressive issue of the socialist journal *Forward* in the Sidgwick Buttery. Irritated by inane chatter of some coarse-voiced workmen, because I couldn't concentrate. Was trying to read about the relations within the left of the intellectuals and the working class.

Bought a brown tweed pinafore dress with flared skirt and a wrap-around plaid skirt (which I made into a cloak) for 10s each from Lisa in the Newnham second-hand clothes mart. This sale caused slight sensation when Ann Mallalieu offered a cocktail dress for £5. Note said 'cost £27 new'. This took most people aback.

Comparing notes, find I and others spend about £30 a year on clothes.

Caroline Lee's mother bought her *Piers Plowman* as a prize for her first, so she won't have to sell her denim suit. I looked like an early Girl Guide or something from the first world war in it, anyway.

27 June 1966: Party at the Stovells...Yorick Wilkes, doing research on the nature of proof, was there. Wearing a super spiv suit in navy with a white pin stripe, spotted tie, broad and gangstery, with a matching hanky in breast pocket (not done except as an outrageous return to the forties). Says suit cost £3 10s in Petticoat Lane and has moth holes. Probably true, as this is smart thing to do, and he'd get there first. He is the best fashion plate I know.

His pretty, amiable wife Flan (Felicity Anne) Snee was there, having taken her final exam to make her a doctor the day before, or perhaps that day...she usually makes his clothes – I remember a lovely mustard and black Robin Hood jerkin job in jersey, and a sort of softly tailored blazer in brown and green stripes. Told him how his recommendation that I should read Lovejoy changed my life. Also met Brian Vickers.

V. W. Grosvenor Myer (1963). Extracts from a diary

IN LOCO PARENTIS

Miss Cole initiated a discussion on topics which included guest hours, informal relations between senior and junior members, and the concept of *in loco parentis*. There was fairly general agreement that for community life to be bearable some rules (particularly those aimed at minimizing noise) were necessary. The senior members of the Committee...stressed that the term *in loco parentis* was never used in Newnham and that no Tutor so regarded herself.

Extract from the minutes of the Joint Committee of Fellows and Students, 7 March 1969

THE ASCENT OF STRACHEY TOWER

I heard that recently the nightly peace of Newnham has been disturbed by intruders who have wreaked considerable damage on some of the College treasures. Things were different when I was up, and respect for property was and still is an unwritten law to the True Night Climber. In the past at least Newnham's complex massif of unweathered brick has inspired little professional interest, probably because the motives for a detected ascent might be misinterpreted and the penalty enormous, and because the older colleges are so much better documented and known. Attitudes to Newnham have been functional and feminine – how to get in as quickly and quietly as possible.

To this end, the Grange Road railings have often been tastefully distorted. But that means of ingress, like the Tennis Court Gates, is really too easy to be considered seriously by the devotee. The devotee wears jeans and may carry a rope, and rarely has occasion to hoist up a despairing ball gown and do combat with the barbed wire.

Both devotee and/or lithe socialite prefer the Rattlesnake Route, graded as Mild Very Difficult, up the left-hand side of the right-hand Peile Gate. Holds are rather sparse, and considerable friction is needed on the descent not to finish with a graceless and noisy splatter into the bush. After that, it's a case of tiptoeing across the gravel and the lawn, begging the dew not to disclose one's footprints, and avoiding pools of light on the grass from windows of the many midnight-oil-burners.

In through X's ground-floor window, with a light gymnastic bound over the tell-tale soft earth and manure of those perfectly tended borders, to the spiny rose trellis and the handhold provided by the window-sill. A quick vault into dark warmth – a rare reward at the end of a rock climb.

The porter once cycled past as I crouched motionless on the top of the Peile Gate, trying fearfully to resemble a cat, spotlit by the head-lamps of a passing car. He bid me a cheery goodnight to my name and kept quiet about it, and my respect for him increased tremendously.

The Hammerklavier Route up the Clough Gate is even worse for exposure to objective dangers of that type. Classified as Very Difficult, it used to involve a direct ascent using the spiked diagonals (oh, the soles of my shoes!) and handholds on revolving spikes at the top. These make a noise like a late Beethoven bass part. The notice warning of 'Serious Accident Danger' placed in 1968 on railings near the gate is no longer true, for use of it has turned the route into a very simple uninteresting scramble.

But times are sadly changing. Not only are vandals climbing into Newnham but also its serious mountaineering potential has been realised by climbers eager to Peak-bag. The *C.U.M.C. Journal* for 1969 records the first ascent of Strachey Tower by McGollum the Foul, Whipple-burger II *et al.* It involved the right pipe by the Porters' Lodge, and various roof levels reached implausibly by throwing a rope round the flagpole. Descent was by laybacking down the already insecurely fixed lightning conductor. The direct chimneys between the concrete blocks have as yet proved unfeasible. And long may they remain so. The more the walls remain free from the rabble of frustrated rock-gymnasts the better. It is, after all, a Ladies' College.

B. Harriss (Beeham, 1965)

LEARNING AND INVENTION

Thus Learning to Invention we have married;
O glad appeasement of a strife long carried,
And to the cause of wisdom cause of danger,
For what can one perform without the other
A tenth so well as when combined together?
Dull Learning steeped in pedantry we find,
Reasons from precedent, not from the mind,
Knows his author's works and can at need recite them,
But never guesses why he came to write them,
Or that a famous poet yet can be
A man or woman much the same as he,
With no more authority for his employment
No more romantic urge than sheer enjoyment;
And so the patterns that some man designed
Making the world a ground-plan of his mind
Are treated as if they were the world itself:
As though you could keep man's nature on a shelf,
And studying it in books, itself adore,
That is, love man, but love his image more.
So finally our learned men applaud
Books upon books, the books themselves ignored.
Let Learning not became a parasite,
Plodding to classify what others write,
But with less reverence and more comprehension
Preserve the old, encourage new invention:
Nor let Invention, overproud in will
Strive for her ends, undisciplined by skill
And by that learning that informs invention:
Tradition and traditional convention.
Fantasy will disfigure her own creation

That has no content but imagination,
No learning, that to self-enclosed humanity
Provides escape from personal insanity.
Then you who our dull scholars would despise,
For fruitless diligence with blinkered eyes,
And think yourselves superior creations
Because you have creative aspirations,
And you who Learning's followers stand confessed,
Rejoice, and lay your differences at rest,
And learn from the union you have seen begun
That Art and Scholarship are best at one.

J. M. Sprince (1968)

Extract from *A Masque of Fallen Women*, produced by the undergraduates as part of the Centenary Celebrations, 1971